Amateur and Proletarian Theatre in Post-Revolutionary Russia

RELATED TITLES

Modern Theatre in Russia: Tradition Building and Transmission Processes
Stefan Aquilina
978-1-3500-6608-3

Russian Theatre in Practice: The Director's Guide
Edited by Amy Skinner
978-1-4742-8441-7

The Sixth Sense of the Avant-Garde: Dance, Kinaesthesia and the Arts in Revolutionary Russia
Irina Sirotkina and Roger Smith
978-1-3500-8740-8

The Great European Stage Directors Set 1: Volumes 1–4: Pre-1950
9781474254113
Edited by Simon Shepherd

The Great European Stage Directors Set 2: Volumes 5–8: Post-1950
9781474254168
Edited by Simon Shepherd

Amateur and Proletarian Theatre in Post-Revolutionary Russia

Primary Sources

Edited by
Stefan Aquilina

methuen | drama
LONDON • NEW YORK • OXFORD • NEW DELHI • SYDNEY

METHUEN DRAMA
Bloomsbury Publishing Plc
50 Bedford Square, London, WC1B 3DP, UK
1385 Broadway, New York, NY 10018, USA
29 Earlsfort Terrace, Dublin 2, Ireland

BLOOMSBURY, METHUEN DRAMA and the Methuen Drama logo are trademarks of Bloomsbury Publishing Plc

First published in Great Britain 2021
Paperback edition published 2023

Editorial matter and selection copyright © Stefan Aquilina, 2021, 2023

Stefan Aquilina has asserted his right under the Copyright, Designs and Patents Act, 1988, to be identified as the editor of this work.

For legal purposes the Translation Credits on p. xi constitute an extension of this copyright page.

Cover design by Charlotte Daniels
Cover image: Soviet communist poster from Russia (© Photo 12 / Alamy)

All rights reserved. No part of this publication may be reproduced or transmitted in any form or by any means, electronic or mechanical, including photocopying, recording, or any information storage or retrieval system, without prior permission in writing from the publishers.

Bloomsbury Publishing Plc does not have any control over, or responsibility for, any third-party websites referred to or in this book. All internet addresses given in this book were correct at the time of going to press. The author and publisher regret any inconvenience caused if addresses have changed or sites have ceased to exist, but can accept no responsibility for any such changes.

A catalogue record for this book is available from the British Library.

Library of Congress Cataloging-in-Publication Data
Names: Aquilina, Stefan, editor.
Title: Amateur and proletarian theatre in post-revolutionary Russia : primary sources / Stefan Aquilina.
Description: London ; New York : Methuen Drama, 2021. | Includes bibliographical references and index. | Translated from the original Russian into English.
Identifiers: LCCN 2020052044 (print) | LCCN 2020052045 (ebook) | ISBN 9781350170995 (ebook) | ISBN 9781350170988 (epub) | ISBN 9781350170971 (hardback)
Subjects: LCSH: Amateur theater–Soviet Union–History–Sources. | Amateur theater–Russia–History–Sources.
Classification: LCC PN3169.S65 (ebook) | LCC PN3169.S65 A43 2021 (print) | DDC 792.0222/09470904–dc23
LC record available at https://lccn.loc.gov/2020052044

ISBN:	HB:	978-1-3501-7097-1
	PB:	978-1-3502-2883-2
	ePDF:	978-1-3501-7099-5
	eBook:	978-1-3501-7098-8

Typeset by Integra Software Services Pvt. Ltd.

To find out more about our authors and books visit www.bloomsbury.com and sign up for our newsletters.

Contents

List of Figures — viii
Acknowledgements — ix
Translation Credits and a Note on Transliteration — xi

Introduction — 1
Stefan Aquilina

Prologue — 31
Platon Kerzhentsev

Part One   Aims and Objectives

1 'The Proletariat and Art' — 35
   Anatoly Lunacharsky
2 'The Proletariat and Art'
   Resolutions proposed at the First All-Russian Conference of
   Proletarian Cultural and Educational Organizations — 36
   Alexander Bogdanov
3 'The Proletkult and Soviet Cultural Work' — 37
   Anatoly Lunacharsky
4 'Ways towards a Proletarian Culture' — 41
   Alexander Bogdanov
5 'The Proletkult – Organization of Proletarian Amateur Performances' — 45
   Platon Kerzhentsev
6 'Craving the Stage' — 48
   Nikolai Lvov
7 'Socialist Theatre in the Years of the Revolution' — 50
   Piotr Kogan
8 'No to Theatre Art, but to Celebration' — 56
   Adrian Piotrovsky
9 'Drama and Mass Performances' — 58
   Viktor Shklovsky

Part Two Amateur–Professional Relations

10 'On the Professionalization of the Workers in the Arts' 63
Fyodor Kalinin

11 'On Professionalism' 67
Valerian Pletnev

12 The Creation of the Proletarian Theatre 77
Platon Kerzhentsev

Part Three Repertoire Issues

13 Repertoire at a Factory Theatre 85
Alexander Mgebrov

14 'The Repertoire of the Proletarian Theatre' 88
Platon Kerzhentsev

15 Notes on Pavel Bessalko's *The Bricklayer* 94
Alexander Mgebrov

16 'Adapt the Plays!' 98
Platon Kerzhentsev

17 *Garland's Inheritance* 102
Valerian Pletnev

18 They Tried to Hide, but Ended Up Fathers 115
Arkhip

Part Four Production Approaches and Examples

19 'After the Holiday' 121
Platon Kerzhentsev

20 Performances during the Civil War 125
Alexander Mgebrov

21 Collective Readings 127
Alexander Mgebrov

22 'Collective Creation in the Theatre' 130
Platon Kerzhentsev

23 'Strife between the Arts' 136
Platon Kerzhentsev

24 'On Futurism' 139
Fyodor Kalinin

25 'Creative Play. The Improvisational Method of N. F. Skarskaia' 144
P. P. Gaideburov

26	'Experiment in the Staging of Émile Verhaeren's Poem "Insurrection"' *Valentin Smyshlaev*	151
27	The Results of the New Theatre *Platon Kerzhentsev*	158
28	The Proletarian Actor *Valentin Tikhonovich*	165
29	'The Dramatization of a Living Newspaper' *Moscow Proletkult*	167
30	'On Staging Agit-Trials' *Moscow Proletkult*	174
31	'Club Stage – Competition of Living Newspapers' *N.N.V.*	178

Part Five Training

32	'On the Work of the Theatre Department of the Moscow Proletkult' *Valentin Smyshlaev*	185
33	Dramatic Laboratories *Platon Kerzhentsev*	189
34	'A Unified Studio of the Arts' *Moscow Proletkult*	193
35	'On Theatre Work at the Clubs' *Moscow Proletkult*	199

Epilogue: The Construction of Amateur Theatre *Nikolai Evreinov*	206
References	210
Index	213

List of Figures

1. Petrograd Proletkult, unnamed and undated. Note the performers wearing simple clothes and the sparse staging. Courtesy of the State Central Museum of Contemporary History in Russia.   7
2. Cover of Platon Kerzhentsev's *Tvorcheskii teatr*, 1920 edition. From the editor's private collection.   10
3. Pavel Bessalko, author of *The Bricklayer*. Courtesy of the State Central Museum of Contemporary History in Russia.   15
4. Blue Blouse performance, *At Our Institution*, undated. © A. A. Bakhrushin State Central Theatre Museum, Moscow.   22
5. Blue Blouse performance, unnamed and undated. © A. A. Bakhrushin State Central Theatre Museum, Moscow.   23
6. Moscow Proletkult May Day Celebrations, 1919. Note the performer engaged in what looks like a reading, while being elevated on a rudimentary platform and in close proximity to the audience. Courtesy of the State Central Museum of Contemporary History in Russia.   80
7. May Day Agit-Automobile, undated. Courtesy of Lynn Mally.   123
8. The First Workers Theatre of the Proletkult. Scene from the performance *The Road Ahead*, 1926. © A. A. Bakhrushin State Central Theatre Museum, Moscow.   162
9. Living Newspaper, Central Club of Builders, *Building Site*. Source: *Rabochii i teatr*, 1927, no. 15, p. 18. From the editor's private collection.   172
10. Living Newspaper, Union of Textile Workers, *The Weaver*. Source: *Rabochii i teatr*, 1927, no. 15, p. 19. From the editor's private collection.   173

Acknowledgements

Possibly because I have myself often worked in amateur and community contexts, the story of amateur theatre in post-revolutionary Russia has always fascinated me. It was, and still is, one of the most challenging historical contexts that I have worked on. Elsewhere, I have looked at ways through which to elevate in importance these amateur realities by, for example, foregrounding the value of their practices as opposed to the cruder theatricality adopted. My objective with this current project was to capture the voices of the main protagonists of the scene – Kerzhentsev, Pletnev, Kalinin, Smyshlaev, Lvov, Piotrovsky, Mgebrov and others. I also wanted to reproduce writings which testify to the often rough-and-ready performances that were taking place in the clubs, on small stages, outdoors, in cafeterias or stuffy rooms, etc. These performances remind us, and I am writing this in late March 2020, of the importance of commitment, application and communal solidarity.

Thankfully, I myself form part of several supportive communities, who have all contributed in their own particular way to the gestation of this project. First of all, I am fortunate to work in a very dynamic environment, the Department of Theatre Studies of the School of Performing Arts (University of Malta); my colleagues – but especially Prof. Vicki Ann Cremona, Prof. Frank Camilleri, Dr Mario Frendo, Dr Marco Galea, Dr Philip Ciantar and Dr Lucía Piquero – have always been very supportive of my research and generous with their time and feedback. On the international scene, colleagues like Prof. Jonathan Pitches (University of Leeds), Prof. Paul Fryer (Stanislavsky Research Centre) and Prof. Laurence Senelick (Tufts University) have also been sympathetic of my efforts to work on Russian theatre – very often, they have provided me with the models and standards to follow. For this, and much more, I remain thankful. A special word of thanks goes to Lynn Mally, whose work in the field was not only an essential reference point but also an inspiration.

The research going into this book has also profited markedly from two research fellowships which I received in 2018 and 2019, namely the William Evans Fellowship (University of Otago, New Zealand) and the Ros Dixon Fellowship (National University of Ireland, Galway). Both fellowships allowed me a change of scene in order to concentrate on the book, and scholars like Dr

Susan Little, Prof. Stuart Young, Prof. Hilary Halba, Prof. Patrick Lonergan and Prof. Elizabeth Tilley were particularly welcoming. I would also like to thank the amazing team at Bloomsbury who have supported the project from its first day: these include Mark Dudgeon, Peter Warren and Lara Bateman. Special thanks also go to the translators who have worked on the texts: Natalia Fedorova, Yulia Belozerova, Maria Kabanova, Anastasia Lesnikova and Alex Trustrum Thomas. I would also like to thank Franklyn Cauchi, Mario Aquilina and Victoria Ysotskaia for their various contributions to the project.

Finally, this project would not have been possible without the love and support which my family unconditionally give me on a daily basis. As always, this book is dedicated to them; to my wife Yulia and our two boys, Matthew and Daniel.

Every effort has been made to trace copyright holders of all copyright material in this book. Any omissions brought to my attention will be rectified in future editions.

Translation Credits and a Note on Transliteration

Translation credits are as follows:

English Language Translation ©Avatar Ltd./Anastasia Lesnikova
Prologue, Essays 1, 3, 5, 11, 14, 16, 19, 22, 23, 29, 32

English Language Translation ©Natalia Fedorova
Essays 10, 24, 25, 31, 34, 35

English Language Translation © Maria Kabanova
Essays 17, 26

English Language Translation © Yulia Belozerova
Essays 12, 18, 27, 28, 33, Epilogue

English Language Translation ©Alex Trustrum Thomas
Essays 2, 4, 6, 7, 8, 9, 13, 15, 20, 21, 30

For reasons of custom and convenience, I have rendered names familiar to English-speaking readers in their anglicized forms (e.g. Anatoly Lunacharsky, not Anatoli Lunacharskii, Alexander Ostrovsky instead of Aleksandr Ostrovskii) and dropped hard and soft signs in names (e.g. Lvov, not L'vov). As per standard practice, when referring to original sources and book titles, I adhered to the Library of Congress system of transliteration (e.g. I write *Proletarskaia kul'tura*).

Entries in the volume that carry a formal title in Russian are reproduced with that title in single quotes (e.g. Lunacharsky's essay 'The proletariat and art'). On the other hand, sections from books are given a title, and in this case no quotes are used (e.g. Repertoire at a Factory Theatre). Titles of plays are in italics.

Introduction

Stefan Aquilina

Soon after the October Revolution, a young aspiring actor with some acting experience garnered from attending the studio of Fyodor Komissarzhevsky drifted towards Cherkizovo, a small village near Moscow. What took him there was the promise of work. The village's drama circle had invited him to stage Gogol's *The Marriage* with a group of local amateur actors. Surprisingly, he said, amateur theatre performances were becoming popular among local communities. The play was put on in the tiny and cramped village club, where the stage was lit by kerosene lamps. Fifty years later, the actor, now a seasoned professional, was astonished to hear that a record of the performance had been kept and that the programme was saved for posterity in the museum of the new city that grew on the same grounds. That young actor was Igor Ilinsky, one of the greatest performers of the Soviet stage.

In some ways, Ilinsky's story is atypical of the amateur theatre taking place after the Revolution. Few actors coasted from the amateur stage towards professional pastures, though some undoubtedly did. In other ways, however, Ilinsky's recollections remain very representative of the broader amateur scene that developed after the Revolution. For instance, that he, a young actor with some training, acted next to amateur actors in a tiny rural village was quite a normal occurrence. Ilinsky also remembered the enormous craving that the workers and peasants had for the rough-and-ready productions that were hastily staged for their cultural entertainment. He did not forget other productions of Gogol and Chekhov in which he took part or his reading of Mayakovsky's poems. He performed in railway stations, in canteens, factories, barracks, for Red Army units, and often in the workers' clubs. He performed with little or no rehearsal time and in unheated rooms (Ilinskii 1984: 164–5).

This volume gathers primary sources about the kind of post-revolutionary amateur theatre described by Ilinsky. The essays are sourced from the first decade after the Revolution. Taken together, they tell a story of unabashed optimism in the creativity of the working classes. They speak of the use of theatre to carve a public role and political voice in the construction of a new world. The sources, however, also exhibit the flipside of the scene, or the sombre difficulties faced by the amateur actors in their work, the incessant calls to raise standards through professional help, and ultimate infiltration from above that transformed what had begun as an autonomous and heterogonous activity into controlled state propaganda. Other anthologies do exist which collate together essays about culture in early Soviet Russia, but this is the first collection that specifically addresses the proletarian theatre produced by the workers.[1] It captures both the theoretical articulations on the practice, produced by luminaries such as Platon Kerzhentsev, Valerian Pletnev, Alexander Mgebrov and Valentin Smyshlaev, as well as the more fleeting descriptions and first-hand accounts of the actual productions staged. As a result, the potential of collective practice, theatrical inventiveness and topical relevance will be highlighted. In this introduction I will expound on the range of the collection and draw links between the various essays, the vast majority of which have never been translated before.

Why should we do amateur theatre?

The collection is divided into five parts, namely 'Aims and Objectives', 'Amateur-Professional Relations', 'Repertoire Issues', 'Production Approaches and Examples', and 'Training'. Part One introduces several of the personalities which sought to define amateur theatre and its place within the broader discourses about proletarian culture that were developing at the time. The essay 'The Proletariat and Art' is a good place to start. It puts a spotlight on the person who more than anyone else was responsible for the way that the arts developed in early Soviet Russia, namely Anatoly Lunacharsky, head of the People's Commissariat of Enlightenment (Narkompros). Debates about proletarian culture could be extended and detailed, or sharp and concise. Lunacharsky's essay (n. 1 in the collection) is certainly of the second type. It relates directly to another short entry bearing the same title (n. 2), this time by Alexander Bogdanov, one of the most influential cultural articulators of the time and at one point Lenin's direct

---

1 For example, see von Geldern and Stites (1995) and Clark and Dobrenko (2007). The main text in English on post-revolutionary amateur theatre is Lynn Mally's *Revolutionary Acts – Amateur Theatre and the Soviet State* (2000). Equally important is her study of the Proletkult (Mally 1990). Both books were essential reference points in my work on this collection.

competitor to the leadership of the Bolshevik Party. It is interesting to compare these two essays to immediately underscore diversity as a defining characteristic of post-revolutionary proletarian culture as well as theatre.

Lunacharsky's essay was published in July 1918, while Bogdanov's text collates the resolution he proposed at the First All-Russian Conference of Proletarian Cultural and Educational Organisations, which was held between 15 and 20 September 1918 in Moscow. Even though the two texts were produced in such close proximity to one another, their discussion about the connection between the proletariat and art shows substantially different focuses. Lunacharsky stressed the relationship between the proletariat and the artistic works of previous eras – plays, work methods, novels, poems, pieces of music, paintings, but also theatres, orchestras, ballet companies, museums and so on, entities, in other words, marked by professionalism and specialization. These cannot be simply transposed onto the post-revolutionary times, because of the marked differences in ideological backgrounds. However, the artistic products of previous eras were not to be completely dismissed either, as some of the most extreme voices of the avant-garde were claiming. This is a point which Lunacharsky developed further in the essay 'The Proletkult and Soviet Cultural Work' (n. 3):

> There are people who believe that any distribution of 'old' science and 'old' art is an indulgence of bourgeois tastes, a cultural curse and the contamination of the young socialist organism with the blood of rotting junk.
>
> There are relatively few radical representatives of this delusion. However, the harm which they bring could be great. [...] I repeat for the thousandth time that the proletariat must be *armed with the entirety of human education*. The proletariat is a historical class. It must go forward because of its past.
>
> To discard the science and art of the past because of their bourgeois roots is as absurd as dropping machines in the factories or railways because of the same reason. (p. 39; emphasis in the original)

The question whether the treasures of previous generations should be either discarded or transformed and assimilated, therefore, was an important one. For the theatre, it related to the role which world-renowned practitioners like Konstantin Stanislavsky might take in the construction of a new theatre or the funding and repertoires of institutions like the Imperial Theatres and the Moscow Art Theatre itself.[2] It also related to the relative usefulness of the pre-revolutionary intelligentsia.

---

2 Collectively, these and other theatres became known as the Academic Theatres, which in 1919 passed directly under the control of the state.

In his conference resolutions Bogdanov did mention the relationship between the proletariat and the artistic treasures of the past, adding that the latter can be assimilated only if critically interpreted and processed by the former.³ His emphasis, however, was on collective work and creation. This implied having proletarian organizations and institutions, including, therefore, amateur theatre, built on comradely cooperation, or the workers coming together to pool resources and skills, generate ideas and products together, and operate within an environment that valued collective criticism. Like Lunacharsky, Bogdanov developed further this subject in another essay, titled 'Ways Towards a Proletarian Culture' (n. 4), where he linked creativity directly to collective work. Collective work was seen cutting across all aspects of human endeavour, be they in economics, science, politics, or the cultural and artistic sectors. It was thus treated as a kind of monism, a binding thread 'uniting all the organizational experience of mankind in its social work and struggle' (p. 43).

The relationship with the professional theatre of both past and present and the role of collective creativity became two contentious grounds of the amateur theatre in the 1920s. The former recurs in various other essays in this collection, most particularly in Part Two, and in individual essays that suggest or even document instances when the plays of Gorky, Chekhov, Hauptmann, Rolland and others were performed to or by the workers (Part Three). One such essay is an extract from Alexander Mgebrov's autobiography, here titled 'Repertoire at a Factory Theatre' (essay n. 13). Cultural theorist Platon Kerzhentsev, on his part, provided a longer list of possible works in his essay 'The Repertoire of the Proletarian Theatre' (essay n. 14) and, elsewhere, some concrete indications on how to adapt current plays (essay n. 16; see below). Collective work, on the other hand, appears under various guises in the essays of Part Four. These guises include Mgebrov's collective recitation in Petrograd and Kerzhentsev's adoption of group work as a production method to create performances. The latter's approaches can also be considered as the most developed attempt to transfer Bogdanov's theories to amateur theatre.

While the first four essays in this collection see Lunacharsky and Bogdanov debate broad meanings of the all-encompassing 'proletarian culture', the remaining essays in Part One shift the discussion squarely to amateur theatre. Such a placement signifies amateur and proletarian theatre as a bracket within the larger debates on culture. In the early post-revolutionary years 'proletarian

---

3 For a discussion on this critical processing, with concrete examples, see Aquilina (2020: 113–8).

culture' was a malleable term that meant different things to different people. It was used to connote the exposure of the workers to artistic contexts that were traditionally closed to them or the production of artistic products seeped into a proletarian ideology. It was also used to refer to a proletarian everyday culture that indicated, for example, which books to read, how to dress, raise children, talk in public, and so on. Theatre came to play a prominent role within these debates about proletarian culture, as a vehicle that could both create as well as transmit the culture of the working classes.

An essay (n. 5) by Platon Kerzhentsev on the Proletkult opens this cluster of essays. Kerzhentsev became a controversial figure in the history of post-revolutionary theatre and its relationship with the state. Initially a vocal supporter of the workers and their artistic creativity, he eventually morphed into a major critic and player in the attack against formalism that characterized the 1930s.[4] Typical of this attack was Kerzhentsev's active participation in the closure of Meyerhold's theatre in 1938.[5] His theories about collective creativity, developed in the first years after the Revolution, however, have a lot to commend them for. They were developed on lines not too dissimilar from what today we might refer to as devised performance.[6] Kerzhentsev publicly defended the Proletkult, contributed to several of its boards and served on the editorial team of the organization's newspaper. The Proletkult was a cultural organization formed on the eve of the October Revolution with the aim of creating a proletarian culture. Its claims of independence soon brought it into conflict with the party, which could hardly accept the existence of an autonomous cell that appropriated for itself and in very loud terms a territory as important as culture (see also essay n. 3). Lenin vehemently detested this organization. Still, the Proletkult did much in the 1918–21 years to create literature, music, art and theatre cells in factories, clubs and workers' districts across the country. Amateur theatre activity increased markedly during the Civil War, and within this explosion the Proletkult became a national movement and major cultural player.[7] However, it is important to underline that the Proletkult was only one part or bracket within the wider movement of amateur theatre, a section or bracket within a much larger tapestry. In the discussion below as well as in the essays chosen I often make reference to the Proletkult only because its work was more visible and, consequently, better documented than other instances

---

4 For a detailed reconstruction, through primary sources, of the 'anti-formalist campaign', see Clark and Dobrenko (2007: 229–48).
5 See Braun (1998: 284–8).
6 This is a discussion that I develop elsewhere, in Aquilina (2014; especially 40–2).
7 By 1920 some 400,000 members could be counted within Proletkult ranks (Mele 1991: 10).

of amateur practice. The voices of the often transient groups were, in fact, much more difficult to capture and their actors often nameless (see Mally 2000: 18).

In his essay 'The Proletkult – Organization of Proletarian Amateur Performances', Kerzhentsev underlined the independent and autonomous attitude which amateur theatre nourished in the workers. Skill and resources were often rudimentary, especially during the first years of the Revolution. Typical of amateur practice in general, workers often had little choice but to congregate together to maximize on the materials that were at hand. If costumes were inexistent, everyday clothes were put on. If the group did not have theatre lights, lamps and torches were used instead. When formal plays were lacking, scenarios were composed and improvised on (Figure 1).[8] Such a do-it-yourself attitude even gave amateur theatre one of its early names. I say 'one of' since several terms were used to describe the activity of the workers as theatre producers. These included the Creative Theatre, the Socialist Theatre, the Proletarian Theatre, the Class Theatre, but also 'club and factory theatre', 'neighbourhood theatre', 'mass theatre' and 'worker-peasant theatre'. One term that did not find much currency was that of *liubitel'skii teatr*, which might be the term closest to the English 'amateur theatre', but which '[i]n the early Soviet period, [it] connoted all that was bad in amateur activities, such as posturing for good parts and wasting time in frivolous leisure-time pursuits' (Mally 2000: 23). 'Do-it-yourself' is the rather clumsy translation of *samodeiatel'nost'*, meaning 'independent initiative' (Swift 2002: 184), i.e. the attitude to be proactive, creative and to do things yourself. It is in this sense that Kerzhentsev used the term in his essay. To translate *samodeiatel'nost'* into English I have adopted Mally's tested practice of using 'amateur theatre' (2000: especially 23), in the understanding that in the post-revolutionary context amateur theatre as *samodeiatel'nost'* contrasted with what Kerzhentsev referred to as 'the most deadly, [...] superficial and ill-

---

8 One particularly detailed description of amateur theatre appears in Nina Gourfinkel's chronicle *Théâtre Russe Contemporain* (I will make reference to an Italian translation; 1979: 127–9). This description is of a later performance, staged in 1926, by a group of workers who called themselves The Ship, underlining that the do-it-yourself practices and a rough-ready presentation were mainstays on the amateur stage. The play revolved around the figure of Lenin. Illumination was a major problem as no light rigs were available, so the actors held electric lamps in hand through which they illuminated their bodies and faces. Various parts of the stage were also lit in the same way. Gourfinkel described the clever effects which the actors created with these lamps, such as asymmetrical shadows, the impression of moving machines, of rotating wheels, and of a great number of workers. Musical effects were created through the use of a piano, harmonica and drums, augmented by plates, brooms and paper sheets. For example, brooms were used to create the sound effect of a train entering a station, while the Aurora's cannon shot was recreated through a strong drum hit. 'Finally', Gourfinkel (1979: 129) wrote, '[t]he various resources that were used to create these various effects were put together to create the music of the Soviets.'

Figure 1 Petrograd Proletkult, unnamed and undated. Note the performers wearing simple clothes and the sparse staging. Courtesy of the State Central Museum of Contemporary History in Russia.

considered theatre dilettantism' (p. 191).[9] A do-it-yourself amateur theatre, on the other hand, drew directly from the Russian tradition of treating theatre as a morally edifying practice (Aquilina 2020: 7–9).

To this understanding of amateur theatre I also add the 'proletarian theatre' tag to underline its class-based focus. It was not just any kind of amateur theatre, but an amateur practice that saw workers come together (sometimes under the direction of professional instructors) to create performances, on material directly relevant to their everyday life, and presented to a workers-based audience in spaces readily accessible to them. The two terms – 'amateur' and 'proletarian' – also appear in the literature as being intrinsically linked. Alexei Gan, who was responsible for the mass spectacles in Moscow, argued that 'the proletarian theatre is the work of the workers themselves and the peasants adjacent to its

---

9 In another essay, Valerian Pletnev spoke of a dilettantism that 'shallowly skims the pinnacle of art without delving deeper' (p. 68). It is this dilettantism which Kerzhentsev, Pletnev, Lunacharsky and other theoreticians steered away from.

ideology' (Blum et al. 1922: 50). He, in other words, distanced proletarian theatre from professionalism to bring it close to amateur practitioners, or workers and peasants. Russian theatre historian Alexei Gvozdev also established the idea that new theatrical cultures develop out of the amateur performances of emerging classes. He supported this with studies about ancient societies, the Middle Ages and the Renaissance. Gvozdev also invoked the history of the Moscow Art Theatre, the reforms of which were seen to have matured in the bowels of amateur theatre. Consequently, he concluded, the proletarian theatre was to grow out from the amateur circles of the Soviet youth, especially those working in the factories (Tarshis in Gvozdev 1987: 7).

A debate about the value of amateur and proletarian theatre is developed in the essays authored by Nikolai Lvov (n. 6), Piotr Kogan (n. 7), Adrian Piotrovsky (n. 8) and Viktor Shklovsky (n. 9). Amateur theatre did not receive unequivocal support. In the essay 'Craving the Stage', Lvov underlined the theatre's pull on the people. This pull was a result of the natural tendency in humans to want to experience a new and brighter life, which comes as no surprise considering that the post-revolutionary years were especially hard, marked by war, starvation, lack of fuel and the near-collapse of the economy.[10] Piotrovsky saw this craving as an opportunity, as the basis to construct a new proletarian life marked by cultural participation. In his eyes, amateur theatre was a space where practitioners sought not only to depict life, but also to transform it. Shklovsky, on his part, saw this as wishful thinking, as the explosion of amateur theatre was nothing more than the spread of a rash or disease. He was wary of the fact that amateur theatre made people wallow in an illusion. It diverted the workers from tackling the difficulties of real life. To him, therefore, amateur theatre amounted to escapism. Among this cluster of theoreticians, Kogan regarded amateur theatre as the basis on which to build the theatre of the future. His essay is also revealing of the fact that the theatre section within the Narkompros had soon tried to understand the breadth and nature of amateur theatre. In the essay in fact he made reference to a questionnaire sent around the many workers' and peasants' circles, and information about the kind of plays staged was collected. Undoubtedly, this was an early effort by official cultural organs to try and keep tabs on a cultural movement which they understood as being only ostensibly under their control.

---

10 Fyodor Komissarzhevsky described these years as a 'living hell' (Komisarjevsky 1929: 2).

Who will help us?

As mentioned above, the essays in Part Two are brought together by a concern about the relation between amateur theatre and its professional counterpoint. They are authored by Fyodor Kalinin (essay n. 10), Valerian Pletnev (n. 11) and Kerzhentsev again (n. 12). While the emphasis in this collection is clearly on non-professional practitioners, it also needs to be said that amateur theatre in post-revolutionary Russia constantly rubbed shoulders with professional realities. Sometimes it is even impossible to draw a clear line between the two. Within the Proletkult, for instance, amateurs and professionals freely mixed together, with the former wanting to receive solid direction and the latter desiring work and remuneration. When the Arena of the Proletkult Theatre staged Romain Rolland's *The Fourteenth of July*, for instance, the main roles were taken by seasoned actors, while the workers took on the choral parts (Zolotnitskii 1976: 310). In the case of the mass spectacle *The Mystery of the Liberated Labour*, staged in Petrograd in 1920, most of the two thousand performers were conscripts from the army, but then important Petrograd directors and set designers like, among others, Yuri Annenkov, S. D. Maslovskaya and Vladimir Shchuko, composed the scenario and took responsibility for the staging (von Geldern 1993: 157–8). Other examples abound in literature.[11] Elsewhere, I have argued that proletarian theatre often functioned as an amateur-professional hybrid: the workers brought in the content of the dramas, contents that were relevant to their class, while the professional directors provided the compositional skill necessary to transform this content into performance material (Aquilina 2020: 114–6). It is this blurring condition between amateur practitioners and professional specialists, on lines of 'who was exactly doing what', which is perhaps the biggest historiographical difficulty when studying the scene.

The essays provide a theoretical underpinning to these amateur-professional configurations. Pletnev articulated his position in some length. A joiner by trade, he quickly rose in the Proletkult's ranks to become its national president in 1920, a position he kept until the institution's demise in 1932. He wrote several plays which became popular on the amateur theatre stages (Mally 1990: 102–3; a section of one of these plays, *Garland's Inheritance*, appears in Part Three

---

11 For a further developed example see James von Geldern's discussion on the staging of *The Overthrow of the Autocracy* (1919) at the Theatrical-Dramaturgical Studio of the Red Army. The performance developed as 'a play at revolution, a make-believe revolt by soldiers who had participated in the real one'. They were directed by Nikolai Vinogradov, a professional director of some experience who was also influenced by Meyerhold (von Geldern 1993: 125–7).

Figure 2 Cover of Platon Kerzhentsev's *Tvorcheskii teatr*, 1920 edition. From the editor's private collection.

as entry n. 17). In the essay 'On Professionalism', Pletnev recorded part of the debate on the relative merits of professionalism:

> [There are those who] insist on the necessity of organising central studios in all the fields of art. In their opinion, the most talented persons must be chosen, through strict trials, from among the students coming from both the centre and the suburbs. It is argued that these individuals should be released from their factory jobs, given a stipend from the government, and work solely in the field of art. (p. 45)[12]

This is a possibility which Kerzhentsev also acknowledged, though in his extract from a chapter of *Tvorcheskii teatr* (The Creative Theatre)[13] he did argue that the shift from amateurism to professionalism was to be treated as an exception rather than the norm, and an undesirable one at that (Figure 2). Pletnev, on his part, suggested the training of workers in technical skill, which professional practitioners have in abundance. It was important, however, that this exposure to bourgeois specialists did not detach the workers from the production processes of their workplace. Without a connection with the workplace, proletarian theatre would lose its ideological basis.

Pletnev's essay also sheds light on the complexity of the debates on proletarian theatre. In other words, he spoke about theatre in an informed manner that contrasts with the simplicity that characterized much amateur productions. For instance, he heeded a word of caution about the development of proletarian experts. These experts were necessary to take the place of the intelligentsia, but they could not be produced on order. Rather, the workers needed the time necessary to go through all the required stages of artistic development. Through these thoughts Pletnev moved close to Stanislavsky's own preoccupation with the organic growth of a scene, a character or a performance, but also of an actor's talent or theatre scene in general. Pletnev wanted the proletarian artists to engage with their practice in a persistent and continuous manner, again recalling Stanislavsky's theories about the actor's work upon himself. This consistency

---

12 That this shift from amateurism to professionalism did indeed take place is confirmed by David Zolotnitsky: '[T]he actors of the Proletkult very soon had to leave their place at the machine and firmly take a job on the stage. They could not combine both. Participants in the central studios began to receive scholarships to the amount of an average wage' (Zolotnitskii 1976: 291). This does not mean, however, that the Proletkult was a wholly professional institution, but only that some of its most talented elements moved on to become professional players. Amateurism in the workers' groups remained the grassroots of the Proletkult's theatre work. Leach, in fact, says that the typical practice at the Proletkult was to have 'a teacher leading about fifty participants, in classes broadly based on his professional experience' (Leach 1994: 69; see also 143).
13 This was an important book which between the 1918 and 1923 went through five editions. Extracts in this collection are taken from the fifth edition of 1923.

was necessary 'to give up trying to hatch a proletarian artist in six weeks, in the same ways that chicken hatch', since 'the growth of an artist in his thought and technique is incessant' (p. 74). A process-based acting formation would allow the form and content of proletarian theatre to become an indivisible whole.

Kerzhentsev was particularly adamant in his support of amateurism: 'The real and only creators of the new theatre are those actor-workers who will also remain at their lathe' (p. 78). Like Pletnev, he viewed the worker's attachment to his workplace as a necessary condition for proletarian theatre. It was this attachment that provided the worker with the skill necessary to process professional practice, i.e. the awareness to choose what was technically helpful while discarding ideologically harmful material. Kerzhentsev derided the technical skill of professionals, though it has to be said that he was not always consistent on this matter (see entry n. 31 in Part Five). A 1932 Olympiad of amateur theatre, organized in Moscow by the trade unions in collaboration with the Communist Party, the Narkompros and the Komsomol, brought in plain sight the technical shortcomings of the amateur stage of the time, a vestige of the work carried out in the 1920s. Plays staged at the Olympiad appeared full of stereotypical characters, superficial plots and weak aesthetics. The advice given was for the workers to improve their technical skill through professional training and supervision (Mally 1993). Ten years before that, however, Kerzhentsev rang a very different bell:

> One should not overestimate the importance of technical formation. It is necessary and indispensable, but the theatre revolution will not take place because of it. [...] The right guidelines for the theatre are more important, as are the right keywords, and the immediate enthusiasm for what is carried out.
> (p. 79)

Amateur theatre certainly changed a lot in the fifteen years or so between the Revolution and the 1932 Olympiad, but the questions raised still recurred across the many forms of amateur theatre evident after the Revolution.

The more extravagant statements and theories given in Parts One and Two here explicate the potential and reach of amateur theatre. However, they pale in comparison with the humbler and more down-to-earth artistic products which the workers achieved in practice. Cultural theorists exalted the self-sacrifice of the workers, the creativity of the actors and the inroads which the proletariat was expected to make. The practical accomplishments in terms of repertoire and performance never reached such lofty heights. Even Kerzhentsev's supposed practical methods were hard to implement, and only his 'more specifically dramatic ideas [...] [managed to] inform revolutionary theatre practice'

(Leach 1994: 24). These ideas included the status of the actor as a creator, the tight relationship with the spectator, the aforementioned need for continuous formation and the use of unconventional performance spaces. The Proletkult's supposedly more polished work also failed to gain much positive appraisal. Such criticism weighed the scene down because it carried political significance that went beyond theatre: a simple and crude performance was equated with a simple and primitive understanding of the Revolution itself.[14]

Which repertoire should we stage?

Part Three collects essays that discuss the repertoire. They also foreground the relative impact of the Revolution on the proletarian theatre itself. A lot of theatre was being produced during the revolutionary era, but theoreticians like Lvov still felt distressed because a post-revolutionary repertoire had failed to appear.[15] It was as if the Revolution had not touched the theatre. Kerzhentsev confirmed this:

> The first year and a half of the Revolution did not bring any updates to the Russian repertoire. Even the theatres that fell into the hands of the sovdeps followed a well-beaten path in terms of the repertoire. Proletarian drama clubs, which sprung up like mushrooms after rain, did not rush to perform new plays, the spirit of which would be close to the working class. Instead they rushed to old bourgeois, third-rate stage rags.
>
> (p. 88)

As a stopgap solution many amateur activists staged pre-revolutionary plays. Kerzhentsev himself compiled a list of about forty-five such plays, which included works by the ancient Greek tragedians, Shakespeare, Molière, Lope de Vega, Ibsen and others (essay n. 14).

Writing again a year later in the newspaper *Vestnik teatra* (essay n. 16), Kerzhentsev reiterated his concern about the failed appearance of a proletarian repertoire. Consequently, he underlined the need to redo and adapt old plays.

---

14 This accusation was also directed towards professional directors like Meyerhold, whose stereotypical depictions of class enemies were seen as counter-revolutionary. They dulled the receptivity of the audience to the dangers of these enemies (Braun 1998: 198).
15 'In most cases the proletarian theatre does not create any new theatre, but simply imitates the templates of the professional stage. All the circles, the Red Army, the workers and the peasants put on countless productions of Chekhov, Ostrovsky and all of the vaudeville nonsense' (Lvov quoted in Zolotnitsky 1976: 292).

Pletnev might have argued that in proletarian theatre form and content were to create an indivisible whole (see above), but Kerzhentsev believed that it was actually important to separate the two from each other. This was necessary in order to rework the plays. Kerzhentsev's elaboration of Verhaeren's *The Dawns* offers one concrete example of this separation. Some elements of the play's content were still relevant to a post-revolutionary audience. These included 'the strict pathos, the deep symbolism, the author's genius in historical generalization, and other features of this modern and sagacious play' (p. 98). The crowd, however, was considered too passive and Erenian, the hero, too hesitant. These elements needed to be carefully unpicked and updated. On a formalistic level, the play was deemed overlong and lacking in stage action. Whole sections again needed to be isolated from the rest and removed. Ultimately, Kerzhentsev wanted 'to keep the play safe, but at least make it articulate, dynamic and economical with words' (p. 99).

Alexander Mgebrov was one director from the professional world who made quite a name for himself with his productions of proletarian plays. A former collaborator of Meyerhold at the theatre of Vera Komissarzhevskaya and of Nikolai Evreinov at the Ancient Theatre, Mgebrov was ideally suited to introduce non-representational forms of performance. Before joining the Petrograd Proletkult in 1918, he briefly headed a factory theatre where he staged plays such as Herman Heijermans's *Wreck of the Ship 'Hope'*, Gorky's *The Lower Depths*, and Hugo von Hofmannsthal's *Electra* (see entry n. 13). He mentioned that these performances were very well received by the workers, who showed 'true sincerity and uplift' (p. 85). Perhaps inevitably, given the politically volatile times, the performances often became entwined with what was happening outside of the performance spaces. An evening programme featuring *Electra* and an extract from Émile Verhaeren's poem 'Insurrection', for instance, was 'interrupted' when halfway through the performance a group of workers filed into the hall, and a speaker rallied the audience to take up arms in defence of the city against the German advance during the First World War.

One proletarian, i.e. post-revolutionary, play which Mgebrov recommended and produced was Pavel Bessalko's *The Bricklayer* (Figure 3). A former railway worker, Bessalko was first exiled to Siberia in 1907 but then fled to Paris where he met Bogdanov, Kalinin, Lebedev-Poliansky and Lunacharsky. He returned to Russia in 1917 and soon after joined the Bolshevik ranks (Zolotnitskii 1976: 297). *The Bricklayer* was easy enough to understand, accentuating Bessalko's wish to write for mass consumption (in Goldman 1977: 361). The play is allegorical in

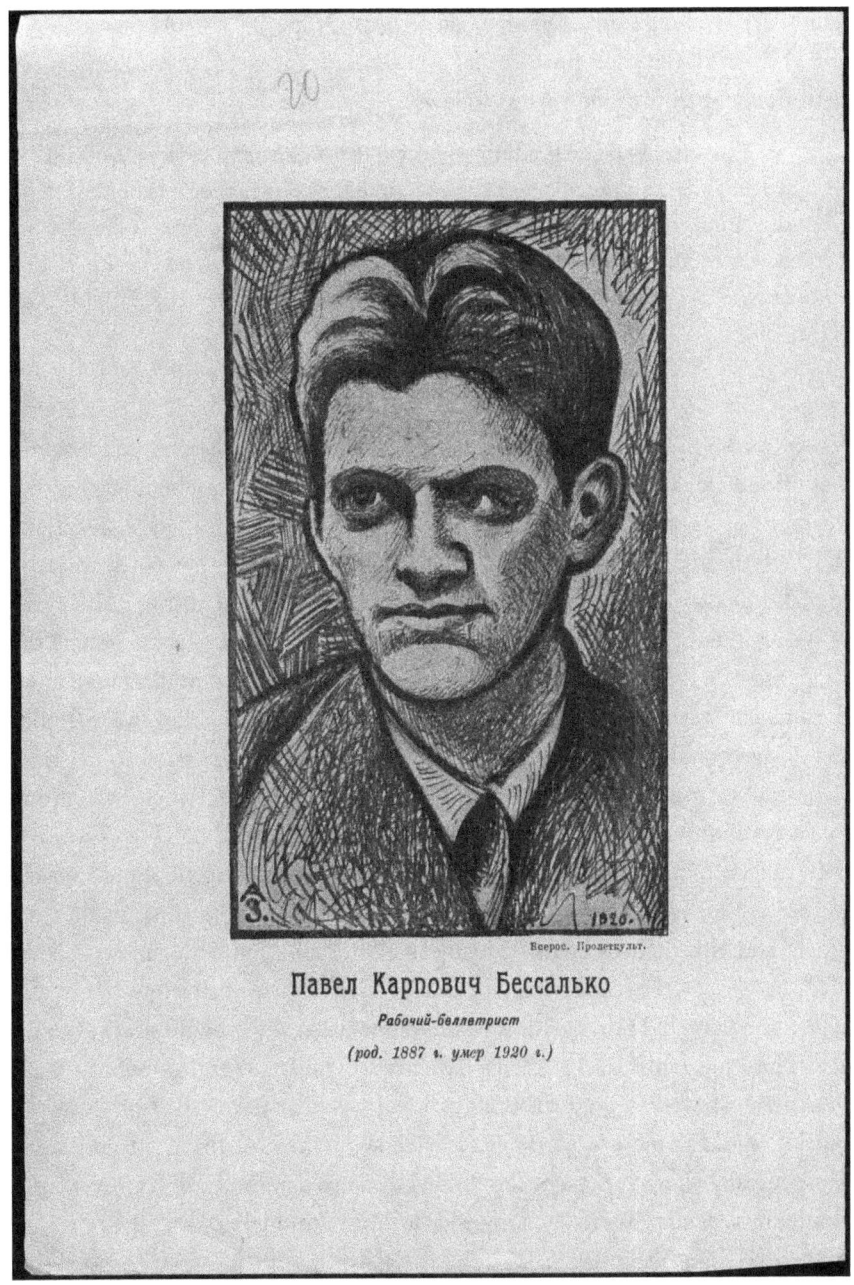

Figure 3 Pavel Bessalko, author of *The Bricklayer*. Courtesy of the State Central Museum of Contemporary History in Russia.

nature. It narrates a conflict between an architect, a specialist in plans and design and the bricklayer, the brave worker who executes these designs. Entry n. 15 reproduces Mgebrov's message as follows:

> [W]ho is the real builder? Is it the architect with his drawings, the architect who only knows desk work and never dares to go to the construction site, to the top of the buildings which his drawings erect, the architect who cannot help but feel dizzy on these peaks? Or is it the one who actually climbs these peaks, [the bricklayer] who stacks bricks, who goes near the sky itself and actually risks his life?
>
> (p. 94)

Mgebrov also provides some indications on the staging of the play. Mass action was included, even though it was not in the original play, highlighting the flexibility of the post-revolutionary repertoire, where workers made alternations to scripts to suit their needs.[16] Song and the sounds of hammers were introduced to make the play light and energetic, in contrast with the pedantic and stiff entry of the architect. The fall of the architect from the tower was represented by the dropping of a doll, exemplifying the use of symbols as a common practice on the amateur stage. In another instance, when staging 'Insurrection' in December 1918, Mgebrov used shouts, stamps, runs and the frenzied passions of abstract figures, all surrounded by a blazing red glow, to symbolize an active crowd fighting for its revolutionary ideals (Zolotnitskii 1976: 249). Beyond Mgebrov's work at the Proletkult, the use of simple symbols on the amateur stage became a means to reach to an unsophisticated audience while still retaining some of theatre's magic and imaginative draw. When describing another performance taking place in Moscow, Kerzhentsev made reference to the use of a wall to signify the separation from old times. This wall was enthusiastically brought down by both actors and spectators (p. 158). The audiences of the amateur theatre movement in general, as well as the Proletkult as its representative microcosm, however, quickly outgrew the use of symbols: 'The symbolism of fire, iron and stone was generally characteristic of the Proletkult since its inception. However, after habitually repeating itself, such imagery lost both immediacy and the power to influence' (Zolotnitskii 1976: 313).

---

16 Mally gives another example of an adaptation of *The Bricklayer*, carried out by a Red Army unit. In this version, a scene was added where representatives from all nations brought gifts to the bricklayer to thank him for his work. The performance also ended with the *Internationale* (Mally 2000: 39).

To give a concrete idea of the kinds of plays making the rounds, two examples are included in this volume. Both are from a slightly later date, 1923 and 1924 to be precise. This is to be expected. Robert Leach argues that while 'innumerable plays [...] were hastily duplicated and sent for performance to different parts of the country' (Leach 1994: 38), only a rather disappointing list of plays remains from the years of the Civil War. Apart from *The Bricklayer*, these plays include Pavel Arsky's *For the Red Soviet* (reproduced in von Geldern and Stites 1995: 22–8), P. Kozlov's *Legend of a Communard* (see Mgebrov 1932: 480–500) and Alexander Vermishev's *Red Truth*. Another popular dramatic form was the *agitki*, agit-prop sketches containing a clear propagandistic message (Mally 2000: 37–9). The plays reproduced here are in comparison more developed, though they still strike our eyes for their clear-cut characterizations and simple structures. The first is an extract from *Garland's Inheritance* (Act 1), a play by Valerian Pletnev, based on scenario which he himself had composed with Sergei Eisenstein (n. 17). The other is a short sketch penned by an author simply referred to as Arkhip (n. 18). The play titled *They Tried to Hide, but Ended Up Fathers* is about a trial of a man who refused to accept his paternity. He even convinced his friends to testify in front of the judge that they had relationships with his former companion. The judge's decision favoured the woman: all men were made responsible for the child's welfare. This example joined other efforts that addressed the issue of divorce, the treatment of female spouses, the difficulties of child-rearing and the status of women in general (Mally 1996).

How do we create the performances?

Following this incursion on the repertoire, Part Four shifts attention to the production approaches used by the amateur practitioners in the creation of their performances. It also gathers recollections and descriptions of specific performances to shed light on the aesthetics of the amateur stage. The part opens with an essay by Kerzhentsev titled 'After the Holiday' (essay n. 19). The essay describes the street decorations set up in Moscow to celebrate the 1918 anniversary of the October Revolution. Though not specifically on amateur performance, or even on theatre in general, I include this essay to refer to a number of critical yardsticks to evaluate post-revolutionary art, including therefore amateur performance. These yardsticks included a careful selection and composition of diverse elements which, however, still create unity and harmony within a given work of art, the use of uplifting material and a certain resemblance (Kerzhentsev called it familiarity) with real life. Further criticism is voiced by Fyodor Kalinin in his 1919 essay titled 'On Futurism' (n. 24). Mally described futurism as 'a blanket term indiscriminately (and inaccurately) applied to impressionism, cubism, nonfigurative artistic forms, and various types of literary and theatrical experiments' (Mally 1990: 145). It came under a barrage of criticism over its pre-revolutionary origins and the supposed difficulty faced by the workers when trying to comprehend its artistic products. Kalinin insisted that proletarian art should steer away from experimenting with futurism because it predicates form over content. Foreshadowing the criticism that would engulf the avant-garde from the late 1920s onwards, Kalinin underlined that 'to consider form by itself means to engage in metaphysics, empty chatter and, of course, this will have nothing to do with Marxism' (p. 64). The proletariat actors, therefore, should steer away from it.

The second essay in Part Four (n. 20) brings the discussion back to amateur performance by indicating the breadth of theatre work that was taking place at the same time of Kerzhentsev's and Kalinin's essays. This was the time of the Civil War, when a veritable 'theatre epidemic' engulfed the country (Mally 2000: 17–46). A consequence of the emancipatory momentum created by the Revolution, amateur theatre created by the workers grew exponentially, much beyond the small scene that was evident before 1917.[17] As Konstantin Rudnitsky says, '[t]here was no club or factory without a theatre' (1988: 45). Extract n. 20 is taken from Mgebrov's autobiography, where he shows that these amateur groups were constructed on very shifting grounds, with their ranks often getting depleted when members were conscripted in the army. The groups, however, still found themselves in the midst of a whirlwind of work. They performed for Red Army units, in clubs, in the open air, in tearooms, in basements and in any other space where political instigation was deemed necessary. The actors working with Mgebrov also performed for free, because performances 'existed as a deep, comradely community, where unforgettable moods and inseparable associations between audiences and performers were sensitively intertwined. It was a continuous, solemn celebration of creativity, energy, and enthusiasm' (p. 126).

Collective creation, first raised at a cultural level by Bogdanov (see Part One), is picked up again in essays 21 and 22. It is transformed into a production approach to create theatre performances. The essays, authored by Mgebrov and Kerzhentsev, juxtapose two approaches to collective work. In working with his performers, Mgebrov immediately noted their lack of skill and experience.

---

17 On the thin amateur scene before the Revolution, see Swift (2002: 181–204).

Proletkult students shared his enthusiasm for theatre, but 'none had stage experience [...]. [They] were amateurs, and more amateur than most' (von Geldern 1993: 31). Consequently, he chose to stage evenings of collective recitations, based on poems by Aleksei Gastev, Walt Whitman and Vladimir Kirillov. These collective recitations involved the rhythmic use of voice, verse and physical expression and embodiment. Whole poems were set to this collective work, which allowed Mgebrov to find quick and interesting compositions on the stage. What he meant by collective work is evidenced by a short description of the processes used. Lines of poetry were divided among a large number of participants; subsequently, they were fragmented into smaller units like words, half phrases and syllables. Some of the fragments were spoken collectively, others individually, while others still were attached to movement patterns or static tableaux. The effect created is reproduced as follows:

> On a high platform, surrounded by a hundred raised hands, in the pose of a large monument, stood the reader of the poem, bare-chested and wearing a leather apron. While reading he was accompanied by distant music and the whole scene was flooded by a strong red glow.
>
> (p. 128)

To create his effects, Mgebrov also made use of anything that was within his and the performers' reach, including chairs, tables, benches, machines, flagpoles, available clothes and so on.

Kerzhentsev's theories about collective work cut much deeper than Mgebrov's practice. The latter, working in a context that was not dissimilar from that of a production house – he worked against a strict deadline, for example – essentially moulded his actors in predetermined vocal and physical patterns. Kerzhentsev's theories, directed towards a studio and experimental culture which the Moscow Proletkult embraced, aimed at empowering the participants. He argued that putting mass scenes on the stage was not enough. Workers were, on the other hand, to be placed within the collective environment of a proletarian theatre production process through which they could embody a collective ethics or attitude, what Kerzhentsev described as 'not only inner affinity and a certain organization, but also unity of spirit, a sense of kinship, common tasks and, above all, a pervading thought for the best interests of the whole' (p. 131). The value of collective work, therefore, was directly experienced within the practice-based and hands-on environment of a theatre process.

Collective creation in the theatre functions when it eschews specialization, that hallmark of professional theatre where the roles of the actor, director, musician, dancer, make-up artist, costume designer, scenographer and playwright are clearly delineated and rarely interchangeable. Amateur theatre, on the other hand, upheld a different principle: participants were to involve themselves in all aspects of production. This approach, difficult though it was to put in practice, was unique to Kerzhentsev. It was seen as the basis on which to build a broader collectivism between the different arts. Kerzhentsev believed that the bourgeois system had created strife between the arts, whereas theatre should be the logical home for artists to bring their endeavours closer together. The Moscow Proletkult was attempting such a synthesis in its theatre, music and literature departments, though more was expected in the area of the formation of the new proletarian actor (see essay n. 23). An entry that speaks in some detail about the characteristics of this proletarian actor was written by Valentin Tikhonovich, an early interlocutor for *samodeiatel'nost'* (Mally 2000: 23), but here used to underline the improvisational, synthetic, class-based, collective and organizational qualities of the proletarian actor (see entry n. 28). These qualities render the proletarian actor a creator, independent of both the text and the director.

A practitioner whose work drew much from Kerzhentsev's theories was Valentin Smyshlaev. Smyshlaev was a member of the Moscow Art Theatre and its First Studio, where he was trained in Stanislavsky's system. Given that he also served as the director of the theatre of the Moscow Proletkult, it stands to reason to think that he was also aware of Kerzhentsev's theories.[18] In his essay 'Experiment in the staging of Émile Verhaeren's poem "Insurrection"' (n. 26), Smyshlaev evidenced a multifarious use of collective creativity. His collective work on this production should be read in parallel to his 1921/22 acting manual *Techniques to Process a Stage Performance*, in which he articulates the centrality of collective creation to theatre processes as follows:

> The stage-director should clearly understand that the essence of the creative work in the theatre is not in despotic methods, where pawn actors are placed on the stage as he likes, where they are made to speak in different voices for some reason that he prefers – no, the stage-director should make it clear that the form of art we call theatre can withstand art criticism only on condition that the creative work is strongly based on collectivism.

---

18 Smyshlaev's work has often been side-lined in the scholarship on Russian modernism. Conversely, I have argued that his work deserves much attention, especially when evaluated as a hybrid between a Stanislavsky-informed practice and the then current theories on collective practice, including Kerzhentsev's (see Aquilina 2020: 63–96).

> The essence and secret of theatre art is in this very collectivism, in the acting 'community', in the friendly comradely solidarity of all the individuals working in the collective.
>
> (Smyshlaev 1922: 11)

The use of group improvisation and collective discussion, decision-making and criticism nurtured this comradely environment. All these practices make an appearance in Smyshlaev's description of the work on 'Insurrection'.

'Insurrection' was staged on 6 November 1918 for the opening of the theatre of the Moscow Proletkult. The process going into the performance revolved around what the participants could bring to the proceedings. It was they, in fact, who chose to work on Verhaeren's poem, and not Smyshlaev. The work took off in a very visual manner, with the group creating a stage image based on the word 'chaos'. Group improvisations were then used to develop a basic scenario, which for reasons of space I did not reproduce here. The production process then oscillated between the voicing of personal recollections (from the participants, who had themselves experienced the events of 1917 and, in some cases, those of 1905) and the technical composition of the performance, expertise which Smyshlaev could provide given his background in professional theatre. Actors were also assisted in giving life to their roles. To do so they used what Smyshlaev called 'the method of today', where participants imagined a day in the life of the characters they were playing. The actors were also encouraged to write down these 'fantasies' or 'dreams'. The usefulness of 'the method of today' was substantial: instead of drawing from the participants' limited technical skill, it made the most of the actors' imaginative capabilities, underscored as those were by their own experiencing of the events. The mass and crowd scenes were also given attention, but instead of drilling the actors, as Mgebrov would have done, Smyshlaev again used collective improvisation to nourish the feeling of being in a crowd, 'that special feeling when one person in a crowd is linked to the whole group through some very special strings' (p. 155).

Both contemporary and current literature about amateur theatre evidence the widespread use of improvisation. This is hardly surprising, given that improvisation also resurfaces in Russian modernism as a tool to engender a collective attitude, develop acting skills and create performance material (Aquilina 2020: 80–3, 119–20). In the case of amateur theatre, the potential of improvisation to create dramatic texts or looser performance scenarios was particularly valued. Typical scenarios would involve brave workers sacrificing

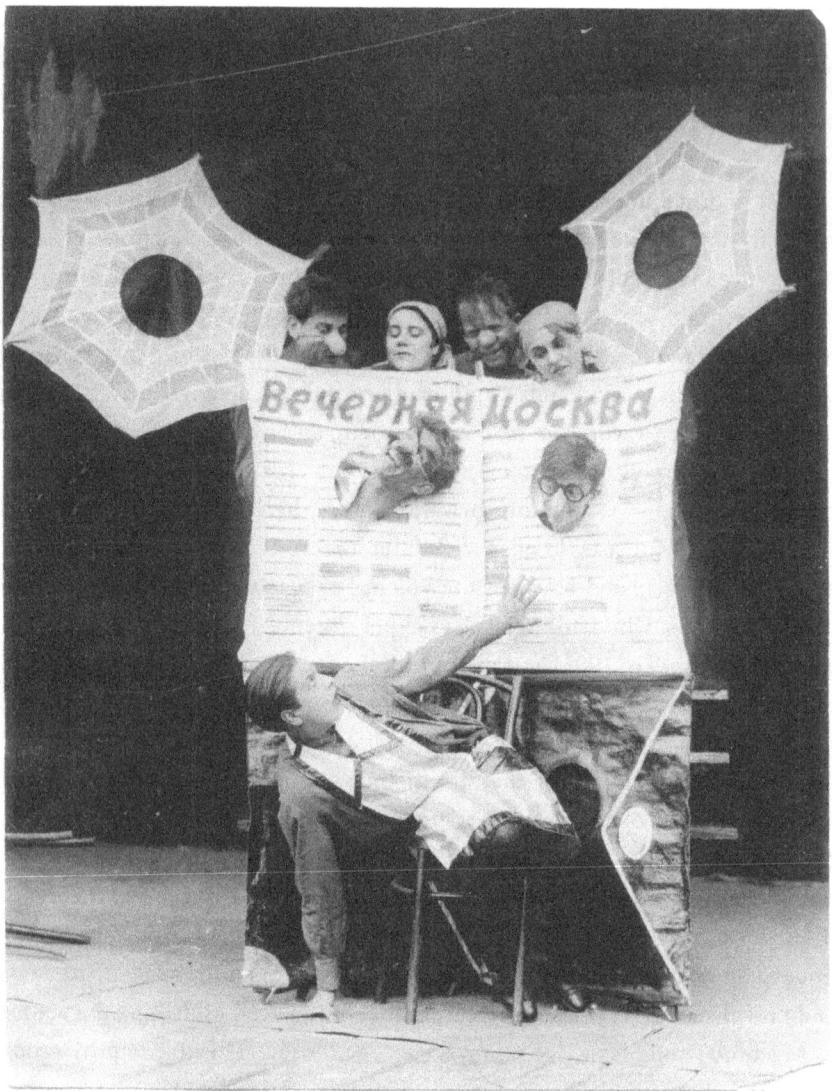

Figure 4 Blue Blouse performance, *At Our Institution*, undated. © A. A. Bakhrushin State Central Theatre Museum, Moscow.

themselves for the common good (Gourfinkel 1979: 138–9). Commedia dell'arte was at times invoked as a model (essay n. 14). Reflective of their developed understanding of theatre, theorists did not see improvisation as a free-for-all endeavour. Kerzhentsev, for instance, remarked that 'in contrast to conventional improvisation where the interpreters have complete freedom' (p. 160), improvisation within workers' groups needed proper guidance

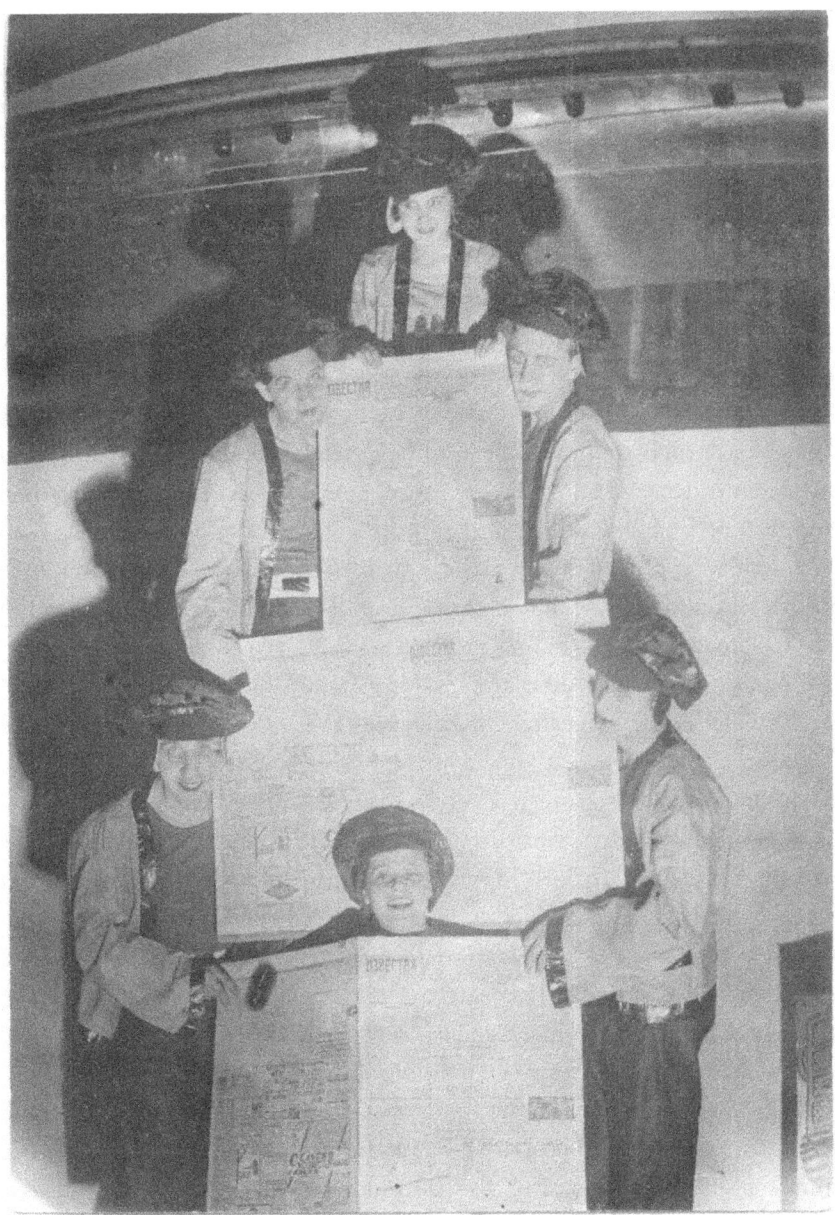

Figure 5 Blue Blouse performance, unnamed and undated. © A. A. Bakhrushin State Central Theatre Museum, Moscow.

to remain within pre-established parameters. The use of improvisation is represented here by Pavel Gaideburov's essay 'Creative Performance. The Improvisational Method of N. Skarskaia' (n. 25). Written in 1919, the text documents an improvisation-based method used at the Mobile-Popular Theatre, which Gaideburov founded as early as 1903 under the name of the Popular Theatre. (The method was also used at the Red Army Studio; see von Geldern 1993: 125.) Nadezhda Skarskaia, who gave the method its name, was Gaideburov's wife and co-founder of the Mobile-Popular Theatre. Gaideburov and his actors conducted classes at the Adult Education Department of the Narkompros, which is where the Skarskaia Method was again adopted. James von Geldern described this method as a 'step-by-step instruction that introduced neophytes [newcomers] to the essentials of theatre' (1993: 123). It stressed instinct, emotion and the release of innate creative energies rather than technical skill, on lines not dissimilar from the imaginative potential unleashed by Smyshlaev's method of today. The essay itself underlines the applicability of the Skarskaia Method within factories, 'evening schools for teenagers, and in various proletarian and children's clubs' (p. 145).

The Proletkult was described above as one bracket within the larger landscape of amateur theatre. Other entities had a similar position. Another bracket was the movement known as the Blue Blouse (Figures 4 and 5). The first Blue Blouse company was formed in 1923 under the auspices of the Moscow Institute of Journalism. It gained its name from the blue work overalls worn by its players. By 1927 it had transformed into a veritable movement made up of thousands of Blue Blouse groups, out of which maybe four or five were professional. The Blue Blouse manifested many of the qualities of amateur theatre, including its reactivity to surrounding contexts and crude aesthetics: 'Blue Blouse is a flexible, vivid, juicy, hard-hitting and mobile theatre, performing under any conditions' (Stourac and McCreery 1986: 3). And '[w]e are against bright beauty and realistic sets and decorations (no little birch trees and rivers), no clumsy props and set' (30). One example of the Blue Blouse aesthetics is given by Nina Gourfinkel – to stage a scene on a boat in *Stenka Razin*, a Blue Blouse collective simply sat down on the floor and mimed the action of rowing (Gourfinkel 1979: 131).

Blue Blouse groups specialized in living newspapers, which appeared in great numbers on the amateur stages of the mid-1920s.[19] As the name suggests,

---

[19] Robert Crane argued that '[w]ithout the thousands of ordinary people who used their material to become theatrical activists themselves, the Blue Blouse would have remained a fairly unremarkable variety theatre performing in Moscow's bars and cafeterias' (Crane 2011: 1).

living newspapers presented the news of the day that were typically found in newspapers. It embraced the use of dance, music, poetry, cabaret, circus skits, farce, satire, types and folk elements in order to enliven its presentations and 'to reach out to unsophisticated viewers, appealing to their emotions as well as their intellect' (Mally 2000: 70). The practice is described here in an eponymous essay (n. 29). This essay originally formed part of a larger collection titled *Iskusstvo v rabochem klube* (Art at the Workers' Clubs). The publication of that book in 1924, from which essays 34 and 35 here are also sourced, was coordinated by the Moscow Proletkult. Several authors contributed to the volume, although the authorship of specific essays remains unclear.[20]

The essay describes the living newspaper as an instrument of agitation, propaganda and social work. It is also reflective of the shifting attitudes towards amateur theatre. Initially lauded for its spontaneity, amateur theatre was by 1924 seen in urgent need of proper guidelines and concrete direction. Mally says that during the years of the Civil War the quality of amateur performers 'was usually indifferent, actors had little time to prepare and they had few props or costumes. But a polished presentation was not essential for audiences or actors – the important thing was that the performance was taking place at all' (Mally 2000: 11).[21] By 1924 a class-based participation was, however, not enough. Consequently, the living newspaper needed substantial modification because, notwithstanding its popularity, its 'quality stayed at a freezing point. [...] Instead of variety and anarchism in the organization a system was needed, with a definite and accurate structure' (p. 168). Concrete instructions were offered, including the use of directors to provide coherence, the adoption of clear dramatizations, the careful articulation of tasks and objectives and the application of slogans. In line with the desire to offer clear direction, the *Iskusstvo v rabochem klube* volume followed this theoretical text with a concrete example (Pletnev 1924: 72–95).

---

20 The introduction of the volume only gives the surnames of the authors in the following note: 'The parts [of the book] are worked as following: Theatre – by comrades Kravchunovsky, Neznamov, Zlatov, and Strekalov; Art – by comrades Zhmudsky and Tarabukin; Literature – comrades Sillov and Vinokur' (Pletnev 1924: 3). The collection was edited by Valerian Pletnev, which explains the reference used here.
21 Even on the pre-revolutionary scene, Swift (2002: 198) wrote that 'it was not the skill displayed in the performances but the fact that they were created by and for workers that seems to have mattered most'.

Will training help us raise standards?

To raise standards, training was universally recommended. Part Five, therefore, gathers essays that tackle the artistic formation of the workers. Smyshlaev's essay (n. 32) 'On the Work of the Theatre Department of the Moscow Proletkult' underlines the studio dimension of the institution. In contrast to the chaotic work of the first wave of amateur theatre, the work led by the Proletkult was to be carefully organized, at least in the capitals. For this reason, Smyshlaev suggested relevant boards and committees, and proper representation for the workers. The essay is also valuable because of the comprehensive training programme which it suggests at the end, comprising of a list of stage exercises in improvisation, sessions in plastic and decorative arts, diction, voice work, as well as site visits to museums and lessons in theatre history. Smyshlaev adds that these 'methods were primarily based on the work of the Moscow Art Theatre, which generally provide room for initiative and self-revelation' (p. 187). Smyshlaev already had experience in teaching workers, when he was invited in September 1917 to give acting lessons to a theatre group organized by the Union of the Youth of the Third International. This school provided free lessons in acting processes and related subjects, on the basis of Stanislavsky's system, which Smyshlaev noted was quite popular among the participants (Anrusenko 2004: 75–6, 94).

Amateur actors, infatuated as they typically are with the stage, often wish to sidestep training in order to plunge directly into performance work. This hurriedness is also mentioned in Smyshlaev's essay: '[T]he student-workers obviously and understandably would rather proceed directly to the creative work' (p. 187). Proper training and preparation, however, strengthen the creative work and, as a result, convince critics, students and audiences of its value. Training was important to consolidate a position within a very competitive artistic scene and at the Proletkult it worked in parallel with the rehearsals. A unique training method which Smyshlaev suggested was that of 'the second day performances', where actors not participating in a particular play would be given the chance to improvise their impressions of the production. This would maximize the impact of the actors' formation: apart from the direct acting experience garnered by the participants in the 'second day performances', the original actors would also receive feedback and criticism on their work.

Smyshlaev's concrete suggestions for a training programme (he even provided a timetable) contrast with the more visionary picture painted by Kerzhentsev.

In his extract, here titled 'Dramatic Laboratories' (n. 33), Kerzhentsev repeatedly underscored the importance of the proletarian and his formation actor. This was the first condition to create the proletarian theatre,

> because every theatre is based on the creative actor, in the same way that literature is based on poets, paint on painters, etc. We have to admit that at the moment we have no actor for the proletarian theatre. But we are expecting him and working to create him.
>
> (p. 189)

Tying with Smyshlaev's worry that amateur actors were strongly drawn by the lure of the stage, Kerzhentsev argued that the proletarian actor was to be created in the studio or laboratory rather than on the stage. He, in fact, spoke of dramatic circles and contrasted these to dramatic laboratories. The former were the rough-and-ready groups of the theatre epidemic which, under the leadership of some third-rate professional actor, turned to the production of shoddy entertainments for the workers to enjoy. Ilinsky described the productions of these circles as 'real hack work' (Ilinskii 1984: 164). Dramatic laboratories, on the other hand, were training-based entities intended to penetrate the circles to reform them from within. The training at the dramatic laboratories was to be led by professionals, Kerzhentsev now complied, drawn from the younger generation who were less ingrained in their habits and more open to the struggle of the proletarian class. The expected result was the creation of the proletarian actor, the performer who has developed his own technique, who was knowledgeable of the ABC of the theatre, who understood and accepted the demands made of him, and who could show initiative and autonomy. As expected, these laboratories were to be 'organized as a sort of artistic community, in which all members live a common and comradely life. The laboratory instructors are simply older comrades' (p. 192).

A curious essay is the one titled 'A Unified Studio of the Arts' (n. 34), which originally also appeared in the volume *Iskusstvo v rabochem klube*. The essay describes how workers' clubs should incorporate a studio offering broad training in a number of disciplines, including physical education, eurhythmics, voice training, verbal and written speech, choral singing and ideological subjects. This training was to be obligatory for all participants, to offer a basis on which more specialized work in theatre, art, music and literature could then take place. In line with the more prescriptive slant of the times in general and of the volume in particular, the essay also offers a concrete lesson plan, comprising of material directly emerging from these disciplines. Recommendations given include training in gymnastics, breathing, musical literacy, biomechanics, diction, stage exercises, how to mount living newspapers and so on. What is curious is that this training was expected to impact beyond the studio into the workers' everyday life:

> The goal of a workers' club is the harmonious and comprehensive development in its members of those conditions that are necessary for building a proletarian life. [...]
>
> **A number of disciplines are obligatory** for the artistic work of a club. This follows from the fact that in studying these disciplines the attention is not on a purely aesthetic upbringing and education, and not on specialization, but rather on their direct implementation in everyday life. (bold emphasis in the original; p. 193)

The aim of the Unified Studio, therefore, was to use artistic formation to improve the way that workers carried themselves and participated in everyday life, in terms of their verbal and written skills, psychomotor abilities, general health and reactivity to the surrounding environment. Training, therefore, formed human beings, proletarians in this case, predating what today we would refer to as transferable skills.[22]

In parallel to the Unified Studio, the volume *Iskusstvo v rabochem klube* also describes the theatre-oriented work carried out in the theatre sections of the clubs (essay n. 35). Workers' clubs carried an important role in the Soviet regime as loci for the creation of solidarity and communal sharing. As Gourfinkel wrote, the club 'teaches workers how to work together. They cultivate group spirit' (1979: 94). The clubs served three concrete tasks, namely as a space where workers could meet, gain information on work and state regulations and relax and entertain themselves. The essay argues that the theatre work at the clubs does not aim to create actors whose skill was on a par with that of the professionals. It rather sought to contribute in a theatrical manner to the life of the club, to its problems and tasks. Participants were trained in the use of theatre to celebrate revolutionary feasts, for instance, or in the production of trials or living newspapers in response to what was happening at the club or the world outside. This connection between the theatre work and the life and demands of

---

[22] A more extended discussion of the Unified Studio of the Arts is given elsewhere (in Aquilina 2020: 118–25), where theories on everyday life by Henri Lefebvre and on education by Robert M. Gagné are used to substantiate the existence of a line or transmission channel between artistic training and everyday life. See also Aquilina (2012: especially 305–8).

the club was considered necessary. Otherwise, the training would run the risk of becoming an end in itself. In view of this, appeals to transform the classes into a separate theatre or any sort of conservatoire or school were to be resisted.

The essay ends with some suggestions for the training programme. The emphasis here was on physical training, not only because 'in the theatre, the material is the actor's body and voice' (p. 202), but also because physical flexibility and endurance were considered basic qualities for any kind of work. This physical emphasis contrasts with what is described as the Moscow Art Theatre's 'system of psychological naturalism' and its emphasis on 'experiences'. Meyerhold's biomechanics provided an alternative that was rooted in the construction and analysis of movement. As a result, the training featured eurhythmics, acrobatics, voice work and an exposure to theatre forms. Stage exercises and improvisations were also recommended to create dramatizations, but plastiques were rejected because of their emphasis on beauty rather than expediency.

Conclusion

The volume *Iskusstvo v rabochem klube* offered other concrete examples and recommendations explicating the directions which theatre work at the clubs was to take. For instance, two examples of agit-trials are given. Agit-trials dramatized mock events as a way of exalting revolutionary heroes and condemning the enemies of the Revolution. They first appeared during the theatre epidemic years but reached the height of their popularity in the mid-1920s. Both individuals and concepts, like Fascism, could be put on trial (Pletnev 1924: 100–39). Again, lack of space does not allow me to reproduce these examples. However, I would like to underline that the prescriptive rather than visionary tone of the essays in the *Iskusstvo v rabochem klube* volume, in addition to the concrete examples, well-defined guidelines and clear programmes given, shows that amateur theatre in the second part of the 1920s was rapidly changing. From a space for self-activation, choice-making and collective creativity, amateur theatre became a tool for cultural programming. The story of amateur theatre in the first ten years or so after the Revolution, in fact, is a story where overseers of amateur theatres 'took all possible pains to determine that amateur art would become methodical, controllable, and regulated, eliminating any stark contrast with the professional' (Mally 2000: 15). Mally says this about the scene at the beginning of the 1930s, but certainly concrete inroads towards such regulation had already been made during the second half of the 1920s.

As an Epilogue, I chose to end this collection with an extract from a national conference on theatre convened by the Agitprop Division of the Communist Party in the spring of 1927. Ostensibly, the conference was about the role of professional theatre, but amateur theatre also received a substantial amount of coverage because of its tight link with the working masses. By then, amateur theatre was often referred to as 'club scene' or 'club theatre'. The main intervention on club theatres was given by Nikolai Evreinov (no relation to the famous director Nikolai Nikolaevich Evreinov, author of the book *The Theatre in Life* and director of the Ancient Theatre). I have edited Evreinov's contribution to about half of its original length in order to underscore the status which amateur theatre carried at the time. Most revealingly, and in line with the more prescriptive attitude of the second half of the 1920s, the use of improvisation to create proletarian plays and performances had vanished. The repertoire of the clubs, in fact, was expected to feature adaptions of full-length plays and formally written, i.e. already vetted, play texts, written specifically for the club stages. Evreinov manifested an even more prescriptive attitude towards amateur work in the last part of his intervention, where he offered several guidelines through which club theatres were to improve their work. What underscored these guidelines was obvious – get professional help – giving a denouement to early post-revolutionary amateur and proletarian theatre which Kerzhentsev, Pletnev, Smyshlaev and others writing ten years before would not have wished for.

Prologue

Platon Kerzhentsev

Source: *Revoliutsiia i teatr*, 1918, sections from chapter 1, pp. 5–12

Which theatre did the Soviet government inherit? First of all, there were the governmental, former Imperial Theatres: two for opera, two for drama and a French theatre. In the capital there were a few grand theatres representative of a high bourgeois culture, which were also known abroad. In the provinces there are many good theatre troupes.

All theatres, private and governmental, show signs of tiredness, of dated and fading stamps. The most famous theatre among these (the Moscow Art Theatre) has moved away from its experimentation to a classic, calmly balanced stage. Fresh innovations (Komissarzhevsky's studio,[1] the Kamerny Theatre,[2] Evreinov's[3] experience, Meyerhold's productions) showed a definite bias towards form, towards 'theatricality'. At the same time, and more than ever, the total isolation of the best theatres from the masses was felt.

Theatre audiences became isolated in the narrow circle of the 'top ten thousand'. Going to the opera, to the Studio of the Art Theatre, or to some other interesting play became a rare privilege for the richest and for the chosen few.

The Russian theatre, which had once flashed in front of the whole world with its achievements, has now turned into a dead end that has no way out. Talk of a 'theatre crisis', 'the death of the theatre', etc., started once more.

[…]

---

1 For a discussion about this studio see Pitches (2019: 95–6).
2 The Kamerny Theatre was a chamber theatre at the centre of Russian modernism and avant-garde. It opened in Moscow under the direction of Alexander Tairov (1885–1950). For more information see Worrall (1989: 15–75).
3 Presumably this is a reference to the work of Nikolai Evreinov (1879–1953; no relation to the Nikolai Evreinov featured in the epilogue of the book). In the pre-revolutionary years Evreinov had made a name with his stagings of Medieval (1907) and Spanish (1911) drama (Leach 1994: 11–16). In 1920 he was responsible for the staging of the mass spectacle *The Storming of the Winter Palace* in Petrograd.

Soviet workers identified three initial tasks: safeguarding proven theatrical achievements; encouraging new searches; and involving the masses in the theatre.

[...]

At last, a lot of attention has been given to the democratization of the theatre, in the sense of bringing it to the masses. The doors of the theatres were for the first time opened to the proletariat, and Moscow Art Theatre's plays as well as those of other good theatres started to be shown in the regions or, if remaining at the centre, to the workers.[4]

The artists themselves, who initially were often sceptical of the new audience, quickly got convinced that the new spectators are much more grateful, much more vibrant, and truly relate to the theatre more than the previous bourgeois spectators ever did.

However, there is no guarantee that the masses will indeed be introduced to the theatre. There is no guarantee that the Revolution will create its own new and particular theatre. It is important to see the creative appearance of a new theatre class, of new social groups.

The workers' and peasants' desire to create their own theatre emerged strongly after October. Everyone who has been observing their lives can tell of the number of independent drama studios which emerged, studios which are working on theatre plays even though they are without any guidance. Improvisations or plays created and written by the participants are typical of these studios.

The workers' desire to create their own theatre indicated their instinctive dissatisfaction with the form and content of bourgeois theatre.

---

[4] Stanislavsky spoke about the difficulties encountered during these early performances to the proletariat, but also of the sharp attention which the workers brought with them (Stanislavski 2008: 324–8).

Part One

Aims and Objectives

'The Proletariat and Art'

Anatoly Lunacharsky

Source: *Proletarskaia kul'tura*, no. 2, 1918, pp. 23–4

1. Art can be called universal to all mankind only when the value of its masterpieces, throughout the centuries and of all nations, becomes the shared contents of mankind's culture.
2. But nobody can deny the clear differences in the arts of the various ages and nations.
3. We, Marxists, know that these differences are explained not by vague ideas – national spirit, century or climate – but through a social order that is based on class relations.
4. Sometimes art is a clear expression of the ideology of a particular class, and sometimes it experiences the cross-cutting influence of several classes; class analysis of a work of art is the most fruitful method for its, i.e. the work of art's, research.
5. The art of one class is not always the same. Typical examples in the evolution of a class' art include the germ, the period of aspiration, classicism, realism, romanticism of despair, mysticism.
6. All stages in the evolution of the art of a particular class are coloured with that class' psychology.
7. The coming of proletarian art emerges from these points.
8. The independence of proletarian art is not expressed in artificial originality. It suggests the acquaintance with all kinds of art of the previous cultures.
9. The intelligentsia is already playing a big part in the birth of proletarian art by creating a series of transitional works.

'The Proletariat and Art'

Resolutions proposed at the First All-Russian Conference of Proletarian Cultural and Educational Organizations[1]

Alexander Bogdanov

Source: *Proletarskaia kul'tura*, no. 5, 1918. Original downloaded from https://document.wikireading.ru/10052 [accessed 15 September 2019]

1. Art organizes social experience through living images, not only in the field of cognition, but also in the field of feelings and aspirations. As a result of this, it is the most powerful tool for organizing collective forces, in a class society where the forces are class forces.
2. The proletariat needs its own class art for the organization of its forces in social work, struggle and construction. The spirit of this art is labour collectivism: it perceives and reflects the world from the point of view of the labour collective and expresses the connection with its feelings, its struggle and its creative will.
3. The treasures of old art should not be accepted passively. If that happens, they would educate the working class in the spirit of the culture of the ruling classes and thereby in the spirit of submission to the structure of the life that created them. The proletariat must critically take the treasures of old art, in its new interpretation, and reveal their hidden collective foundations and their organizational meaning. Then they will become a precious legacy for the proletariat, a weapon in its struggle against the same old world that created them and an instrument in the creation of the new world. The transmission of this artistic heritage must be carried out by proletarian criticism.
4. All organizations, all institutions dedicated to the development of the new art and the new criticism, should be built on comradely cooperation, which directly educates their workers towards the direction of the socialist ideal.

Adopted unanimously with 1 abstention.
20 September 1918

---

1 For a detailed discussion about the conference see Mally 1990: 45–50. Substantial effort went into the organization of the conference, which was held in Moscow and attended by some 330 delegates and 234 guests, most of whom hailed from working-class organizations. In retrospect, much of the debate taking place at the conference was typical of the times and the scene. Delegates discussed the autonomy of the Proletkult (a matter also raised by Lunacharsky in his essay 'Proletkult and Soviet cultural work', reproduced here), the need for a proletarian science, organizational and financial matters, the relationship between art and the workers and so on. A governing board for the national Proletkult was also elected. Transcripts from the conference were published by the Moscow Proletkult in 1918.

'The Proletkult and Soviet Cultural Work'

Anatoly Lunacharsky

Source: *Proletarskaia kul'tura*, no. 7-8, April–May 1919, pp. 1-3

When a few of my comrades and I organized a conference on questions of proletarian culture, a few days before the revolution, I pictured the meaning and role of the organization which would come out of the conference, and which was later to be called Proletkult, quite differently from how the organization eventually developed.[1]

At that time the government was purely bourgeois,[2] and in the beginning the proletariat had to find its own cultural ways through a non-governmental, and partly anti-government, initiative.

The young organization had important aims: to raise the bar of the mental, ethical and aesthetical levels of proletarian education, while aiming at independent creative work. It aimed at creating proletarian class standards in such areas, standards which are different from the rest.

From the very beginning I was pointing out a complete parallelism: the party – in the political area; the professional unions – in economy; the Proletkult – in the cultural area.

Now everything has changed. We have to think carefully. On one side, what should be the relations of the Communist Party towards the Soviet government? What are the laws that govern the professional relationship between the Sovnarkhoz[3] and the other economic authorities of the Soviet state? What is the borderline between the Proletkult on one side and the Narkompros on the other?

I will not discuss these first two questions now. I will just mention that no one thinks of finding the party redundant or wishes to replace it by having a merger between the Central Committee and the Sovnarkom (Soviet National

---

1 Lunacharsky is here referring to a conference of proletarian cultural organizations that took place in Petrograd the week before the storming of the Winter Palace. The conference delegates 'met to discuss the role of fine arts and education in the working-class movement' (Mally 1990: 29). The role of the intellectuals proved a particularly sticky point, foreshadowing a broader debate on the role of pre-revolutionary professionals and art that would be picked upon by Fyodor Kalinin, Valerian Pletnev and Platon Kerzhentsev, among others (see Part Two). The definition of proletarian culture was an even more contentious point, which created a split in the conference. For more information about the conference see Mally (1990: 26-31).
2 This is a reference to the Provisional Government led by Alexander Kerensky.
3 Sovnarkhoz, usually translated as Regional Economic Soviet, was the organization which managed a particular economic region. Every Sovnarkhoz was subordinated to the Supreme Soviet of the National Economy.

Committee),[4] a presidium of the *Central Executive Committee or anything of such kind.* Nobody even thinks of saying that the party and the Soviet government lead parallel work.

It must be clear to everyone. That is the way it is, that is the way it is supposed to be, that this work is done by the conscious communist proletariat, the vital parts of which are currently both the Soviet party and the Soviet power.

The proletariat, being in control of the government and in possession of the entire cultural heritage of the country, must naturally create agencies which ensure that schools of all types, libraries, museums, theatres, concerts, exhibitions, magazines, etc., are turned into instruments of proletarian enlightenment.

What is understood by this term: 'proletarian enlightenment'?

It means, first, the distribution of the universal values of science and art, without which one cannot be considered a knowledgeable person, without which a proletarian remains a barbarian, and without which he will be unable to efficiently wield either the power or the instruments of production which he has conquered.

This is a gigantic task.

And we must add another task: we must also assign the title of proletarian enlightenment to the process of spreading pure proletarian ideas, first to the poorly educated segments within the proletariat itself, then to the masses of peasants and the segment of the population involved in physical labour and, finally, to the intellectuals.

Does the proletariat have an undisputed ideological heritage?

Yes, in some areas, it has. The most developed parts of Marxism, especially in the areas of sociology and economics, less so in the areas of history and philosophy, can currently compete for their rightful place, *the principal place*, in universities, libraries, etc.

The backbone of our practical, political programme is our marvellous heritage, which must be made known to everyone through our political propaganda. Therefore, it must be conducted through all government agencies.

However, even if we consider all these purely proletarian elements, which the government digests and delivers to the masses, we will see that they still only represent a relatively small fraction of the contents of a state cultural programme.

Who can deny then that when teaching science, for example, we must use all our experience? Perhaps, we will be able to slightly alter the methods of education, but even that task is very time-consuming.

---

4 The Sovnarkom was a government institution formed soon after the October Revolution. It amounted to the executive committee of Bolshevik ministers. For detailed information see Rigby (1979).

In the area of art, we must never, under any circumstance, let the proletariat be ignorant of all the wonderful products of human genius.

Here we come across two extremes, about which we must definitely warn any proletarian agents who begin work in state culture.

There are people who believe that any distribution of 'old' science and 'old' art is an indulgence of bourgeois tastes, a cultural curse and the contamination of a young socialist organism with the blood of rotting junk.

There are relatively few radical representatives of this delusion. However, the harm which they bring could be great. It should also be noted that some hardworking followers of proletarian culture needlessly whine in unison with the futurists on the physical annihilation of all old culture and that the tempo of the masses should be restricted. This is claimed through unconvincing experiments to which their own art is reduced.

No, I repeat for the thousandth time that the proletariat must be *armed with the entirety of human education*. The proletariat is a historical class. It must go forward because of its past.

To discard the science and art of the past because of their bourgeois roots is as absurd as dropping machines in the factories or railways because of the same reason.

The other extreme is when those people who are getting involved in scientific and artistic cultural work claim that the real proletarian work is achieved by adding some Marxist sociology and communist programme and that this will get us what we are looking for.

We must resist this at all times. The great proletarian class will in time upgrade culture from top to bottom. It will establish its majestic style, which will be reflected in all areas of art. It will insert its own soul into it. The proletariat will change the very structure of science. Even now we can already predict which way its methodology will be heading.

If we made the government spread only new things, solely proletarian things, we would collapse the proletariat into barbarism. We would cut away its roots, and nobody would be surprised if the fruits of proletarian creation in the areas of science and art turn out frail and stunted.

The government's task is to spread truly indisputable knowledge, which the proletariat has so far conquered in only few areas that are directly related to its struggle, and to fertilize the proletariat field with that rich material which it inherits.

However, if after this we claimed indifference to *independent proletarian requests*, to the proletariat's efforts to create their own art forms and their own ways in science, then we would be making a most unfortunate mistake.

Thus, both of these tasks are clearly and specifically highlighted. The Proletkult must, in no instance, consider completed the first sprouts of proletarian art and proletarian thought (except for the figures of scientific socialism). In no way should it attempt to replace previous works of art with these first sprouts. Similarly, its agencies should not concern themselves with familiarizing the entire sphere of 'human education'. In the first case it would demonstrate a most careless case of arrogance, which must be left entirely to the futurists. In the second, it would intrude into its own work the other side of its struggle, the nationwide work of the state.

Therefore, the Proletkult must concentrate all its attention on studio work; on outlining and supporting original talents among proletarians; on creating guilds for writers, artists, working-class scientists; on the creation of various studios and living organizations in all areas of physical and spiritual culture, with the indispensable goal of developing those independent seeds of freedom which can be found in a proletarian's soul.

A proletarian or, more accurately, a worker-peasant government, cannot treat these types of young organizations without the greatest trust and greatest care since, with time, these kinds of organizations will spread the light and warmth which will, eventually, significantly outshine everything inherited by us so far. This will create, within culture, that new world which we founded in politics and which we made possible in economics.

Therefore, I believe that the aspirations of, for example, the Board of Education of the Mossovet[5] to destroy the Moscow Proletkult are entirely illegitimate. Moreover, the many opposing viewpoints give it no chance of success. It would be a complete absurdity to forbid Moscow's proletariat the same organization for the independent development of cultural values which is now available in almost every city. Not to mention that destroying this thriving and fertile Proletkult is, fortunately, too big a task for the Mossovet.[6]

---

5 The Mossovet was the name given to the Moscow City government during the Soviet period.
6 On further references to the debates surrounding the Proletkult see Platon Kerzhentsev's essay 'The Proletkult – Organisation of Proletarian Amateur Performances', also in Part One.

'Ways towards a Proletarian Culture'

Alexander Bogdanov

Source: *Proletarskaia kul'tura*, 1920, no. 15–6. Original downloaded from https://document.wikireading.ru/10054 [accessed 20 September 2019]

Theses

1. Creativity of all kinds – technical, socio-economic, political, daily, scientific, artistic – is a type of work and therefore also consists in organizing (or disorganizing) human efforts. This is nothing but labour, the product of which is not a reproduction of the finished sample, but something 'new'. There is not, and can never be, a strict border between creativity and simple labour; not only are there all the transitional stages, but often one cannot even say with certainty which of the two designations is more applicable.

Human labour, always relying on collective experience and using collectively worked-out methods, is in this sense always collective, no matter how narrow its individual aims and its external and indirect forms are (that is when it is the work of one person and only for himself). Such is creativity.

Creativity is the highest, most complex form of labour. Therefore, its methods come from labour methods.

The old world was not aware of this general social nature of work and creativity, nor was it aware of the connection between their methods. It dressed creativity with a mysterious fetishism.

2. All methods of labour – and with it creativity – lie within the same framework. Its first phase is a combining effort; the second is the selection of its results, the elimination of what is inappropriate. In 'physical' work material things are combined; in the 'spiritual', images are, but as the latest psychophysiology shows, the nature of the efforts that combine and select is one and the same, known as neuromuscular.

Creativity combines materials anew, not according to the usual pattern, which leads to the selection of more complex and more intense images. The combination and selection of images are incomparably easier and faster than that of material things. Therefore, creativity often proceeds in the form of 'spiritual' labour, but by no means exclusively so. Almost all 'random' and 'inconspicuous' discoveries were obtained by the method of selection of material combinations and not through preliminary combination and selection of images.

3. The methods of proletarian creativity have their basis in the methods of proletarian labour, that is, the type of work that is characteristic of workers in the newest large-scale industry.

The features of this type are (1) the combination of elements of 'physical' and 'spiritual' labour and (2) a visible, not hidden or masked, collectivism as its very form. The first depends on the scientific nature of the latest technology, in particular on the transferral of the mechanical side of effort to the machine: the worker is increasingly becoming the 'leader' of iron slaves, and his work, in an increasing proportion, is reduced to 'spiritual' efforts – attention, consideration, control, initiative and the role of muscular tension are relatively reduced. The second depends on the concentration of labour in mass cooperation and on the convergence of specialized types of labour by the power of machine production, which increasingly transfers the direct, physical specialization of workers to machines. The objective and subjective uniformity of labour increases, destroying the partitions between workers, and with this uniformity, the actual compatibility of labour becomes the basis of comradely, that is, consciously collective relations between the workers. These relations, with their results – mutual understanding, mutual sympathy and the desire to act together at the same time – are expanding, going beyond the factory, the profession, the production, to the working class on a national and then global scale. The collectivism of humanity's struggle with nature is recognized.

4. Thus, the methods of proletarian labour are developing into *a monism* and *conscious collectivism*. Naturally, the methods of proletarian creativity are also developing in the same direction.[1]

5. These features have already expressed themselves clearly in those areas where proletarian creativity has so far been manifested, primarily in economics, in the political struggle and in scientific thinking. In the first two areas, this constantly manifested itself in the unity between the structure of the organizations which

---

1 Conscious collective work as the basis of proletarian theatre was picked up markedly by Platon Kerzhentsev, both as a theoretical framework and also as tentative practical method for the workers to create their own performance work. Collective creative work eschews professionalism, nourishes an all-round performer and involves the future audience in the production process (see the essay 'Collective Creation in the Theatre', in Part Four). Robert Leach (1994: 22–5) identifies Kerzhentsev as the one who more than anyone else sought to transfer Bogdanov's ideas expressed here to amateur theatre.

the proletariat created – the party, the professional and the cooperative, which all showed the same type, the same comradely, consciously collective principle. It was also reflected in the development of their programmes, which in all of them steadily gravitated towards one ideal, namely the socialist one. In science and philosophy, Marxism was the embodiment of both the monism of the method and the consciously collective tendency. Further development, on the basis of the same methods, should develop a universal organizational science, a monism uniting all the organizational experience of mankind in its social work and struggle.

6. In the field of domestic creativity, since it goes beyond the limits of economic and political struggle, the proletariat has so far proceeded spontaneously, but still along the same lines. This is evidenced by the development of the proletarian family, from the authoritarian structure of the peasant, from philistine to comradely relations, and the universally established proletarian form of politeness, that is 'comrade'. Since this work will continue to be conscious, it is quite obvious that its methods will be imbued with the same principles: it will be the work of a harmoniously holistic, consciously collective life.

7. In the field of artistic creation, the old culture is characterized by the uncertainty and unconsciousness of its methods ('inspiration', etc.), their isolation from the methods of labour, and from the creative methods in other areas. Although the proletariat is still taking its first steps, the general tendencies characteristic of its art are already clearly outlined. Monism affects the desire to merge art with working life, to make art an instrument of active aesthetic transformation along the entire line. Collectivism, at first spontaneous, and then more conscious, appears vividly in the content of artistic works and even in the form of an artistic perception of life, illuminating the image not only of human life, but also of nature: nature, as a field of collective labour; its connections and harmonies are like embryos and prototypes of collective organization.

8. The technical methods of old art developed separately from the methods seen in other sphere of life – the technique of proletarian art must consciously seek and use all those methods and materials. For example, photography, stereography, motion picture, colours, phonography, etc., must find their specific place as new means in the system of artistic production. It follows from the principle of monism of methods that there cannot be methods of practice and science that do not find a direct or indirect application in art, and vice versa.

9. Conscious collectivism transforms the whole meaning of the artist's work, giving it new stimuli. The artist of past times saw in his work the revelation of his own personality; the new artist will understand and feel that a great whole is being created in and through his art, and this whole is the collective. For the former, originality is an expression of the self-worth of his 'I', a means of exaltation; for the second, it means a deep and wide capture of collective experience. Originality becomes an expression of its contribution to the active participation in the work and development of the life of the collective. The first can half-consciously strive for life's truth – or evade it; the second must be aware that truth, that objectivity, supports the collective in its work and struggle. The former may or may not appreciate artistic clarity; for the second, art is nothing more than accessibility to the collective, in which there is a living sense of the artist's efforts.

10. The awareness of collectivism, the deepening of the mutual understanding of people and the connection of feelings between them will make possible the development of direct collectivism in creativity, that is, the direct cooperation in it of the many, up to the level of the mass. This will be incomparably wider than what it has been till now.

11. In the art of the past, as in its science, there were a lot of hidden elements of collectivism. Opening them, proletarian criticism enables the creative perception of the best works of the old culture. These are seen in a new light, leading to an enormous enrichment of values.

12. The main difference between the new creativity and the former one is that now, for the first time, it understands itself and its role in life.

'The Proletkult – Organization of Proletarian Amateur Performances'

Platon Kerzhentsev

Source: *Proletarskaia kul'tura*, no. 1, 1918, pp. 7–8

The Proletkult has not been around for long – its work is only just now getting better – and yet there are people who are already against the existence of this organization, people who have their doubts regarding the expediency and necessity of its work. There is a controversy going on around the Proletkult. It is argued about. It is denied or not recognized. It is not believed in.

However, while listening even vaguely to these attacks and denials, one will notice the complete unfamiliarity which the Proletkult's opponents have with its tasks, plans, hopes and potential. In fact, a large fraction of these objections against the existence of Proletkult is based on this simple unfamiliarity with the question at hand.

Into this category falls the common question: why should the Proletkult even exist, when all its concerns for a proletarian school, literature, science and tasks are already performed by the Ministry of Enlightenment[1] and countless other cultural and educational Soviet organizations?

This argument only touches the formal, external side of the question and ignores completely the heart of the problem. Yes, of course, the Proletkult is working and will continue working in the same area of education, in matters that are scholarly, literary, scientific, theatrical, etc., but its approach, its methods, its tasks, differ considerably from the methods of other cultural and educational organizations and agencies of all kinds.

Leaving aside a full and detailed description of the Proletkult's tasks (our readers can find this information further on in our journal), I will name one of the typical features of its method. The Proletkult strives to awaken proletarian creation in the areas of science and art and to help with its detection. It wants to find and establish the sprouts of a new culture which have already made their way through the thickness of the old bourgeois cultural layer. Amateur performances of the masses are taken as the foundation of its work.

---

1 The People's Commissariat for Enlightenment, known as the Narkompros and headed by Anatoly Lunacharsky.

In this sense, it should be said that proletarian art attracts special and exclusive attention from the Proletkult, and artistic beginnings are foundational to its work. Amateur products of the masses in the area of creating new cultural values guarantee the strength of a new proletarian culture.

Naturally, the expression 'proletarian culture' should not be taken in the narrow sense which the opponents of the Proletkult attribute it. We do not think that proletarian culture, art or science can solely be the creative product of the proletariat. This ordinary and totally false interpretation is analogous to the misconception that was once shared, that the political and sociological ideology of the proletarian, which only fulfils proletarian tasks, appears only in the minds of the workers. Just like the ideology of the working class, socialism was created by those who came from the bourgeois class but who took the side of the proletarians. In the creation of a new proletarian culture, a large part of the work can be done by the representatives of other classes who take on the ideology of the working masses.

Viewing cultural work as an endeavour that requires creativity and independence, the Proletkult performs its actions in completely different and special ways. For example, what happens at other cultural-educational organizations or school sections in the area of literature?

They introduce works of literature from past centuries; they highlight (maybe even from a class point of view) the evolution of elegant literature; they give a sociological and an artistic analysis of contemporary literature. The Proletkult wants to do something completely different. It seeks to discover and unite those writers, mainly from proletarian circles, who create themselves elegant literature in the spirit of a new socialist culture.

We must begin to try and create the conditions for artistic creation and prevent the dying out of those sprouts which, perhaps, are still weak, but which can develop, grow strong and produce exceptional valuables. It is precisely for these goals that the Proletkult will have to create clubs for poets and writers, in which they will be working on creating a new art in a friendly cooperative and critical environment. The best works will be published in the form of compilations and almanacs, or printed in magazines. Thus, a kind of literary studio will emerge, the kind of school of art which the bourgeois order knows nothing about.

Similar cultural cells, which unite all those who want to fulfil their aspirations in creating a new culture, will appear in other fields as well. The Proletkult School of Art should not be a place for the sole teaching of drawing. All those who seek a new art that is close to the proletariat in spirit, and those who create it, will be united under its roof. The head of the art department will look for all those workers who devote their spare time to drawing or who spend long hours in art galleries. They will help the vague instinct of art in the masses to emerge in the areas of painting, sculpture and architecture.

The Proletkult's theatre department does not focus solely on the familiarization of the working-class suburbs with model plays of a theatre or a studio. It will not create troupes of professional actors who would produce socialist or revolutionary plays. This task should be handled by the government, by the artistic education department of the Soviet and other similar organizations. The Proletkult will unite the activity of the proletarian drama clubs and help dramaturges from the working classes find new forms and content for the upcoming socialist theatre.

Thus, the Proletkult will use the creative beginnings of amateur performances as the foundation for all its fields of work. It will have to create the context in which anyone who wants to exercise his creative instinct in the areas of science, literature, theatre, school, etc., can find the opportunity to create freely and work in a friendly and amicable environment.

No other organization puts this as its task.

Obviously, the creative work to create a new culture cannot proceed at too quick a pace, and it will not be able to give immediate and striking results.[2] The enemies of the Proletkult will have many opportunities to gloat at the alleged fruitlessness and obscurity of the work carried in the creation of the new culture. However, this gloating will not embarrass those who unite around this new organization. The creative path is a difficult one, but it leads to solid and joyful results.

Through hard, methodical work, the Proletkult will create a new cadre of workers around itself and produce the values of the new culture which will be included in the treasury of time.

---

2 For a longer discussion about the prolonged time necessary to develop a new culture see Valerian Pletnev's essay in Part Two 'On professionalism'.

'Craving the Stage'

Nikolai Lvov

Source: *Vestnik Teatra*, no. 56, 1919, p. 8

At one point, Evreinov compared the stage to sticky paper.[1] Inexperienced young men and women are drawn to the stage like flies who, on experiencing its intoxicating charm, can no longer leave the theatre, escape or leave from its tenacious embrace.

The craving for the stage is usually explained as a wide-spreading folly, a caprice of the bored bourgeois intelligentsia: they have had enough of everything in life and all of its pleasures. The disappointed young man aspires to the theatre, to the stage, in order to enter the circle of artistic bohemian life, to find new impressions for their frayed nerves.

But only the blind enemy of the theatre can say this, in turn resolving in a superficial manner a complex psychological question. The pull towards theatre is rooted much deeper than that in the very nature of man.

The desire to experience the new, and to feel previously unexplored feelings, is very natural – to transfer into someone else's image, to live someone else's life, in another world, which you have created during the stage transformation and in the midst of electrical lamps. Such is the strong pull which keeps a person in the theatre.

And now, when new ideas have been thrown among the broad masses of the people, when new opportunities for life have opened for them, now an unrestrained rush to the stage immediately inflamed these classes. At the theatre they find an outlet for their aspirations, for a different and brighter life. They have the opportunity to broaden their spiritual world with new and unexplored experiences.

A person witnesses this craving for the stage as soon as he comes close to a new actor, a new theatre maker.

---

1 Lvov is probably here making reference to the director Nikolai Nikolaevich Evreinov, famous for experiments in symbolism and eventual author of the book *The Theatre in Life* (1927); see also footnote in Prologue. This Evreinov bears no relation to the other Nikolai Evreinov, who in 1927 was at the head of the national cultural division which organized an important theatre conference on the then current state of Soviet theatre. Material from Evreinov's contribution at that conference appears in the Epilogue.

Here are the exams at the Proletkult Theatre Studio. A young girl wearing a kerchief reads in a timid voice the fable *The Monkey and the Glasses*.[2] The teacher asks this simple question: 'Have you ever done anything in the studio before?' She answers: 'No, I am just two weeks in from the village. It was there that I performed in plays.'

Sometimes from the provinces, from the backwoods, people come to Moscow with one purpose: to train in the theatre arts.

Such a newcomer has not known for a long time where exactly he wants to go. He does not understand the difference between a theatre, a school and classes with an instructor. Finally, one phrase resolves all doubts of the Muscovite to whom the newcomer has turned for instruction: 'I want to play on the stage.' Here is his dream. That's why he left his home and rushed headlong to Moscow, not fearing hunger and cold.

And here is another example. Not long ago, a letter arrived in Moscow, to the address of the 'troupe of theatre lovers'. The letter was saturated with the author's passionate desire to perform in the theatre. This letter is so curious that it should be quoted in full:

> I humbly ask the troupe of theatre lovers if it is possible to accept me into your troupe. I am currently 32 years old [...], my physique is correct, but the head is small. I am married by civil marriage to a citizen. She is from the Yaroslavl region and of a small stature. I studied at the local school, and after graduation I went into the military.
>
> During and after the military training, I participated for about six years in performances, acting roles of significant complexity.
>
> Is there any material that you need from me? Any documents or identification card? Please describe your conditions for acceptance into the troupe and how one can get authorization to travel to your company of comrades. In solidarity, N.

The above letter is, of course, a curiosity. But there are parts of it that are very sincere and touching, showing how strong the craving for the stage is in such obscure 'theatre lovers'.

And this 'theatre lover' is not alone. In the provincial corners, in the provincial wilderness, languishing in everyday life, such 'theatre lovers' sit and dream of a bright life which they can experience only on the stage.

---

2   This popular early nineteenth-century fable tells the story of a monkey with eyesight that was getting worse and worse with age. The monkey heard that glasses could solve this problem, but on getting a pair it finds itself unable to use them properly. In frustration, the monkey breaks the glasses. See https://www.masteryourrussian.com/russian-fables/ [accessed 1 February 2020].

'Socialist Theatre in the Years of the Revolution'

Piotr Kogan

Source: *Vestnik Teatra*, no. 40, 1919, pp. 3–4

'What does the history of ideas prove, if not that mental activity is transformed along with the material?'

These are the unforgettable words of the *Communist Manifesto* which during these two years of the Revolution inspired all the ideologists of proletarian culture. A radical breakdown of material relations is taking place before our eyes. It must lead to a spiritual transformation. A new science must come. The emergence of a new art is inevitable, and with it the birth of a new theatre.

During the honeymoon of our Revolution, problems were posed on a large scale. 'The whole socialist culture is a new branch of the great tree of universal human culture. It has flowers in an abundance that was never seen before, and the sweetness of the promised fruits,' wrote Lunacharsky. 'We should not compromise, but firmly, without hesitation, standing on the class point of view, we will create our own culture,' said the talented poet-worker Samobytnik-Mashirov at the first All-Russian Conference of the Proletkult.[1]

No other single form of creative activity attracted such attention as the theatre. Over the course of two years, numerous lectures were given on the issue of socialist theatre. Public debates were held where heads were bashed, and fierce debates took place about the directions of proletarian theatre. During this time extensive literature developed, precious evidence that the inexhaustible creative forces lurking in the soul of the proletariat allowed him, despite the struggle that was unprecedented in history, to take serious steps towards the conquest of this form of art, this form of art which is the most powerful factor to influence the feelings and will of a person, and which the general consensus believes that in the old bourgeois society it experienced a crisis.

It is quite natural for the mass to strive for the theatre. The theatre, even the chamber one, still contains an orgiastic origin. A crowd converges between its

---

1 Presumably, Kogan is here making reference to the Bolshevik worker and Proletkult organizer Aleksei Samobytnik-Mashirov, who had also participated in the organization of the first Proletkult conference. Samobytnik-Mashirov strongly adhered to the idea that the Proletkult should rely on a new proletarian intelligentsia (Mally 1990: 96). In a longer bionote, Mally explains that Mashirov gave himself the pen name 'Samobytnik', which means 'original' or 'distinctive'. He was born in St Petersburg in 1884 and was involved in political activism from a young age. This activism led to his exile from 1905 to 1908. On his return he began to write proletarian literature and later served as the president of the Petrograd Proletkult (Mally 1990: 101).

gilded walls. Even if separated from the stage by a ramp, the audience still remains a participant in the play. Theatre, even when distorted by the false bourgeois individualistic culture, is still the most powerful stimulus for the collective experience of mass delight. And the unprecedented revival of theatrical life in Russia is naturally explained by the colossal scope of our Revolution, which awakened the masses to the desire to realize themselves as a great whole. The people, and especially the more active and creative elements, instinctively feel the significance of the theatre as a light that illuminates the darkest and most intricate meanders of the thorny path ahead.

During the years of the Revolution, tremendous work has been done in the construction of a worker-peasant theatre.[2] True, there is no ingenious creation, no theatrical spectacle has been revealed in which the greatness of the events taking place would find a worthy embodiment. There will be no new theatre until there is a new form. No efforts and guesses by the theorists, even deep and serious ones, can create this form until poetic inspiration reveals it to us. But does it follow from this that we should sit back and wait for its natural birth? Every new artistic phenomenon is the result of a collective request and of collective efforts; it is not a hot-headed whim. And today, more than ever, the mass is involved in the creation of artistic works. We are entering a new era in the natural distribution of work, even in the field of poetry which has so far been shrouded in mystery and considered the kingdom of the elect few. And these searches, this intense theoretical work, these successful and unsuccessful experiences of improvisations, collective performances, mass shows, processions and festivals, new teaching methods, theatre studios where the proletarian youth come in their masses – all this is a powerful fermentation. All these collective efforts are not only the harbinger of a new theatre, but also the necessary work to create those conditions without which its emergence is unthinkable. The appearance of a new form of art has always been accompanied by this intense work of the collective. Only our science of the individualistic era, which focused its attention on personality, created an optical illusion that prevented us from seizing the process of the birth of creativity.

---

2 The 'worker-peasant theatre' was a division within the Narkompros formed in 1919. It was short-lived, however. While its first leader, Valentin Tikhonovich, believed that workers and peasants had a lot in common, the first conference of this theatre exhibited the division between these two social groups. At this conference, which took place in November 1919, a vocal faction even argued that 'peasants could be helpful only insofar as they subordinated themselves to workers' (Mally 2000: 22). The division disbanded a year later. An essay by Tikhonovich on the proletarian actor is given in Part Four.

On the day of the second anniversary of the October Revolution, we wanted to at least share some of the impressions created by this work.

First of all, the quantitative side is striking. The future historian will note that during the bloodiest and most brutal revolution, all of Russia was acting. In the section for examining the worker-peasant theatre at the theatre department of the Narkompros more than a thousand theatre circles were registered in factories and villages. This figure is probably a small part of the actual amount. Sometimes local intellectuals take part in the creation of the circles, but more often we are dealing with a pure composition of the circle, whose members are workers or some peasants, or both together. Clubs are proud that they do without professional help (the decorations are painted by the workers, the costumes prepared by female workers, workers also constitute the directors, actors, musicians, conductors and so on).

These numerous circles, which currently cover the whole of Russia, flare up, go out and light up again, like fireflies. The repertoire, the questions, the petitions and requests with which they shower the centre – all this provides rich material. You can draw a complete picture of 'non-professional' acting in Russia. There are no manuals, make-up, no literature, canvas, or scenery. Peasants and workers beg for the necessary material to satisfy their theatrical hunger. They instinctively feel that theatre is the most faithful and direct way to familiarize oneself with the gains of human thought. The centre can only partly meet these sincere cries, whose extraordinary perseverance can only be compared to cries for bread. The general devastation and lack of materials prevent us from responding to this cry for bread. All sorts of 'honoured' and undeserving actors, who conduct theatre business in our country, distribute public funds exclusively among professional theatres and do not hide their contempt for this mighty outburst of the people, for this 'bad grade' amateurism that has spread throughout Russia.

Meanwhile, these millions of theatre lovers played a great cultural role. Usually the initiative for the creation of a circle belongs to young people and most often to the communist youth. Inert elements of the village, especially the elderly, do not have the confidence and love for these 'mischievous' ventures. The theatre's power is so strong that this 'venture' quickly draws the entire population, and within two months the most ignorant and clumsy citizens of the village begin to admire this new guest. Performances are crowded with spectators. It is here, among the images of art, that the rural population realizes for the first time that the Revolution brings with it light and joy. There were cases when reconciliation with the new life began through the theatre, when the first promising glimpses of a thoughtful attitude towards the great social tragedy of our days were born in the soul of dark and prejudiced masses.

The repertoire of these theatres is not only determined by requests from the audience, for several reasons. They choose simple things that do not require expensive materials, short plays, sometimes plays without female roles (there are still places where parents do not allow their daughters to perform on the stage) – these are the conditions in which the people fulfil their need for theatrical spectacle. And despite all the difficulties, justice must be given to the sound instinct of the people; plays by serious writers and the classics prevail. The people's need for healthy laughter is most often satisfied by staging Chekhov's vaudevilles, which went around all the peasant hut-theatres. They play Gorky, Tolstoy, Heijermans (*Wreck of the Ship 'Hope'*), Miasnitsky[3] and whoever else. But, in general, we hardly see any vulgar plays. Here are some of the figures (according to the survey held by the TEO of the People's Commissariat for Education). The questionnaires of nineteen purely workers' circles give the following information about the repertoire: Chekhov is mentioned nine times, followed by Ostrovsky (7), Gorky (3), Tolstoy L., Chirikov, Andreev, and S. Belaia[4] (2), O. Dymov, Kosorotov, Semenov, Teffi, Averchenko, Gogol, Pisemsky, Hauptmann, Heijermans, Chuzh-Chuzhenin, Evdokimov, Rassokhin, Fedorovich, Smerchinsky, a local author (surname not specified), Arsky,[5] E. Karpov, de Courcelles, delle Grazie[6] (1). Of Chekhov's work, *Uncle Vanya* is mentioned only once, as the rest are vaudevilles. If we take into account that the success of these vaudevilles is not due to the particular properties of Chekhov's work, but in general to the popularity (and uncomplicated staging) of the vaudeville, then Ostrovsky would have to take the first place. He takes the first place in all the other circles (except for one, the smallest circle), that

---

3 I. I. Miasnitsky was a popular playwright whose works were performed at the Korsh Theatre towards the end of the nineteenth century. Largely forgotten today, he made a name for writing comedies on topical issues, with his plays featuring merchants, bureaucrats, retired soldiers, servants, wannabes from the intelligentsia and provincials wishing for life in the city (McReynolds 2003: 58–60).

4 Sofia Belaia's popularity warrants a brief reference. She was a provincial actress and theatrical entrepreneur who before the Revolution also wrote a voluminous number of plays, often in a melodramatic fashion that brought out the hardships of the workers. Her plays were seen as artistically weak before the Revolution, but after 1917 they gained extensive visibility on the amateur stage, especially when she reworked them to focus on class struggle and the status of women. *The Unemployed*, one of her most popular plays, depicts a worker whose injury at the workplace leads to suicide (see Swift 2002: 109 and 129).

5 Pavel Arsky's short one-act play *For the Cause of the Red Soviets* (1919) depicts the White enemy as an evil player who stops at nothing, not even the murder of defenceless women and children, to seize power back from the hands of the Soviets. The play ends with an impassioned call to arms of a Red soldier, directed not only at his comrades on the stage but also, and more importantly, at the comrade soldiers in the audience. It is reproduced in Geldern and Stites (1995: 22–8).

6 Most probably this refers to Marie Eugenie delle Grazie, a German novelist, essayist, poet and dramatist. Her 1900 play *Schlagende Wetter* (*Firedamp*) is a naturalistic play that shows the exploitation of mine workers by their owners, underlining the separation between the two classes (Wilson 1991: 484–5).

is in the purely peasant circles, the worker-peasants groups, the mixed groups (intellectuals and workers and so on). For example, in eighty questionnaires of theatrical work by peasant circles the following are mentioned: Ostrovsky 38 times, then Sofia Belaia (23), Tolstoy L. (13), Gogol (12), Semenov (9), Nikitin (6), Andreev (5), Gorky (3), Osetrov (3), Samburov (3), Pushkin, Polushin, Gorbunov, Chirikov, Klepikov, Khomutov, Podnosov, and 'local authors' (2). The following are mentioned once: Molière, Grigorovich (*Fishermen*), Stakhovich (*Night*), Remizov (*Wolf's Teeth*), Nekrasov (*The Evening of Recitation*), Lisenko-Konych, Epifanov, Merezhkovsky (*Romantics*), Dobrovolsky (*Expropriator*), Kraseva (*Shaved Arkhipka*), Miasnitsky (*Uncle's Apartment*), Rutkovsky (*Web*), Klepikov (*In the Lowlands*), Velikanov (*Blue Beard* – a farce), Tikhonov (*Over the Edge*), Naidenov (*The Seventies*), Lebedev (*Ladybug*), Fedorov (*Az and Firt*). One questionnaire simply says 'Plays from everyday life'. In some others the following plays are mentioned but without giving the authors: *Long Live Freedom* (1), *Guest* – a translation from Swedish (1), *Workers* (1).

The many requests for literature include plays 'that cover issues of modern life, questions of the Revolution, the life of the peasant and the worker'. Due to the poverty of revolutionary dramatic literature,[7] the village and the factory are content with the rather flat works of Sophia Belaia, who writes revolutionary dramas even if not without art. Her works like *People of Fire and Iron*, *The Unemployed*, *Proletarians* and other ad hoc plays depict the heartlessness of the bourgeoisie and the sufferings of the exploited. These are straightforward plays that depict the unforgettable grievances of the recent past. They are very popular and successfully staged.

Such is the general picture of the theatrical movement that spontaneously arose among the lower classes of the people. The Revolution liberated the masses and pulled them out of the shackles of ignorance in which the Tsarist government and its minions held the peasants and workers. The theatre played an important role in these years when the people rushed towards the light. For good or bad, it was a spontaneous impulse and the creation of the people themselves. We hardly helped them. The 'generals' of the artistic world are convinced that the art of the future is not in this erratic spontaneous outburst, but in elaborate experiments and desk work, which they try to use against artistic taste.

The interest in the theatre that has awakened among the masses is key to the renewal of our future theatre. But even now, the influence of the Revolution in the search for the form of the socialist theatre is noticeably felt. This influence

---

7 This is a point addressed by various authors in Part Three. See especially Platon Kerzhentsev's essays.

is manifested in several directions. First of all, a huge theoretical work has been done. The ways of the theatre of the future are explored by the best experts on the subject. Kerzhentsev's books, especially *The Creative Theatre*,[8] should be noted. It contains interesting information on the attempts in collective creativity and mass performances in the West, a number of articles published in other newspapers, the 'Protocols of the First All-Russian Conference of the Proletkult', etc. In these works, the main issues related to the problem of socialist theatre are thoroughly studied, while the concept of folk and class theatre is defined. Other issues discussed include the question of professionalism, collective creativity, the use of improvisations, the adaptation of plays and the attitudes towards the existing repertoire.

Along with the theoretical work, a great deal of artistic activity is underway. The following are to be noted: the interesting achievements in collective recitation by V. K. Serezhnikova, Mgebrov's attempts in Petrograd,[9] Smyshlaev's dramatization of Verhaeren's 'Insurrection' at the Moscow Proletkult,[10] the improvisation in the studios of the Proletkult and so on. Not everything was successful in these experiments, but there was much in them that was wonderful. One thing is certain: the source of creativity is on this path; here burns true inspiration, and the ardent faith in the creative forces of the people. From the classical repertoire, everything that matches the needs of the moment is extracted. They put on plays by Schiller, Shakespeare, Hauptmann, Verhaeren, delle Grazie, Heijermans, Lope de Vega (*Fuente Ovejuna*), everything where the masses speak, where they long for freedom and fight against oppression.

The 'honoured' artists consider the socialist theatre as an unborn child. But how many 'collectives' occupying the best theatres in Moscow can now be called a corpse?

A child will be born – we know that. But the corpse will never rise again.

---

8 *Tvorcheskii teatr*. This proved an enormously popular book, one which between 1918 and 1923 went through five different editions. The last two editions were heavily expanded, meaning that a study of the different editions of *Tvorcheskii teatr* can shed light on the way that amateur theatre and its theories developed throughout those years.
9 See relevant extracts from Mgebrov's autobiography in Parts Three and Four.
10 A detailed description of this production is given in an essay by Smyshlaev himself reproduced in Part Four. See also a description of Smyshlaev's studio work at the Proletkult in Part Five.

'No to Theatre Art, but to Celebration'

Adrian Piotrovsky

Source: *Zhizn' iskusstva*, 19–22 March 1921, page unidentified.

In a recent issue of *The Life of Art*,[1] Viktor Shklovsky likened theatrical circles to scarlet fever and to a deserter's delirium, refusing to see in them possible material for the 'building of a new way of life'.

It is gratifying to see that there is a dispute around these circles. It should have been understood, for a long time now, that their activities will determine the immediate destinies of our art. They will do so more than the academic theatres combined.[2]

Nobody now doubts the spontaneous appearance of the circles. There is only one question: Is this appearance painful or vital? Is it a rash, or a burst of health? Do you want to know the answer? Look at the individuals and at the circles. From which majority do the theatre groups come, from the sick and the weak? From the segments of society left behind by life? No, they are formed from the best and the strongest, from the communist youth, the best of the Red Army, the sailors. These are the people who most actively participate in society.

The theatre has many faces. It could become a monastery. Such a monastery was, for example, the eighteenth-century pastoral theatre, the last venture of the aristocracy, which hid its doomed head under the large hats of the shepherds.

In the hands of professional actors, such a theatre is a work of art like any other. As the business of the theatre lovers, it becomes part of everyday life. Then its reactionary nature speaks about illness and heralds the death of its previous form.

Such a theatrical disease was the dilettantism of the French aristocracy and the dilettantism of recent years in Russia.

At the heart of both of them there is an imitation, a dressing up and a pretence to be someone else, a departure from life, the monastery.

Is this the theatrical nature of the current Republic, pouring itself out in the creation of the theatrical circles? No. The best, strongest circles are alien to the desire to escape from reality.

1 *Zhizn' iskusstva* in Russian.
2 The academic theatres were the Bolshoi, the Maly, the Moscow Art Theatre, its First and Second Studios, Tairov's Kamerny Theatre and the Moscow Children's Theatre. The government recognized these as custodians of the Russian theatrical traditions and thus rewarded them with initial financial support (Braun 1998: 160).

Instead of performances in wigs and make-up, the best, spontaneously created front line, navy and youth circles prefer 'trials', 'mysteries' and all kinds of 'dramatized improvisations' of meetings and barricades.

The workers are carrying out a revolution. The Red Army is fighting. The plots of these dramatizations are simple; the methods of their construction are not complicated. Basically, they are based on one constantly varying device – *not imitation* of life, *but its transformation*. Exacting theatre lovers frown, and they are absolutely right. There is no theatre here; citizens are theatre lovers; there is no art at all!

Workers and Red Army men in the best theatre circles remain workers and Red Army men. They are looking for a theatrical action that does not change but actually transforms the face of their class. They are looking for actions which make the Moscow-Zastava workers become world heroes, and the recruits from the red-rural camps the victorious troops of the Revolution.

Such is the path of the theatrical circles in its extreme schematization. It experiences a number of distortions, because of the infection of petty bourgeois dilettantism, which is conveyed by the sticky hands of instructors who have a petty bourgeois ideology.

It changes because, in their interest and social composition, circles are extremely diverse.

But in general, this path is clear, and of course this path is not towards the theatre. It is situated outside of the theatre. It is not art. It is life. This path is to celebration, to the appearance of a transformed and more beautiful everyday life.[3]

Of course, the interaction between a transformed life and art is inevitable. The future will show that it is not rooted in the recently developed slogan of theatrical neo-realism, with its three-sided decorations, but in the super-realism of the celebration which is rooted in a transformed everyday life.

Now let one thing be clear. The thousands of theatrical circles scattered throughout the country are the fighting units that are revolutionizing daily life. Their weapon is a transformative, non-imitative, theatre play.

---

3 Everyday life has an important place in both pre- and post-revolutionary cultural debates. In their analysis, Christina Kiaer and Eric Naiman contrast the 'material, repetitive, unchanging and therefore deeply conservative activities associated with the domestic sphere and the body' with *bytie*, a transformed everyday life with activities that are 'progressive, inventive, emotional, spiritual, and transcendental' (Kiaer and Naiman 2006: 10). In post-revolutionary Russia this transcendental, i.e. transformed and improved, everyday life was linked not to spiritual realms but to ideology. It was in the everyday and routine-like activities of everyday life that the grand transformations brought forward by the Revolution were to be understood and lived out. See also Fitzpatrick (1999).

'Drama and Mass Performances'

Viktor Shklovsky

Source: *Zhizn' Iskusstva*, 9–11 March 1921, page unidentified.

Adrian Piotrovsky suggests (in *Petrograd News*) the use of drama groups for organizing participants in mass performances.

Indeed, no one knows what to do with these dramatic circles. They breed like bacteria. Neither the lack of fuel, nor the lack of food, nor the Entente – nothing can delay their development. Frightened leaders try in vain and suggest the most diverse ways to replace these circles. But these circles are unshakable.

'And what if they close you down?', the circles are asked. They answer: 'We will perform the vaudeville in secret!'

And Russia performs and performs. There is some spontaneous process of transforming living material into the theatrical. And then there is Evreinov, proposing that '[e]very minute of our life is theatre'.[1] Why do we need theatre when we have a theatre at every minute?

Piotrovsky understands the desire to use these theatre groups in work, if only to take them away from the vaudeville, from the masquerade, and the dressing up.

I think this is impossible. Theatrical circles just want to dress up and play masquerade. […]

Life is hard; its severity cannot be hidden. And in this difficult life, we must not be like the Selenites (the first people on the moon), planted in barrels, from which only those tentacles useful to the collective are allowed to grow. We are in the realm of necessity, and through it goes our road towards the future.

A man would always be glad to go where everything was easier, where they could think of nothing more than soft pillows, and where people drank warm water. But that road of yesterday is, of course, locked. And now people run to the theatre, to the actors, and according to Freud's thought on psychosis we thus hide in some kind of mania, like in a monastery. This means that instead of the difficult reality that is real life we create for ourselves an illusion of life, an illusion of reality.

---

1 See relevant footnote in Nikolai Lvov's essay 'Craving for the Stage'.

You remember, in all probability, the description of the theatre in Dostoevsky's *Notes from the House of the Dead*.[2] Covering a shaved head with a wig, wearing a costume, moving into another life – that was what captivated the convicts in the theatre. Dostoevsky says they turned out to be good actors. This is because in the old days hard labour removed the strongest part of the people.

Popular mass performances strongly show the joy of the crowd in affirming the present day and its apotheosis. They are legitimate when no one is looking at them from a window or from a special tribune. Otherwise it degenerates into a parade, into a fortified ballet and into an orchestra of horn music. And that's why it is not a masquerade or theatre.

Popular mass performances are the business of life. Drama clubs are a psychosis, escapism, the Selenite's dream about limbs.

These millions of circles cannot be closed – one cannot forbid a person his ravings. They are like the rash of a disease, and as such, they deserve the attention of sociologists. But you cannot use them to build a new life. It cannot be built from the delirium of a deserter. That is too cruel.

---

2 *The House of the Dead* is a semi-biographical novel published by Dostoevsky in 1860-2. It depicts the life of convicts in a Siberian prison camp.

Part Two

Amateur–Professional Relations

'On the Professionalization of the Workers in the Arts'

Fyodor Kalinin

Source: *Proletarskaia kul'tura*, no. 7–8, 1919, pp. 29–31

As soon as the workers' participation in cultural development became common practice in Soviet Russia, and as soon as it began to spread to the sphere of the arts, the question was immediately raised about turning the workers with a particular calling for the arts into professionals: writers, artists, actors, musicians, etc. This is quite natural. If we would like to seriously and, most importantly, consciously facilitate the building of proletarian culture; if we want to ease the process of liberating the proletariat from bourgeois culture and, particularly, from the bourgeois art; then the discovery of a proletarian ideology and a proletarian culture can only happen with the serious mastery of artistic technique, which requires time and hard work. No one would deny the need to learn techniques and methods achieved by humanity in its long and diverse history, completed by the bourgeois society. This may raise a question about how to take and digest these techniques. Not only in art, but even in a simple craft, one needs to know how to use a particular instrument, and it is only this knowledge that makes it possible to display with maximum freedom and lightness the most complex and intricate conceptions of a rich soul. We repeat: the negative attitude towards learning technique is impossible to imagine, and no one is planning for it. Encouraging workers to become art professionals is met with embarrassment and reverential fear from the other side. The opponents of professionalism are concerned that workers, after being separated from their machine tools and physical labour, would distance themselves from the working class and its interests and therefore would lose the specifics of their class. These opponents are also concerned that the workers will lose the capability of accepting and digesting socialist ideology, which is that specific quality no other class or stratum of society possesses to the same extent.[1] In order to be more convincing, the opponents of professionalism step back in the history of the labour movement and use its shameful stigmas as live illustrations. They use as examples the representatives of the working class, the professionals of political and economic movements:

---

1 This is an opinion which Platon Kerzhentsev expresses in a section of *Tvorcheskii teatr* reproduced in n.12 as the entry titled 'The Creation of Proletarian Theatre'. See also Valerian Pletnev's essay which follows immediately here, where he argues that the main problem posed by professionalism is that it removes the proletarian from the production process.

Noske,[2] Ebert,[3] Scheidemann[4] and others. 'These are your professionals,' our opponents say triumphantly. 'They lost connection with their machines and tools, forgot the ABC of socialism, and turned into the worst enemies of the labour movement.'

These live illustrations are very irritating and make us experience burning hatred as a result of their treacherous betrayal of revolutionary interests. It is thought that this fact alone would have shown the proponents of professionalism the errors of their position. But it only seems so to those with a superficial and non-Marxist thinking. These illustrations are another kettle of fish, and they have nothing to do with us at the moment. All of us Marxists know that truth is concrete, and we do not think about it outside of a specific time and place. Noske, Ebert, Scheidemann and similar scoundrels became professionals in the capitalist society, not in the Russian Socialist Federative Soviet Republic. Even our opponents understand that this makes an enormous difference, not a small one.

What is the matter? How come that our opponents, Marxists themselves, have not noticed such a difference? Had this been the only point, the opponents of professionalism would have likely sensed this difference, if not completely realized it. It is hard to imagine that they missed such an obvious thing. Our opponents' mistake lies in the deeper misunderstanding of the conditions, which are not directly obvious but require the foundations of Marxism to be taken into account in every matter that involves decision-making. The main argument of the opponents is that if the worker becomes professional in the arts he breaks away from the working processes of his factory or plant life. This is their mistake. They make a fetish out of physical labour. They think that the ideology of the working class is defined by physical labour. In reality, it is defined by the mode of production in general and by the position of the working class in this mode of production.

Does a peasant, a craftsman or a small workshop owner work less physically than the factory worker? Their labour may be more complex and diverse than that of the factory workers who mechanically repeat the same operation over and over, day after day. However, for a peasant or a craftsman this does not guarantee liberation from the petty bourgeois ideology. It also does not necessarily facilitate

---

2 Gustav Noske (1868–1946), a German politician of the Social Democratic Party of Germany (SPD), notorious for using military forces to suppresses the uprising of 1919 (Tucker 2006: 1342).
3 Friedrich Ebert (1871–1925), leader of the Social Democratic movement in Germany and President of the Weimar Republic from 1919 to 1925 (Tucker 2006: 631).
4 Philipp Scheidemann (1865–1939), German politician, again of the Social Democratic Party of Germany, who declared the creation of a German republic as an aftermath of the Kiel Mutiny (Tucker 2006: 1016).

the acceptance of proletarian ideology. The point is not only in the worker breaking away from the working processes of the factory but also in the class position he occupies. When Scheidemann and others separated themselves from labour for political and economic work, the economic essence of their position changed significantly. They had the possibility to live a different, well-off life. The General Secretary of the German Trade Unions, with about three million members, was some kind of king. This position provided plenty of temptations to repeatedly betray the cause of the workers, whether intentionally or not. The same applies to those politicians who are continuously elected as deputies in order to fill parliamentary seats. If we had an issue in capitalist society with workers breaking away from their machines and tools to go to a professional art school, we would not have our hand in it but we would not resist it either. Our main front is political and economic, and we cannot take resources from it and divert them to the secondary front. This diversion would be a waste of our already poor resources, and the results would not be fully justified.

The current state in Soviet Russia is entirely different. We gained political and economic power; now we need to strengthen it. This task requires cultural recourses, and we now face the life-size challenge of cultural development.

The Soviet State possesses an ideology and the means for propaganda, but it does not have enough resources of its own to use these to their full extent. Our opponents continue to use our own apparatus against us, if not expressly so then by implication. This way they support the bourgeois ideology which has been crystallized in the works of art, in its dead or living carriers, in all kinds of actors, artists, writers, musicians, scientists …

Art is a powerful tool to strengthen and develop ideology; we need to use it, and, therefore, it is necessary to develop human resources in this area by promoting the most talented.

Our opponents fear that after being fully removed from their workplaces the workers would get under the influence of the bourgeois ideology and forget their status as workers. We do not think so. First of all, their position will not change at all when compared to the one of the factory workers – and this is the most important thing. They will live and study using a subsidy, which at least will not be higher than the worker's salary. Their positions will not be similar at all to those of Scheidemann and Noske in a capitalist state. Besides, in Soviet Russia, as we have already mentioned, the ideological apparatus of public outreach is in the hands of the workers and peasants' government, and the bourgeois influence is undermined. Therefore, there are no temptations of the capitalist state, and no danger in breaking away. To be afraid of the 'embourgeoisement' of the workers who learn the techniques of the arts means to attach too much power to the bourgeois ideological influence and its particular attraction. We have the opposite opinion. If the proletarian ideology destroyed all the fortresses of the bourgeois and took the free road, then its finalization is taking place right now in every area. There is no reason to fear that the bourgeois ideology is more attractive than the proletarian one or that the workers studying in art studios are like a sympathetic audience that easily gets under the corruptive influence of the bourgeois ideology.

We will not be able to create proletarian art if we do not create the conditions for the workers to unfold their rich abilities. If, out of fear of separating a worker from his machines and tools, we contribute to create a source of half-trained dilettantes who, regardless of their lofty natural talents, face the obstacle of a lack of necessary technical skills and, therefore, are slowed down in showing their creative abilities, then this means that our actions will be not only useless but also harmful.

We are convinced that the point of view of those opposing professionalism in the arts will fail and that it will not be supported by the broad working masses. A serious understanding of Marxism and the need to master quickly the apparatus of cultural endeavor will work against this point of view. Besides, it would have been too absurd to allow the bourgeoisie to have all rights and privileges but then deprive the workers of them. It would mean that the workers' government is its own worst enemy and that they cut the branch which they finally sat on after so much effort. No, the working class is not so naive to hand the development of their own culture over to the bourgeois intelligentsia because of the ill-conceived, however sincere, opposition to professionalism.

'On Professionalism'

Valerian Pletnev

Source: *Proletarskaia kul'tura*, no. 7–8, 1919, pp. 31–7

I

The extensive growth of proletarian culture puts before us a number of important questions. The art of proletarian theatre, the new methods of literary and artistic creation, the new directions in art, the relationship to industrial processes, and professionalism – all these questions demand a principal justification to their every step.

In this article we will deal with the question of professionalism.

Students of different studios talk about the impossibility of combining their factory jobs with their work at the studio. The artistic tensions necessary to concentrate on a role, write a novel, or sculpt are drastically reduced by the weariness of a day's hard work, while the work that these students must do is colossal. They must study the particular sphere of art which they work in, work on assimilating and perfecting their technique, and study samples of the past. With an eight-hour work day there is simply no time for all this. Therefore, the work of these students can be called random, incomplete and amateurish. Plenty of effort, time and pure physical strain are necessary to conquer all the values of bourgeois art and adopt it critically. Moreover, these students claim that if we want to create reliable foundations for proletarian culture then the full opportunity to work in the field of art which they are most strongly attracted to is necessary, so that they can give it all their effort and time. Proletarian culture cannot be solid without the relatively rapid integration of artistic techniques in the fight against the powerful influence of bourgeois art culture.

It is necessary to master first the technique of art and only then, armed with technical perfection, commence the battle. Otherwise all the attempts would simply be a waste of time.

The issue of professionalism raised increasingly animated debates at the second conference of the Moscow Proletkult. Two points of view emerged: the first – recognition of professionalism; the other – its rejection.

Representatives of both views agree that it is necessary for the proletariat to conquer bourgeois art and culture, especially its extraordinary technique. The adoption of this technique has to flow through critical analysis – this also raised no controversies. The attention was diverted to a different plane.

The defenders of the first point of view insisted on the necessity of organizing central studios in all fields of art. In their opinion, the most talented persons must be picked, through careful examinations, from students coming from both the centre and the suburbs. These individuals should be released from their factory jobs, receive a stipend from the government and work solely in the field of art.

In this new job they will be under the supervision of art specialists and comprehend scientifically the material and artistic techniques. To create the new proletarian culture, they will grasp critically the old culture's fruits.

The general task of the central studio, according to its followers, is 'the release of the proletariat from the petty-bourgeois swaddles of the "specialists" and the immediate creation of the proletarian's own specialist, proletarian-artists who emerge from the depths of their class'.

Thus, technical education, arming the proletarian-artist with mastery, is the primary step on the path of building proletarian art. Without this there is a risk of falling into dilettantism, shallowly skimming the pinnacle of art without delving deeper.

The supporters of the central studio idea back their position with one other incredibly important argument. Arming a proletarian artist with the conquered technique and the mastery of art cannot occur on a mass scale. It is possible to create leaders and supervisors in the field of art from among the proletarians. This will lead to the release of the 'specialists' from the bourgeois art. The leader of proletarian art will be at the centre of the proletarian spiritual culture.

The proposed foundational stone of all of this construction is as follows: the movement in favour of professionalism grew out of the Proletkult's practical work. It is not an office invention. It was created by life itself, and opposing it would mean ignoring the demands of the time, refusing vitally necessary and, perhaps, historically inevitable phenomena. Unless this movement is put under control, it will pass by the Proletkult. Talents and geniuses will manage to overcome the obstacles in their paths, though they will do so on their own, without the help from the proletarian centre of culture. They will be against the proletarian centre of culture. According to its followers, this is the nature of the question of professionalism.

II

All of us who deny professionalism see the in-depth analysis of this question as necessary. The supporters of professionalism see it clearly: a movement was born among students; it was summoned by life itself, and we must meet it halfway. This understanding is too simple. We believe, just like our opponents, that a proletarian artist must possess artistic technique. A proletarian artist must receive a solid, general and technical education. However ... we approach the issue from another angle. For us it is important to determine the following: how is proletarian culture built? Through cultural education or struggle? If it is the former, then there is nothing to argue about: the sooner and more effectively we succeed in promoting with the proletarian masses the known sum of knowledge and artistic skill, and the sooner we create our own artists, the better. Cultural education is always somewhat apolitical. The concept of class art, class struggle, is rejected by the cultural educators. Art, in their opinion, is common in all humanity, and therefore all the conquests of the old world are equally precious and dear to us, and the sooner we give the masses the opportunity to possess them, the easier it will be to solve the tasks in front of us. However, we, who have lived and are still living by the principles and methods of class struggle, have a different point of view. For us, the art of proletarian culture is a process of struggle. And since this is so, all the issues of proletarian culture are raised and solved by us on an entirely different plane, unlike the representatives of pure cultural education.

Therefore, which tasks do we put ahead of us in the creation of proletarian culture?

At this moment when the class struggle is intensifying, it is especially amusing to talk about a peculiar truce between the proletariat and the bourgeoisie on the grounds of the recognition of art as a common human value, something which stands outside or above classes.

The creation of proletarian culture is a process of struggle with the remnants of bourgeois culture, a struggle where the psychologically harmful influence of the declining bourgeois art on the proletarian masses is defeated. The great revolution spread its wings over the entire world and seized the political and economic sides of life in Europe. The old capitalist order is disintegrating. Revolution destroys the old and opens vast prospects of constructing socialist forms of economy. Along with this, the authority of the bourgeois was overthrown and replaced by the proletariat dictatorship, a class destined to lay the first bricks of socialism. Therefore, it is an architect-class, the creator of a new world.

Soviet power and the socialization of production: these are the cornerstones that the great world revolution is building.

However, while the revolution has changed the areas of economic and political life, and while the autocratic past and the bourgeois authority now seem like a thing of the past, a different situation is seen in the sphere of culture. In culture, the power of the old world is still very strong. And it cannot be overthrown with a bayonet; it cannot be destroyed like the bureaucratic, economic or political order. Bourgeois culture infiltrates our life, all our ways, in the infinite chain of everyday relations. Architecture, theatre, literature, music, art – all these are the values of the bourgeois world. They have their deep psychological influence everywhere, on the streets, in theatres, libraries, museums and exhibitions. Their influence is often unnoticeable. Art is the product of the spiritual, infinitely diverse, multifaceted action of man. It appears to be common to all and familiar to every man. Every man is an artist. This commonality of art forms the basis of common humanity, the classless nature of art. Art lives on the summits, where it cannot be reached by waves of class struggle. This is what the artists of the old world say. This is what our comrades repeat after them, without having realized the basis and complexity of our world view, without understanding that reality determines consciousness, and emotion then follows. The struggle against outdated views, the struggle against the psychological influence of bourgeois culture, the complete annihilation of its remnants, the transformation of a vague and speculative ideology – which the masses are soaked in – into a clear, vivid, class ideology: this is our main problem in creating proletarian culture.

The cultural revolution is only just beginning. The necessity of destroying the bourgeois ideology is only just now being understood by our comrades. Therefore, it is absolutely imperative that we possess clarity of thought, clarity of vision, and a sharp critique and solid foundation of class consciousness. On the basis of these positions, we see the necessity of creating a proletarian artist. If at this very moment – let's assume, rather quickly – we succeed in creating, under the tutelage of 'specialists', proletarian artists who are skilled in technique and the corresponding art forms, would this solve the main problem of creating proletarian culture, which is the creation of proletarian art leaders for our class culture? Categorically and undoubtedly – no!

And here is why.

What is the relationship between technique and form on one side and contents on the other? This is an old and eternally new question. For us, there is no self-sufficient form. Thoughts on it were born during the last stage of the bourgeois art's expansion. 'Senseless' creativity, the worship of form, which was a movement born during the revolution process, shows how strong the inertia of the outdated concepts is.

For us, form comes out of content. What comes out of the thought behind creation always demands a certain form. Try to transform the wild verses of Verhaeren's 'Insurrection' into Nadson's mournful verse.[1] This is impossible because a word in poetry is not a random and independent entity. A thought is words without sound. Words encase a thought into a clear shape, enabling our senses to perceive it. A thought demands from words a certain rhythm and strength. In the same way that it is impossible to swaddle a lion with a child's garments and place it into a crib with a pacifier in its mouth, it is also impossible to force a thought into a shape which does not fit it. And any text is valuable from an artistic point of view only when its shape and contents form a whole.

All modern art is an undeniable proof of this statement. Here is one vivid example. A proletarian set a goal for himself – to capture in a form of art the centuries-long struggle for socialism. All the names of the revolutionaries, which history has conserved for us, must be preserved in monuments. The Council of People's Commissars employed the best artists for this. And what was the result? Marx, with that fiery exterior, a revolutionary to the bone, a flaming tribune, a warrior of thought, is in the hands of artists everywhere transformed into a kind or, in the best-case scenario, a strict little old man. Under the dead blocks of stone, plaster or bronze, there is no sign of Marx's fiery temperament, his great mind and his scorching character. Why is this so? Because to the artists creating these monuments, Marx was a great scientist, even though there were so many of them in the centuries that passed. And not one of the artists has felt Marx the revolutionary. Therefore, a form came about which agreed with the craftsmen's thoughts. Marx's monument-busts are, at best, a rendition of a scientist deep in thought, no more. Marx the revolutionary did not exist to the artists because they are far from the world of fighting, the world of relentless revolutionary fire, the world of creation, the victories and defeats. This happens despite the fact that most, if not all, of these artists are in complete possession of all the techniques of art. We would suggest to those who defend professionalism, and who advocate that the proletarians must quickly master the techniques of art, to look at the monuments erected during the Revolution, and to think about them. The results would be most instructive. Therefore, the creation of a proletarian artist who is simply a technician, skilled in the forms of art, does not solve the problem.

---

1 Semeon Nadson (1862–87), Russian poet and notable literary figure of his generation.

We put thought at the basis of our creation. A proletarian artist with a pure class world view is to us the basis of proletarian art. And foremost in the creation of our proletarian culture we put the creation of such a proletarian artist.

It would be appropriate here to ask a question to the followers of professionalism. Are they sure that the 'specialists' who are in charge of training a proletarian to become an artist will not distort, with their own 'forms', the yet perhaps unsettled psychology of our comrade? We cannot be sure of this.

A proletarian artist, before he begins creating, needs thorough support. The process of creation is a long one. Before identifying an idea in words, sounds, stone, paint, an artist creates and processes the thought in his consciousness. And already this process of mental work, which is a spiritual and internal fire, is for a proletarian artist a process of struggle against bourgeois thought. In this case, pure class consciousness is the fire which cleanses the thought and the creations of a proletarian from all that which is alien and hostile. And only then, when the internal process of creation ends with the necessity to express that idea does he act on the second phase, via the form of art and its technique. It is rather obvious, of course, that the proletarian will be unable to express his inner world without the necessary technical skills, even though he is sensitive at heart and with deep thoughts. He must know how to do that; he must learn the technique of art, though the conditions in which this proletarian artist learns the techniques of art are very important to us.

Social reality determines consciousness. The proletarian's position in society and his role in the capitalist process of production hone his consciousness to oppose the world of capitalist relations. Industrial relations make him an enemy of capitalism. A single force is formed from scattered workers. This force is the proletariat class, imbued by the unity of thoughts, goals and the path to achieve these.

The ideology of the proletariat is born in production. There, its psychology is developed. And the more developed the industrial forces are, and the tighter their organization is, the more likely the collectivism of proletarian forces will be.

In the capitalist process of production, with its endless division of labour, the consciousness of each proletarian is filled with a precise content. A proletarian is clearly aware that his individual strength is of an infinitely small value and that only in tight cooperation with his co-workers is this value able to transcend distances, create locomotives and vehicles, conquer water, create steamers, conquer air and create steel birds that pertly breach the blue serenity of the celestial skies. The first strike of the hammer brings with it the second, and then the third follows. Without the second strike, the third is inconceivable, without the third, the fourth is, and so on. The logical chain that ties together the efforts of hundreds and thousands of workers cannot be broken. The process of production demands unity of action, the collectivism of creation in which one link follows the next.

The process of capitalist production is characterized by depersonalization, the derivation of work to the automatic repetition of a single operation. This turns a proletarian into a small screw in a giant machine, into a small, unnoticeable figure that lacks any individuality.

But along with this 'the modern imperial capitalist locates all symptoms of impersonality, socialisation and, in accordance with this, the collectivistic psychology of the industrial proletariat is formed'.[2] And, more importantly, 'every worker in this system (of capitalist production), more than in any other period, is an indissoluble and essential link in this process, in all of this system'.[3]

If the proletarian is 'an indissoluble and essential link' in the process of production, then the main force in the formation of proletarian class psychology is the process of production itself. The proletarian's psychology is developed and sharpened in the process of production, in the continuous and indissoluble unity of his work with the work of his comrades.

There, the proletarian receives the first and deepest class upbringing. This is the process of capitalism preparing its own committed undertakers, underestimated by us. In denying the individuality of the proletarian, in mechanizing him, capitalism thus creates a most reliable foundation for its powerful nemesis, proletarian collectivism. Class development is not limited, of course, to the process of production. It is simply the main force. Economic oppression also binds proletarians together into a unified force with a unified goal. However, what is processed least of all is the depth of psychology. Here reigns the direct, vital and sometimes narrowly mercantile interest. The basis of the development of the psychological class is given by the process of production

---

2 In the original the following footnote is given: F. Kalinin, 'Ideology of Production', in *Proletarskaia kul'tura*, no. 5, p. 9.
3 Footnote in the original: Ibid., p. 7.

as such. It is only here that the proletarians realize deeply the creative power of a proletarian collective. There, the communal feeling, the bonds of camaraderie, is born. From the mechanical bond between proletarians as units of labour develops the sense of psychological unity. This is not the unity of a mass. It is not the herd instinct, manifested in fierce yet brief flashes. It is collectivism, a continuous organic consciousness of unity that takes the soul of a proletarian to most sacred depths.

Thus the chief evil of professionalism is that it rips the proletarian artist away from the production process.

Torn away from the production process, the proletarian artist falls into a seemingly 'technical' treatment by the 'specialists' who are far detached from a class world view and emotion. The job of these specialists is to constantly influence a proletarian with bourgeois psychology. Along with this, the influence of the production process and the comrades that are in this process bound to him are lost. And this is the moment when a proletarian would particularly need to be in tune with his class psychology, because the creation of culture is not only a simple achievement of bourgeois artistic wisdom but, mainly, the struggle against it.

Supporters of professionalism confuse concepts together. They claim that after turning professional the artist would not pull away from the populace.

We also believe this to be unlikely. However, we repeat that the point is not that the proletarian artist might pull away from the masses. The point is that through professionalism he pulls away from the production process.

By binding the proletarian artist to the production process, our opponents object that we, first, degrade our work to the degree of amateurism and, second, lengthen the process of creating a proletarian artist. Time-wise, they say, we push the arrival of finished proletarian works of art into the far future.

To this we retort with a question: how can one determine where and when will an artist finish his artistic development?

Never and nowhere, under no circumstances, will an artist ever say that he has reached the final line in his art. The growth of an artist in his thoughts and technique is incessant. There can only be two cases when time limits on an artist's creation are set: either the physical death of the artist or the historical demise of the school of art of which he was a member. The latter is, by the way, the most probable, and the inevitable fate, of those modern bourgeois artists that are devoted to the old ways.

Therefore, determining any kind of time frames to art means a lack of understanding of art's dynamism, the very life which gives it birth.

Apart from all this, socialist ethics (i.e. the recognition that physical labour is every citizen's responsibility) in professionalism, in placing a proletarian in a privileged position when compared to others, meets an irreconcilable contradiction.

Finally, the positions and arguments of the supporters of professionalism are directly contrary to the tasks that art puts ahead of itself.

We were always taught that art is a reflection of life. Now it must become the creation of life, and not a dead mirror that reflects in cold blood both the Madonna's godlike smile and Quasimodo's evil grimace.

Here are a few concise examples. Let's take the visual arts. Our task is to make our reality, all our life, imbued with a certain delicateness and beauty. The cup on my table, the tablecloth, the table itself, the cabinet where I keep my books, the book itself, its cover, the walls of my house, the house itself: why cannot and why shouldn't all this be valuable, from an artistic point of view? Why shouldn't all these things be works of art? If we deem this necessary, then what does the production process turn into? Wouldn't a factory be a laboratory where works of art are created? Wouldn't the line between the creator and the doer be erased? Wouldn't the worker and the artist be united in one person? That is exactly what would happen, and that is why we strive to achieve it. And if that is the case, then why is it necessary to remove the proletarian from the production process and direct him to art? Wouldn't it be easier to just bring art to the production process? This must be especially the case because that is what all our artistic aspirations are reduced to. And then art will stop being simply the mirror of life. What is art therefore supposed to be, the creation of a new bright life? What is the purpose of greenhouses for proletarian artists? Let them be tempered in the process of labour; let them be surrounded by the wild winds of class struggle. Then the proletarian artists will show us ourselves in a clearer and deeper manner. They will call the weak and those who doubt the 'clamouring world of struggle' into the struggle of life, 'into its scarlet stream'. Only one thing is necessary, which is to give up trying to hatch a proletarian artist in six weeks, the same ways chickens hatch.

We react negatively to the professionalism which is deeply convinced that it can create artists who are brilliant technique-wise but shallow in their class content. The shapes of bourgeois art are magnificent, but ...

'Beware of Greeks bearing gifts!'

At this time of tense class struggle we must be vigilant, more so than ever. Imagists, futurists, representatives of a deeply reactive and expiring ideology – all these sprang to life, presenting themselves as proletarian artists.

Our main responsibility is to isolate the proletarian artist from them, not mechanically, but psychologically. And what these 'specialists' truly are, at least most of them, was demonstrated with sufficient clarity by Balmont's performance during the 'Arts Palace' strike.[4]

In conclusion, I would like to raise what in our opinion is a necessary question: why was professionalism so actively proposed, and why is it so well defended?

We find the reason for this in the fact that it is not only the ordinary workers in the construction of proletarian culture who have not yet fully comprehended the full scope of truly revolutionary actions, but also many of its other curators. Ahead of us there still remains a harsh struggle; even this is not fully understood.

Methods of creation, methods of critical review, the relation of art to life and life to art – all these are values which must be partly forgotten, while others must be cardinally reassessed. Colossal, ideologically critical work is still ahead of us. And the valuable thing about the question on professionalism is that it makes a number of other issues arise that are both of a practical and principal importance. They live and demand answers. This highlights the vitality and righteousness of the path which we follow. And yet they tell us: 'be careful' but also strong-minded.

Closer to life, deeper into it, oppose that which is old; support that which is new.

One thing must be remembered: the cultural revolution is only just beginning. Our task is to deepen and strengthen it and not to waste our efforts chasing cheap thrills.

---

4 Konstantin Balmont (1867–1942), poet, translator and leading figure in the Russian symbolist movement (Senelick 2007: 34–5).

The Creation of the Proletarian Theatre

Platon Kerzhentsev

Source: *Tvorcheskii teatr* 5th edition, 1923, pp. 75–88

The creation of the new proletarian theatre needs to starts locally, in the districts, because only on this condition can firm and tight bonds be created among its participants, those familial ties that were unknown in the bourgeois theatre. I prefer to call these theatres 'neighbourhood theatres' because they will be born among the neighbours of a proletarian district, the workers at the same workplace or industrial city, people from different professions but who live close to one another, etc. The neighbourhood theatre in the countryside will be created by the inhabitants of the same village or of a smaller rural district.

I attribute a very particular importance to the territorial proximity among those who organize a neighbourhood theatre, because only this condition allows for an active and extensive participation in the theatre. Each neighbourhood theatre will be organized depending on local circumstances. However, the general principle is clear: the masses of the workers have to be involved as much as possible in the work related to the theatre.

[...]

The actors' collective has to be composed of amateurs, of local workers. All those who want to try out their abilities are included in a list, and for each new production the most suitable names are chosen. If this is too large, then the collective can be divided into different groups. The smaller groups are then directed by different directors and in turn perform different dramas.

In no way is a stable company of amateurs to be created. Such a development would immediately distance the theatre from the efforts of all the other workers. The theatre must provide the opportunity to all those who wish to try out their own skills. Naturally, this does not mean that everyone, without exception, will act or that parts will be assigned by a ballot. What it means is that the director is tasked constantly with the formation of new elements, with the search of new actors and with the preparation of those who are inexperienced, instead of only using the services of tried and tested artists. The theatre must remain a continuous laboratory of teaching and learning, in which new actors debut every day, in which there is no division between principal and secondary actors, or main and secondary roles.

For this reason, the amateur actor who today acts in the theatre of the neighbourhood will tomorrow take the stage of the club or the barracks, while the one who yesterday acted a small part at a small school theatre will today play the protagonist in a successful comedy at a district theatre.

I am of the opinion that the principle of amateurism needs to be safeguarded as much as possible. The real and only creators of the new theatre are those actor-workers who will also remain at their lathe. Certainly, some of them will go on to improve and specialize in the field of theatre, but I see this only as an exception and, in all truth, a dangerous rather than desirable one.

Even though at the beginning the amateur theatre of the workers will suffer because of the insufficient technical preparation of its interpreters, it will be distinguished, on the other hand, by its fresh and immediate youth, by the boldness in its experiments, by its passionate momentum.

Bourgeois theatre managed to renovate itself, at least in part, thanks to the reformative action of external amateurs who contrasted with the isolation, corporate spirit and sordidness of the professional actors – the proletarian theatre needs to take account of this past experience.

Workers who are passionate about the theatre will say the following: 'But we are badly trained and inexperienced, we still have to learn, learn and learn more, and therefore we have even more reason to become professional actors and to dedicate all our time to the theatre rather than just the hours of relaxation. It is for this reason that the bourgeois theatre stands firm, because it is supported by the highly developed technique of the professional actors which for us is still unreachable. If we dedicate ourselves entirely to this we will acquire the same perfect technique of the bourgeois actors. And then the proletarian theatre can defeat the bourgeois theatre.'

I do not agree with this objection.

One should not overestimate the importance of technical formation. It is necessary and indispensable, but the theatre revolution will not take place because of it. Was our revolution in economics accomplished by specialists in finances, economics or commerce? The impulse and guidelines were certainly given by them, but all the weight of the destructive and creative work fell on the workers' shoulders, who had no experience in finances or economics. Even our cultural conquests were achieved with the help of the workers who had been to school for only two years.

Technique is necessary, but in a period of revolution it is not the centre of gravity. The right guidelines are more important, as are the right keywords, and the immediate enthusiasm for what is carried out.

[…]

When bringing in new workers, those who love the theatre, one needs at the same time to fight against the 'dilettantes' who treat the problems of theatre art lightly, superficially and carelessly. We need to arrive at the point where the borders between the genuine amateur and the serious professional have disappeared.

But this is not the most important matter. It needs to be remembered that the task of the proletarian theatre does not consist in the formation of good professional actors who can stage successfully the dramas of a socialist repertoire. Its task is the opening of a road for the creative and artistic instinct of the masses.

This also does not mean that the doors of the workers' theatre are to remain closed to the professional actors. Certainly not! They will have a lot of work to do in the instruction of the amateur actors, in the technical preparation of the performances, in the artistic direction and in the gestation of all other theatre areas in which their experience and understanding are helpful. Professional actors who wish to detach themselves completely from the bourgeois theatre will always have a place in that workers' theatre which is searching for new forms and new scenic conquests.

[…]

At the moment, the construction of a neighbourhood theatre building cannot be dreamed of. Existent spaces need to be adapted. However, the transformation, on a new basis, of the old theatre spaces is needed, and it is needed from the beginning. This transformation facilitates the application of new methods and the learning of completely new possibilities. The inert and traditional theatre space must necessarily be left behind.

[…]

The neighbourhood theatre will not need to close itself behind the four walls of the theatre building. It will take its work outside in the streets and squares. It will form small groups of three or five actors who on feast days or in the evenings will go round the city and stage semi-improvised performances in the parks or the streets' corners. They will perform as readers or gather around groups of people who, under a tree or somewhere similar, will hear them read poetry and prose. These wandering groups or individual actors will, perhaps,

Figure 6 Moscow Proletkult May Day Celebrations, 1919. Note the performer engaged in what looks like a reading, while being elevated on a rudimentary platform and in close proximity to the audience. Courtesy of the State Central Museum of Contemporary History in Russia.

go through the city with a mobile stage and perform short scenes outside.[1] The song and music sections of the proletarian theatre will promote choral song on a large scale, which is close to the Russian spirit and very popular in Russia. This has not been disciplined and cultivated enough (Figure 6).

If the neighbourhood theatre manages to gather around itself a large number of actors, painters and other collaborators then it can use all its energies to attempt

---

1 In her account of post-revolutionary theatre, Nina Gourfinkel gives similar examples of street theatre: 'For the 1 May 1919 festivities, Leningrad was literally covered by four mobile theatre companies. One of these companies staged a Petrushka, the text of which was written by Lunacharsky. A year later an original experiment was attempted. In that year, the power station worked with great difficulty. Power cuts were so common that each time the energy was restored a general outburst of joy and cheering ensued. Twelve trams travelled across the city through half devastated streets. They were equipped with open air platforms, and decorated in drapes and with painted canvas. They were transformed into mobile theatres. During the frequent power cuts, the actors, who had changed in the tram, took the stages and gave short presentations of ten to fifteen minutes. In the next years, these experiments were built upon; in Leningrad alone, one could count three hundred mobile companies. A part of these companies travelled the city and mingled with the crowds. They either used platforms which had been prepared beforehand or acted at the same level of the street or pavements, circled by the spectators. Another group of these companies occupied the platforms more permanently. Trucks were used' (Gourfinkel 1979: 125–6).

the staging of an open-air performance. In the beginning, such a performance would only be a simple carnival procession in which masks and symbolic figures ridicule the hated capitalists and represent the triumph of the workers' class in a symbolic, and perhaps naive, form.

[…]

The availability of a sufficient number of stable neighbourhood theatres makes a successful and central socialist theatre possible. This would obviously be founded in the capital cities. I am not imagining this as a model theatre that would absorb the best dramatic forces of the proletariat, but one which from a technical point of view would be the best-equipped theatre. It would offer the district groups the possibility of showing their best work in a larger auditorium and in front of a more exigent public.

The transformation of the central theatre in a theatre with a fixed group of professional actors, even if these are coming from a work environment, contradicts, in my opinion, the essential principle of proletarian theatre – its highly tight link with the masses. I am convinced that a theatre organized along those lines would inevitably lose the link with the masses. It would become a normal and old-fashioned theatre. Only the repertoire would differentiate it from the rest, and not its basic principles. Such a theatre might stage good socialist dramas, but it will not become the creative proletarian theatre about which it has been spoken. For this reason I believe that a central theatre with a fixed group of professional actors would rob the most precious forces from the districts. It would be pushed onto the dangerous path of the professional theatre's interests. In turning professional a theatre group would naturally have its own workshops for scenography, accessories and costumes, with equally professional and paid personnel. And the creative contact with the masses would get lost.

In one word: a central socialist theatre can promote the Revolution only if it is created on the principles of the neighbourhood theatre described here.

Part Three

Repertoire Issues

Repertoire at a Factory Theatre

Alexander Mgebrov

Source: *Zhizn' v teatre tom 2*, 1932, pp. 302–6

Between 1917 and 1918 I lived in a small room with Chekan.[1] Quite a few people from every part of the literary and artistic world visited. Moreover, we, with Fyodor Sologub[2] and others [...] often went to the outskirts of the workers' districts, where all kinds of evenings and concerts were held. The audiences were made of workers, who showed that they were sensitive to Whitman,[3] Verhaeren, and Tagore,[4] and everything in general that came from true sincerity and uplift.

At one point one of our former comrades from the Ancient Theatre wandered into our path. 'Listen, Mgebrov and Chekan,' he told us. 'Why are you sitting here, without a theatre?! Come to work at the factory! There you will be better understood than anywhere else. I am leading the worker's theatre of the Baltic factory.[5] But it is closer to you. Come on! Work!' Chekan and I, without hesitation, rushed to work.

So, finally, after a long break, I drove to the theatre. And what a wonderful theatre it was! It was the first real workers' theatre that I saw in my journeys, a magnificent dream of the future, the entrancing joy of the spontaneous and elemental creativity of the masses.

Essentially, there was nothing at the theatre of the Baltic factory that corresponds to what we mean today by the workers' theatre. Its repertoire was not that of a standard or typical amateur theatre. But, on the other hand, it had considerable interest from the community of workers and those individuals who rallied around it. There were many talented, peculiar and young workers, who in the years that followed vividly showed themselves in the most diverse fields of social, revolutionary and proletarian artistic activity.

1 Viktoria Chekan, Mgebrov's wife (Mally 1990: 112).
2 Fyodor Sologub (1863–1927); symbolist poet and novelist, who as a playwright became closely associated with Meyerhold (Braun 1998: 76–7).
3 Walt Whitman (1819–92), an American author often referred to by Mgebrov in his descriptions of early Proletkult theatre in Petrograd (see other essays) in Parts Three and Four.
4 Rabindranath Tagore (1861–1941), Indian poet, musician and artist. At the time described by Mgebrov here, Tagore was vocally protesting against British imperialism. His philosophy was based on the belief 'that problems which defy solution at an abstract, intellectual level may nevertheless be resolved at the "existential" level of one's everyday life' (Sen Gupta 2005: 1).
5 This is probably a reference to the Baltic Shipyard, which would mean substantial organizational support for theatre production.

The head of the theatre was, as the representative of the Cultural Commission for the Baltic Plant, a Baltic worker, Georgy Pavlovich Nazarov, who later carried out significant work at the Proletkult. He was full of exceptional energy, quick witted, and could be a good actor.[6] But besides Nazarov I recall a whole series of other people who went on to do important things. Of these, the most significant were Drozdov, who was then our prompter, and one of the first organizers of the Red Guard, a worker called Titov, who also proved to be a great and talented military organizer during the Civil War, Eliseev, later a talented actor of the Proletkult and the Heroic Theatre, Khrustalev, and many others.

The point, of course, is not that all these young people managed to prove themselves as important revolutionaries, social activists and organizers. The most remarkable thing is that, undoubtedly, they were all self-made people, significantly gifted by nature. They quickly proved themselves as soon as life gave them the opportunity.

These young people often gathered at my place. I remember them very well, as very shy, modest young people, blushing with every word and movement. But they thought of their theatre with a rare purity and love. At that time, amateur performances played an important role in the theatre. The actors themselves created, under the direction of the artist Bassovsky, both the scenery and the props, and some plays, such as the *Wreck of the Ship 'Hope'* and Gorky's *The Lower Depths*, were wonderfully staged and successfully performed several times. They gathered a large audience of workers. It should be noted that the work was carried out under enormous strain, with which the whole life of that time was penetrated.

A few impressions from the Baltic Plant are completely unforgettable. The most striking of these is the moment of the German advance on Leningrad,[7] which as we know was completely unexpected.

On the day we got to know of this offensive, an unusual performance was taking place in our theatre: *Electra* by Hugo von Hofmannsthal. Afterwards, I read aloud Émile Verhaeren's poem 'Insurrection'. There was a relatively small audience in the hall, but suddenly a long factory alarm sounded, similar to that which is heard in emergencies. I was already on the stage with a torch in my hands, illuminated by its glow, in the costume of a symbolic worker from the barricades. I did not manage to get to the middle of the poem I was reading, as

---

6 Mally describes Nazarov as the theatre's standout student (Mally 1990: 103–4).
7 By the time of the German advance in the First World War, the city had been named Petrograd. The name Leningrad was then adopted in 1924.

tens of hundreds of people filled the hall in an instant. I finished the poem with great enthusiasm, involuntarily gripped by a strange and unknown tension of being in front of an unexpectedly growing crowd.

At the end of the concert, perfect silence reigned in the hall for some time, despite the mass of people. This silence was unusually deep. The people were waiting for a speaker. And then a very modest, simple, short, almost unnoticeable person, an invisible worker, came on the stage. Without raising his voice, with the complete absence of any oratory pathos, he literally said the following: 'Comrades, the news has come that the Germans are advancing on our city. You, yourself understand what needs to be done. Now everyone who wants to defend Petrograd: sign up at the tables. In two hours, trams from here will take you to the station. Whoever has a rifle, take it; who does not, get one!' That was his whole speech.

But it seems to me that not even the most inspired and brilliant speech would have made such a strong impression as the speaker's words.

'The Repertoire of the Proletarian Theatre'

Platon Kerzhentsev

Source: *Iskusstvo*, no. 1 (5), 1918, pp. 5–7

No one will probably argue that the remake of Dickens's *The Cricket on the Hearth*, staged by the First Studio, was for the past few years the most sensational play in the Russian repertoire. All reviewers were delighted by both the production and the play itself. To attend the *Cricket* was a coveted dream of any Muscovite and provincial spectator. Admiring the *Cricket* became a fashionable theatrical trend.[1]

Of course, there are moments of selfless love in *The Cricket on the Hearth* but the play's overall impression can be characterized by the following: a hymn to philistine comfort, a triumphant song of narrow family life, a praise to a warm fireplace, a cricket on the hearth, a child's cradle, ham and wedding cake.[2] All these elementarily vulgar themes are spiced up with sly intrigue, wrapped in a sentimental poetic mist, and have Dickens's usual happy ending where everything works out in everyone's favour: lost sons are found; shaken marital happiness is reinvigorated; evil rich men repent and become kinder; loving hearts are united through marriage.

If we were to picture the apotheosis of philistine happiness, we would not be able to come up with anything better than the production of *Cricket* or of *A Christmas Carol* (Dickens as well), where the praise for the fried goose is no less important than the story of a repenting and mellowing Scrooge.

[...]

The first year and a half of the Revolution did not bring any updates to the Russian repertoire. In terms of the repertoire, even the theatres that fell into the hands of the sovdeps followed a well-beaten path. Proletarian drama clubs, which sprung up like mushrooms after rain, did not rush to perform new plays,

---

1 Staged in 1914, and directed by Leopold Sulerzhitsky and Boris Sushkevich, the Moscow Art Theatre's First Studio adaptation of Charles Dickens's novella *The Cricket on the Hearth* was undoubtedly a major success that came to characterize the Studio's early phase of work. Rebecca B. Gauss described it as 'a celebration of humanity and the human spirit [with] [...] an emotional impact [that] was enhanced by its anti-war slant which made a great impression as war fever spread across Russia on the eve of World War I' (Gauss 1999: 42).

2 The setting of the play depicted the warm and comfortable, if modest, living arrangements of John Periwinkle. The living room for example was dominated by a large fireplace. The narrative developed as a Christmas story dripping with love and solidarity in the face of greed and human evil (Gauss 1999: 43).

the spirit of which would be close to the working class. Instead they rushed to old bourgeois third-rate stage rags. We must admit bitterly that in the field of theatre the working class of the socialist revolution era fell under the influence of bourgeois tastes, and bad ones at that. In Moscow and its provinces, in 1917–18, socialist youth clubs and proletarian theatres under the flag of the sovdeps staged such vulgarities as *Wife for Rent, Fig Leaf* or crude imitations of the art of Evdokimovs (*Unburied*) and Belaia (*Unemployed*).[3] Of course, the influence of second-rate actors, who weaselled their way into superintending the Soviet theatres, and the associated intellectuals, also impacted on these repertoire choices. Whole organizations (for example, the Factory Workshops and the National Theatres of Moscow) tried to stuff the awakened nation with the concoctions of the Evdokimovs, Klepikovs, etc. Moreover, more responsible organizations were interested in the state theatres, in two or three theatres in everyone's sight in the city centre, rather than in the theatrical life of the work suburbs.[4]

It so happened that the issue of the proletarian repertoire and the people's theatre was raised but in no way solved. Some upgrades in this field have been scheduled, but a lot more needs to be done in the near future. The repertoire of proletarian theatre is yet to be created.

What solutions should we present to the problem of the repertoire of the proletarian theatre? In his witty book, Romain Rolland[5] highlights three principles for a people's theatre: 'The first requisite for a people's theatre is that it must be reinvigorating. It must first of all give pleasure, a sort of physical and moral rest to the workman weary from his day's work.' On the basis of this, Rolland, for example, condemns *The Power of Darkness* as a play that 'weaves a sense of gloom on the poor rather than doing them any good'.[6]

---

3 Sofia Belaia; see Piotr Kogan's essay in Part One 'Socialist Theatre in the Years of the Revolution'.
4 Reference to the Academic Theatres. See Adrian Piotrovsky's essay in Part Two, 'No to Theatre Art, but To Celebration'.
5 Romain Rolland (1866–1944) was a French dramatist, novelist, essayist and art historian. He was awarded the Nobel Prize for Literature in 1915. In 1903 he published a popular essay titled 'The People's Theatre', which Kerzhentsev refers to above and in *Tvorcheskii teatr*. In the latter, Kerzhentsev also reproduced Rolland's views on mass outdoor performances. Based on his analysis of Swiss outdoor spectacles, Rolland argued that mass performances should be based on known historical plots and reproduced using large-scale materials: paintings, marches, sacrifices, battles, dances, pantomimes. More poetic parts should be simple, imbued with one feeling. This dichotomy would give the energy, speed and variety demanded by such performances (Kerzhentsev 1923: 85–6).
6 Written by Leo Tolstoy in 1886, *The Power of Darkness* is described by Laurence Senelick as 'a sombre drama of peasant crime and rapacity' (2007: 404).

'The second requisite is this: the theatre ought to be a source of energy. Its obligation is to avoid what is depressing and discourage what is altogether negative; an antidote is necessary, something to support and exalt the soul.'

And third, finally:

> The theatre ought to be a guiding light to the intelligence.[7] Joy, energy, and intelligence: these are the three fundamental conditions of our people's theatre. It must avoid two excesses. The first is moral pedagogy, which seeks to extract lifeless lessons from living works (this is both not aesthetic and useless, since an alert public will immediately scent the bait and avoid it). The second is impersonal dilettantism, the only purpose of which is to amuse the people at any cost. This is a dishonourable thing for which the people won't always thank you.[8]

These remarks, albeit with a few additions and corrections, can also be used for the proletarian repertoire. Theatre has to stimulate the working class towards an energetic life, improve its vibrant revolutionary mindset and enrich one's experiences and field of study. However, anything inartistic, crudely biased and moralizing must be avoided.

First of all, the proletarian theatre has to find plays imbued with a true socialist spirit, which is the revolutionary protest against the binds of capitalism.

We must admit that at this point there are almost no plays of this kind. It's doubtful whether we can find more than a dozen such plays that are even somewhat close to these requirements, not to mention that some of them are not even translated into Russian.

Even if we broaden our requirements and include plays which, in one way or another, do tackle the revolutionary struggles of nations, or scold the capitalist way of life, we would still not have a lot to pick from.

We can mention Verhaeren's *The Dawn*[9] (though the play is imbued with the idea of history that is shaped by one hero, which is foreign to the proletariat), *The Weavers*, Galsworthy's[10] plays (*The Mob*, *Strife*, *Justice* – though notes of 'conciliation' can be heard in *Strife*, and in the other plays a deliberate bias

---

7 In Russia, where theatre was always seen as a means for moral improvement (Aquilina 2020: 7–9), this third requisite would have certainly struck a major chord with cultural theorists like Kerzhentsev.

8 Footnote in the original: Romain Rolland, 'The People's Theatre', pages 83–6.

9 A popular post-revolutionary choice; see how Kerzhentsev recommended certain adaptations to the play in order to make it relevant to the post-revolutionary world, in his essay, also found in this part, 'Adapt the plays!'. Furthermore, see Aquilina (2020: 116–18), where I use the same essay to discuss how adaptation involves what I refer to as 'critical processing', where certain aspects of, for example, a play are retained while others dropped.

10 John Galsworthy (1867–1933), English novelist and playwright, winner of the Nobel Prize in Literature in 1932.

ruins the overall impression), Heijermans's *Wreck of the Ship 'Hope',*[11] Romain Rolland's plays about the era of the French Revolution (*The Wolves, Fourteenth of July, Danton*), plays by the Irish dramaturges, largely unknown in Russia: Lady Gregory[12] (for example, *The Gaol Gate*), Yeats[13] (for example, *The Countess Kathleen*), Octave Mirbeau's[14] satires (*Epidemics, The Purse, Thief, Scruples* and *Jean Roule*), and some of Bernard Shaw's[15] plays (*The Devil's Disciple, Mrs Warren's Profession, The Chocolate Soldier*).

Almost no Russian play catches the eye. There is Gorky's[16] *Enemies*, though theatrically this play is doomed to fail. Andreev's[17] *Savva* is acceptable as a protest against religious superstition.

Of course, not one of the above-mentioned plays can be called exemplary for the socialist theatre. And the proletarian theatre is doomed to fail from the beginning if it gets into the loop of plays like the ones mentioned above. We must also use the treasury of past centuries. Even from the repertoire of contemporary theatre we can select several dozens of wonderful plays, works which have an artistic and social meaning to which the proletariat will relate to in a much better way than the current philistine audience. This classic repertoire will do much towards developing taste, like a necessary education, which is the only weapon against theatrical vulgarity. Theatre managers who become addicted to plays from the working life, and always with a socialist bias, will only push the audiences away from the theatre towards plays like *Unburied* and *Unemployed*.

In a workers' theatre, there must be scents of romantic heroism and the pathos of struggle. However, there must also be carefree laughter and an energetic, uncontainable fun. Let all the eras of the past and all the lines of theatrical creativity pass before the masses. When shown to audiences from the working class, and under the treatment of working-class troupes, this old repertoire can be transformed and seen in a completely new light.

---

11 Herman Heijermans (1864–1924), whose work *Wreck of the Ship 'Hope'* was again closely linked, if not in an entirely positive manner, with the early history of the First Studio.
12 Lady Gregory (Isabella Augusta, 1852–1932), Irish dramatist and co-founder of the Abbey Theatre.
13 William Butler Yeats (1865–1939), also co-founder of the Abbey Theatre and winner of the Nobel Prize in Literature in 1923.
14 Octave Mirbeau (1848–1917), French novelist and playwright,
15 (George) Bernard Shaw (1856–1950), Irish playwright and political activist, winner of the Nobel Prize in Literature in 1925.
16 Maxim Gorky (1868–1936), prominent literary figure in both the pre- and post-revolutionary eras, eventually closely linked to the development of socialist realism.
17 Leonid Andreev (1871–1919), Russian playwright and novelist, whose works ranged from naturalism to symbolism. His plays take a pessimistic outlook on life, with *Savva* being about a young terrorist who tries to blow up an icon (Senelick 2007: 17–18).

The working class and its future socialist theatre will not deny the plays of the past. Beautiful examples of art, past and present, must be included in the repertoire: some Greek plays, Shakespeare's tragedies and comedies (*Hamlet, Lear, A Midsummer Night's Dream* and *Julius Caesar*); Calderon's *Life Is a Dream*; Molière's *The Imaginary Invalid, The Middle Class Gentleman, Tartuffe*; Lope de Vega's *Fuenteovejuna*; Schiller's *The Robbers, Wilhelm Tell*; Prosper Mérimée's *Jacquerie*; Ibsen's *Brand, An Enemy of the People, The Master Builder*, Gogol's *The Government Inspector* and *Marriage*, and others like *The Woods, The Storm, The Dowry, Fruits of Enlightenment*.

Many plays from both the classic and socialist repertoires are yet to be translated or extracted from the archival dust of oblivion. It is not only the repertoire that needs renewal, a lot of work and new discoveries. The theatre in general needs it as well.

For us to somehow try to circumvent this scarcity of the repertoire, we must resort to the hard, ungrateful and challenging staging of novels and stories. As material for production we can point to Wells's[18] novels devoted to a futuristic society, Voynich's[19] *Gadfly*, Zola's[20] *Germinal*, perhaps Felix Gras's[21] trilogy, written in the era of French Revolution (including *Terror* and *White Terror*), Pierre Hamp's[22] works (*On the Rails*, which is still not translated completely), Frank Norris's[23] novels about American bread syndicates, Jack London's[24] short stories and novellas, Upton Sinclair[25] and others.

Short works which would be curious to stage include those of A. Gastev[26] (*Poetry of the Worker's Blow*), Walt Whitman,[27] Verhaeren and others.

Finally, we will have to utilize extensively the principle of improvisation. Commedia dell'arte has all the reasons to be reborn in Russia right now. Let the director or someone give the working-class troupe a few words on some

---

18 Herbert George Wells (1866–1946), English prolific writer.
19 Ethel Voynich (1864–1960), Irish author. *Gadfly*, which is a play situated in Italy of the 1840s when under Austrian yoke, became particularly popular in Russia.
20 Émile Zola (1840–1902), father of theatrical naturalism.
21 Felix Gras (1844–1901), French author.
22 Henri Bourrillon, pseudonym Pierre Hamp (1876–1962), French author.
23 Benjamin Franklin 'Frank' Norris (1870–1902), American author who wrote primarily in the naturalist style.
24 Jack London (1876–1916), a very successful American novelist, journalist and social activist.
25 Upton Sinclair (1878–1968), prolific American author, winner of the Pulitzer Prize for Fiction in 1943.
26 Aleksei Gastev (1882–1941) was an important advocate for what Rolf Hellebust refers to as 'the metallization and mechanization of the proletariat in the first decades of the Soviet Union' (1997: 503). He was particularly popular in the first years after the Revolution as a writer of proletarian poems.
27 Mgebrov's essays in Parts Three and Four make reference to Walt Whitman's works.

topic. Maybe, he will highlight a few types and two or three moments in the development of the plot. Everything else, the dialogue, the development of the plot and its culmination will be improvised by the performers themselves, perhaps with the participation of the public.

The desire to write or improvise one's own plays is incredibly strong right now. There is talk of such improvised plays from a couple of places in Russia, from villages and work settlements. These plays are adored by both the performers and the population more than the plays with a rigid and strict delivery of the text.

This thirst of improvisation reveals a healthy theatrical instinct. When it becomes a little bit more formed, and after going through the ordeal of theatrical experience or schooling, we will have new proletarian dramaturges and the repertoire will be consolidated.

For now, we must admit that the proletarian theatre's repertoire is not yet created.

Notes on Pavel Bessalko's *The Bricklayer*

Alexander Mgebrov

Source: *Zhizn' v teatre tom 2*, 1932, pp. 420–33

'Insurrection' was first staged by the Proletkult at the end of December 1918 on a double bill with the play *The Bricklayer* by Pavel Bessalko. This was just before our trip to the Western front. In writing *The Bricklayer*, Bessalko was undoubtedly influenced by everything that had happened at the Proletkult, putting a lot of its personalities into the play. At the same time, and oddly enough, the play showed an Ibsenian influence, especially through his play *The Master Builder*. At the same time, Bessalko's play is also permeated with a proletarian ideology, one of the main carriers of which was the author himself.

[…]

In the play, Bessalko deduces the type of a new man, the proletarian-builder type, to whom he contrasts the old bourgeois architect. He touches the acute question that is related to the whole of modernity: Who is the real builder? Is it the architect with his drawings, the architect who only knows desk work and never dares to go to the construction site, to the top of the buildings which his drawings erect, the architect who cannot help but feel dizzy on these peaks? Or is it the one who actually climbs these peaks, the bricklayer who stacks bricks, who goes near the sky itself and actually risks his life? These moments are remarkably vivid in Bessalko's play. Here he is a real proletarian. In the rhythm of the whole play, it is felt that Bessalko does not get dizzy from these heights, his spirit correctly guesses the psyche of the builders, not only of the drawings, but of the building itself. The play shows the architect's wife, a woman from the bourgeois class with whom the bricklayer falls in love. I must say that the whole play is designed in symbolic colours. And the bricklayer, the architect himself, and the wife are not real people, but only symbols.

The wife of the architect, a luxurious, beautiful woman, falls in love with the bricklayer and does everything to make this love work. Her husband, citing vertigo, does not dare to climb to the top, but she is attracted by the height and to the mad masons, who are merrily working at the top of the scaffoldings without experiencing any vertigo.

All this is full of symbolism. In Bessalko, as in Ibsen, height is a symbol of human affairs and aspirations. But in Ibsen's *The Master Builder*, the idea is expressed in more abstract terms: it is individualized. Bessalko, on the other hand, interprets everything through class self-consciousness. From the very first moments of the play, he sharply demarcates two worlds, two opposing ideologies. One is the representative of the bourgeois class, an architect who believes that his ideas and drawings make him the real builder. The other is made of the people of another class, i.e. the class of the workers, who only unconsciously fulfil these ideas and plans. However, the ideology of the working classes is that of people who have nothing to lose, because the bourgeois builders only allow them the highest levels and the basements.[1]

This basic idea in Bessalko's play is expressed in sufficient imagery. The young, beautiful enthusiasm of the bricklayer is brightly contrasted with the senile architect. The judge between the two worlds, between both of them, is a woman, the giver of life, who is based on the immediacy of attraction, who is free from dogmatic and false prejudices. The bricklayer's faith in life, fervently affirming the ideology of his class, and based on humanity in the broad sense of the word, wins the heart of the architect's wife, who agrees without hesitation to the bricklayer's demands to leave her husband.

'I cannot love builders', she says to her husband, 'who are not at the top of their buildings, and you are one of them.'

She remains adamant in this decision even when the architect, wounded by her reproach, decides to climb the scaffoldings. 'Do not do that, you will feel dizzy,' his wife warns ironically. But he replies: 'I will prove that the creator is higher than the created ... '

Despite the strong will that seizes the architect, he does not cope with the heights of the scaffoldings and falls down ...

With this, Bessalko seems to emphasize that the bourgeois class must sooner or later die. Nothing in the world can save it from destruction, neither strong will, nor knowledge, nor all the advantages and privileges it won by humiliating all of mankind.

The image of the architect in Bessalko, despite his characteristic lack of words, is sustained to the end. Bessalko managed to remarkably construct the first act of his play. With a few brightly symbolic words and phrases, he immediately introduces you to the very essence of mankind's class struggle. At the same time there is a youthful and stormy enthusiasm, and a sense of humanity in everything, so that you involuntarily pass over certain parts of the play that are

---

1 Mgebrov is making reference to the fact that in the houses of the rich the servants' quarters were often on the lowest and highest floors.

undoubtedly primitive or its accidental contradictions which necessarily emerge when big thoughts are only clothed in symbols.

We staged the first act of the play in spring-like and joyful tones. In order to emphasize the superiority of the new proletarian ideology, which was then rapidly affirming itself, we introduced mass scenes into this act, which Bessalko did not have. His play begins with a conversation between a bricklayer and a house painter holding on to a high wall of a house under construction. In our version, the play began with movement on a large scale. Downstairs, against the wall, the bricklayers are in their work overalls. Hammers are heard. A sonorous song fills the air. There is a lot of movement. A lot of hearty laughter. Friendly productive work is bubbling. The bricklayer is on the scaffolding, above the painter. In the sunlight, his cheerful song rises from above.

Our main task was to give the play a lot of air, light and energy. Therefore, the appearance of the architect, pedantic, dry, narcissistic, buttoned up and fully believing in his superiority over the bricklayers, those insignificant executors of his great plan, was especially emphasized. Scaffoldings rose on the stage. And when the architect, overwhelmed by vanity, climbed them, his figure really flashed higher and higher on the scaffoldings. His fall was portrayed quite naturalistically: a huge doll was dropped from above.

The second act takes the viewer to a simple work room, where the bricklayer and the architect's wife now live together as husband and wife.

The bricklayer draws something on a board. This is a boring day in autumn. There is rain outside (according to the author's remarks). The bricklayer is studying construction. He must take the place of the death architect. He wants to be the new builder, as his class demands. The architect's wife does not really like this. She fell in love with him not for knowledge, but for strength and immediacy, for the fact that his mind was that of a simple worker which had not dried up from mathematical calculations and for the fact that he did not look like the death architect. But this offends the bricklayer. The simplicity of ignorance is objectionable to him. Having met the architect's wife, he can no longer bear the ignorance of savagery. A dispute arises between them, through which the views of the bricklayer become clear. The argument is interrupted by an old house painter, who rushes excitedly into the room, announcing that the revolution has begun. The old painter enthusiastically talks about what is taking place in the streets, and this story prompts the bricklayer and his wife to rush and help the comrades. The end of this act sounds like a stormy appeal, and here Bessalko's directness revealed itself, tearing through the whole philosophy with which he tried to fill this part of the play.

The third act is an apotheosis. It takes place at the foot of the fantastic tower, which the bricklayer dreamed of in the second act and which he has now finally built. Here the bricklayer is a symbol of the victory of a new class. He is surrounded by a crowd of workers who nominated him as the representative of their power. He is greeted in front of the whole world by the chairman of the commune.

The celebration begins by raising the banner on the tower. It is collected by the bricklayer, who boldly climbs the scaffoldings to crown the top of the tower with the banner of the commune. The crowd watches him with great attention.

The images which Bessalko uses to depict the crowd express various moods: not only friends but also the enemies of the working class, doubting and not believing in the victorious march of the proletariat.

The bricklayer reaches the top and fastens the banner of the commune at the top of the tower. This moment is welcomed with enthusiastic cries.

Thus ends this short but vividly symbolic play, the first dramatic work of the late Bessalko, which, in spite of all its primitiveness, revealed the author's undoubted dramatic talent, courage and novelty of approach, and a bright, ardent faith, not only in the future, but also in the present as a fiery rush to the future.

'Adapt the Plays!'

Platon Kerzhentsev

Source: *Vestnik teatra*, no. 36, 1919, pp. 6–8

The author of the article 'The Question of Change' (in *Theatre News*, no. 33) refers with some scepticism to 'V. Kerzhentsev's light hand'[1] and my plan for the radical adaptation of theatre plays.

Our reality is that we do not have a repertoire yet, which is a certainty. Nowadays it is important that we redo and adapt plays.

The author of the article mainly pointed out the need to follow a common style and approach in adapting the plays, so that they do not turn into a whimsical mosaic of gemstones, cobblestones, concrete and stumps. Holy truth! Two different approaches are possible: adapt a play according to the author's conception, or use a play as the basis for creation, adding different material and giving it another tempo or style.

I can give you a specific example to illustrate my ideas. Last spring, the Moscow Proletkult, on my initiative, started to adapt Verhaeren's *The Dawn*.[2] A military mobilization took most of the Proletkult staff to the war front and immediately cut short the idea. Only a general plan of the changes remained, a plan which was created through collective meetings.

In working on Verhaeren's creation, we tried to save the character and topics of the play: the strict pathos that did not have one smile, the deep symbolism, the author's genius in historical generalization and the other features of this modern and sagacious play.

However, we also had some essential objections with which to contend. All throughout the play, the central position is taken by the hero. He is the one who makes history, but the crowd is very passive and from time to time even stupid. The hero – Herenien – is illuminated way too often and there is too much tedious talk. He talks about himself, his work, his dreams, his plans etc.

There are other problems. The hero, who should personify the brain and desires of the proletariat, shows hesitance or half-heartedness. He is willing to make concessions and to negotiate. In our political language, he is a

---

1 V. Kerzhentsev is a pseudonym the author sometimes used (Mally 1990: 111). His real name was Platon Lebedev.
2 Vsevolod Meyerhold directed a famous version on *The Dawn* in 1920, of which Kerzhentsev was particularly critical. See Braun (2016: 211–6) and Braun (1998: 162–5).

'compromiser'. A beautiful scene at the Aventine loses heroic pathos through Herenien's 'menshevism'. How can the play be successful if the proletariat is shown in an image which is not typical of our days?

The first necessary changes were the promotion of the crowd and giving Herenien a different character.

The second set of changes concerned the play's technical form. *The Dawn* is long, massive and more appropriate as literature rather than for the stage. It is clear that first of all we have to cut these long speeches and, secondly, turn the word into action. What about the endless, sluggish and weak scene with Clara? What about Herenien's story about the people's uprising and fraternizing with the enemy (Act III, Scene I)? Can the theatre show this scene? We can and should keep the play safe, but at least make it articulate, dynamic and economical with words.

However, the adaptation and cutting of the play did not complete the work. The need to add something was clearly felt. First of all, in this play, dedicated to the class struggle, there is no representative of the hated enemy against whom the people direct their uprising. A group of generals appear briefly, an impersonal consul passes quickly by, and that is it. The Banks and the Parliament, which are badly mentioned by Verhaeren, only remain as words. The real owners of the Big City stay in the shade. This dramatic method can certainly, at times, be exceptionally impressive. The hero can impress more if he rarely appears on the scene. However, the play has to be constructed accordingly if this is to take place, and the transparent gleams of the psychological attack on the behind-the-scenes hero have to be concentrated. Verhaeren hasn't got it. He fell for Herenien's oratory and forgot about the hero's enemies. That's why there is the need to add a short and terrible scene, the meeting of the Senate, with waving candles and the sound of weapons and the noise of the uprising. There are some strange business figures and others from the parliament. They are wary of words and tight-fisted with money. They are preparing treason and bribes. They are afraid but they do take risks. They are ready to run and do not mind risking all.

This scene will immediately show the figures of the city owners, which in the play are only fleetingly mentioned.

To brighten the private and intimate psychology of the participants in the struggle, a short scene with dialogues between the people in the crowd – mother and son, a couple in love, two friends, etc. – was planned. This was to take the place of the lyrical scene between Herenien and Clara.

Finally, we wanted to make an essential addition to the final part of the play. Verhaeren brilliantly foresaw the fight not only against militarism and imperialism, but also against the parliament. The word 'Soviet' is almost on his lips. Of course, it is difficult to add this term, but we have to dot the 'i' and to further and dramatically push forward the dictatorship of the proletariat. Moreover, Verhaeren glorifies the end of the war and the fellowship between the workers, but all the action is set in one country. Nowadays, we are living in such an international context that it comes naturally to add an international motif to the play. The uprising and victory of the workers happened not only in the Big City, but also in other counties. Herenien's funeral becomes a feast because of the radio news about the victorious revolution in the Mountain Country or the Republic of the Star's flag (Radio news about Hungary arrived at the time of the Party congress).

A general line of the play was planned as follows: the development from chaos and decay (wars, fires, hunger and anger) to synthesis, from destruction to creativity, from war to revolution and peace.

With regard to the staging: the plan was to distinguish four or five main actions and support them with intermediate pieces (behind the city gate, the Senate's Congress, a few dialogues, etc.). Briefly, the play's plan was as follows.

A scene at the crossroads shows the besieged country in flames and chaos, and the enmity between different social groups. The peasants are angry at the townspeople and the workers. The poor hate the farmers. There is the uprising of those who are hungry and tired of the war, but they are without direction. We can see the dawn of freedom in the dead of Herenien's father. We can hear hope and the prediction of victory in the words of the workers. Here we can see Herenien as a son and a leader, and Eno as a person of compromise. In front of the people, two ways are outlined. The crowd follows Herenien to the gate not to take part in the funeral of the old man; no – the village is going to fight; this is the agrarian movement of the revolution. The peasants are eager to fight and join the proletariat in the city (an Aventine strike).

But the city gate is strong. The power of the city owners has not been broken yet. We can see generals and the army guarding the gate. The first scene: militarism is in front of the people.

Somewhere here we can add the Senate scene. The proletarian uprising in the city worries the Senate. Near the city walls there is a peasant uprising. What are the Senate going to do? The soldiers are not reliable. A council suggests the use of provocation, a tested method, or the bribing of one of the national leaders. This is not extended to the clean-fingered and perfect Herenien and Eno. Therefore, this role has to be changed accordingly.

Then there is the Aventine. The central part of the play depicts a crisis. At this point the stage changes drastically. Eno's words move Herenien, who is stubborn and strong-willed. He is against any form of agreement. Eno is weak-spirited and bribed, and dreams of a career. He is for settlement and agreement. When tactics are discussed someone is for terror. But Herenien wins and the October Revolution is conceived. We are on the eve of the uprising.

Two additional moments are placed here: a scene in a trench and the preparation of the organized fraternity. Maybe we can also add Clara and Herenien's short scene here. She came here to find her husband.

A couple of short lyrical scenes follow – before the tragic hour of the revolutionary fight the participants are worried.

The hour of the uprising has come – the peasants join the proletariat of the Big City. The enemy's soldiers kill their officers and join the uprising.

Scenes of fight and victory, and Herenien's death. He is killed by a hand from a corner, probably Eno's.

The last action starts with the grand funeral procession (the leader's body is placed on a high platform in the middle of the theatre hall).

The funeral becomes a celebration of the victory. The news of the proletariat's victory in other counties is heard. The funeral songs change into a victory hymn. All the people (maybe even the audience) are cheerfully singing about the victory of the proletariat.

This is the main outline of an adapted *The Dawn*, the way it was made in our collective meetings. The full adaptation will take place during the process of staging and rehearsal.

Even now I think that, if we adapt the play with courage and determination, Verhaeren's unactable *The Dawn* might become the favourite play of the proletarian audience.

We can make mistakes in the process of adaptation, from which we must learn. I would prefer badly adapted plays to that classical junk we now see at the theatre.

Garland's Inheritance

Valerian Pletnev

Source: *An extract from the play*, Act 1, pp. 5–17

How we acquired *Garland's Inheritance*

Plot – *Pravda* No. 111 on 22 May 1923, article by M. Koltsov. The scenario is edited by V. Pletnev and S. Eisenstein. The scenario is based on an American cinematographic tempo. Text – V. Pletnev.

In general: this is the proof for anyone claiming that we 'do not have a repertoire' – such rich material is in front of these people every day, but one just has to know how to use it.

Act 1, Episode 1

Offices of Factory Modern. Director's office.

MR GLAN: (*Walks around the office*) If it goes on this way we will go bankrupt! (*Picks the phone*) Hello … Dobby … What's up with the advert? When is it going to be ready, damn it!? (*Hangs up*) Idiots!
AGENT: (*Enters*) Good afternoon, Mr Glan.
MR GLAN: Answer?
AGENT: The union will not give us the permit.
MR GLAN: Why?
AGENT: Our competitors …
MR GLAN: And you are walking around mouth open! (*Aside*) Have you spoken to the union's secretary?
AGENT: Yes.
MR GLAN: And?
AGENT: The secretary suffers from honesty.
MR GLAN: Bad secretary! One more step towards the collapse. What shall we do?
AGENT: Go higher.
MR GLAN: To Gompes himself … to the head? But he is not here; he is somewhere fishing for votes. Can we talk to his secretary?

AGENT: Of course.

MR GLAN: Go to him immediately and arrange an appointment for me. Is he suffering from the same … ?

AGENT: Well, no, I suppose. (*Exits*) Will call in an hour!

MR GLAN: Asvert! (*A servant enters and opens a poster so that one can see only the text: Cigars of the death.*)

Episode 2

Offices of Factory Ella. Director's office.

MR STROPP: (*At the phone*) How soon am I going to see them? Modern is giving the advert tomorrow and we are scratching our feet … Printing house? Give them an extra dollar … Don't sleep, damn it! (*Hangs up*) If tomorrow they are going to work like that then we'll go bankrupt …

AGENT: Good afternoon, Mr Stropp.

MR STROPP: Good … Any good news if it is a good afternoon?

AGENT: The union of the tobacco makers is going to sign the agreement with you. Modern was denied.

MR STROPP: Not bad. But we need the approval from the Federation of Labour. And this old devil Gompers is somewhere fishing for votes. Can the secretary approve?

AGENT: No …

MR STROPP: In this case we need to get Gompers.

AGENT: He will be at the office at 5 p.m. The secretary will make you an appointment. I've arranged it.

MR STROPP: Does Modern know about Gompers's arrival?

AGENT: I think not.

MR STROPP: Well, and how is Mr Glan?

AGENT: Very bad. Furious as never before. Getting ready for a fight with you. He wants to see Gompers.

MR STROPP: Really! He cannot see Gompers before us.

AGENT: Don't worry! I am supposed to arrange Mr Glan's appointment with Gompers.

MR STROPP: Great! (*Phone rings*) Hello! Yes? Great! (*To the SECOND agent:*) Prepare the car at half past four. (*Takes the phone*) Hello … Smith? Give the agent 250 dollars. Prepare the new employment act and the advert for the new jobs. Yellow!… 10–15 per cent. (*Hangs up*) Car, quarter to five. Let's go!

GOMPERS'S SECRETARY: (*At the phone, speaks with Mr Stropp*) Ella?… Mr Stropp? Great! Samuel Gompers is expecting you at 5 p.m.

MR STROPP'S SERVANT: (*At the phone*) Hello. 1-14-b … Modern? Mr Glan?… Gompers will be at the office at 5 p.m. Mr Stropp is off to see him … A meeting … At 5 p.m. …. All the best!

Episode 3

Office of Samuel Gompers, Chairman of the American Federation of Labour

GOMPERS: (*Enters fast. Takes off his cloak and cap with glasses*) The reds organized the unemployed and a cruel attack was carried against me.

SECRETARY: In our decent district?

GOMPERS: Yes … This virus spreads everywhere. We can expect anything from them. (*Sits at the table*) What do you have? Speak briefly.

SECRETARY: Emergency. The situation with the tobacco factories Ella and Modern.

GOMPERS: Do they want a permit?

SECRETARY: Yes. The union refused Modern and gave the permit to Ella.

GOMPERS: Why do we have to deal with it?

SECRETARY: There is some yellow workforce at Ella factory.

GOMPERS: OK! Then we won't approve the agreement.

SECRETARY: But the yellow only do the heavy work.

GOMPERS: So what? And how many healthy young men are unemployed and sell their muscles to the Bolsheviks? Kick away the yellow and shut our people up. We cannot indulge these yellow pigs. (*Knock at the door*)

SECRETARY: Hello … The Director of Ella.

MR GLAN: (*Enters*) Mr Gompers?

GOMPERS: How can I help you … ?

MR GLAN: Glan, director of factory Modern.

GOMPERS: Please …

MR GLAN: (*Sits down*) I hope you are aware of our situation? … The tobacco makers' union refused to give us the permit.

GOMPERS: Yes, I know.

MR GLAN: Great! I wonder if you, Mr Gompers, are aware of the fact that Ella uses yellow labour.

SECRETARY: Yes, we know. There are some yellow unskilled workers.

MR GLAN: You are wrong. The Chinese are also operating some of the machinery. They also work with the cigars.

GOMPERS: Even cigars?
MR GLAN: Even cigars. Such union's policy surprises us. To let the yellow work. Is that their cigar you are smoking? The Chinese sometimes glue them with their own saliva … Well, with the tongue …
GOMPERS: The federation hasn't considered this question yet. Of course we are against the yellow labour … (*Makes a gesture for the secretary to leave*)
MR GLAN: You should understand … The fact that the unions support the yellow labour, especially during the elections, is not good for you. We have 3,500 workers …

Episode 4

At the shop. Windows are open. Light fabric curtains protect the goods from the sun. Shop assistant is on the stage.

Backstage a loud sound of two car sirens is heard. Then, a crash. Mr Stropp flies onto the stage pushing away the goods. The chauffeur falls through the window.

REPORTER: (*Runs in, writing very fast*) Both cars smashed. One flew into the busy shop. Two are killed, six are injured, some badly.
POLICEMAN: (*Runs in, leans towards Stropp*) Alive! He is just unconscious.
SECOND POLICEMAN: (*Next to the chauffeur*) Both are alive …
SHOP ASSISTANT: My goods, My goods! Oh, my God!
POLICEMAN: (*To the SECOND*) Ask for the motor! (*To the shop assistant*) Don't worry, Madame. We'll draw up a report now.

Episode 5

Samuel Gompers's office

MR GLAN: (*Continues the conversation*) We will increase the pay by 5–15 per cent, we will organize medical inspection and, with your help, I hope we will keep good relations.
GOMPERS: Yes, if the tobacco maker's union will agree to that.
MR GLAN: I suppose your word will be taken into account.
GOMPERS: I will pass a word, of course. But there is no guarantee that it will solve the case in your favour.
MR GLAN: We hope it will. Very grateful for your help. Good bye!

GOMPERS: Good bye!
(*Mr Glan leaves*)
GOMPERS: (*To the secretary*) The permit should be transferred to Modern. Phone the tobacco makers.
SECRETARY: They may not agree.
GOMPERS: If so ask them to come to me.
SECRETARY: Tomorrow? In the morning? In the afternoon?
GOMPERS: Morning is better.
MR STROPP: (*Comes in fast*) Mr Gompers?
GOMPERS: (*Formally*) Who am I talking to?
MR STROPP: The director of Ella factory.
GOMPERS: Which enjoys yellow labour?
MR STROPP: I am sorry … But …
GOMPERS: And the tobacco maker's union has 5,000 unemployed?
MR STROPP: But the union agreed … We pay more … The yellow are involved only in unskilled labour …
GOMPERS: And some skilled jobs … Cigars for example …
MR STROPP: It's a lie!
GOMPERS: I am very sorry. I have no time. Until your factory has a single yellow worker the Federation won't help you with the permit.
(*Mr Stropp turns fast and looks at the secretary in an angry manner; the secretary shrugs and follows him.*)
GOMPERS: (*Writes down*) Modern Factory 3,500 votes. Not a lot, and it's never too many.

Episode 6

MR GLAN: (*Examines posters. The servant opens them in front of him.*) This should be placed in the City. These are for the railway stations and piers. That one in Tamany Hall. This? Well, not bad! Mr Stropp will enjoy it. 'Cigars of the death'. Sounds good.
CHAFFEUR: Mr Glan … I am banned from driving for three months for crashing into Mr Stropp.
MR GLAN: (*At the phone*) Hello. Dobby? … Give the chauffeur 200 dollars and keep him in the garage … How to register it? … Health expenses for injuries after the accident with Mr Stropp.
CHAFFEUR: It was a good job that I sent him straight into the shop. It costs more, Mr Glan.
MR GLAN: Well, well! Thank Mr Stropp that he let you make money out of him.

CHAFFEUR: But you promised more.

MR GLAN: But I give less. Turn left and move away!

DOBBY: (*Enters*) Mr Glan, Miss Adeline asks you to spare some time. Mr Bodwen came and they want to talk to you.

MR GLAN: Mr Bodwen? What does he need? I have no time for chitchatting.

DOBBY: What shall I answer?

MR GLAN: I will phone her when I have time. Order the sticking of the adverts, and hire twenty motors for two days. Launch the sales for six new types. The percentage of the first type in the new stock should be increased by 15 per cent. Don't waste time. We should finish with Mr Stropp.

Episode 7

Offices of Ella Factory. Director's office.

MR STROPP: (*Walks around the office*) I don't understand anything … We will close the factory and chuck out 2,500 people for Mr Gompers … unemployed. (*To Garland*) How do you like such a scenario?

GARLAND: (*Fixing electric wires*) Unemployment is not a gift, neither to us nor to the Federation.

MR STROPP: But you will have it. We haven't got the permit. We use yellow labour. As if Modern doesn't!

GARLAND: The union is now aware of this.

MR STROPP: What does your union know? If Sam-drink-tea of San-pin-lin cut his ponytail and called himself John, he will still not turn white … Do a good check-up. You can ask the union to do so.

GARLAND: We will talk to the union.

MR STROPP: The sooner the better. (*At the phone*) Hello, Smith? Postpone the announcement to hire more workers. Give the lists for the sections … only half of the new batch of goods should be processed. Yes, yes … Workers? … Let them know!… It's not a secret, the policy of Mr Gompers … (*to Garland*) Here is the result of your head's acts. Unemployment …

GARLAND: For us this is not the first time.

Episode 8

Union's club. Cinema. Dancing.

GARLAND: Hello, John! A bottle of cider from you for the wage increase.

JOHN: Hello, Garland! No problem. Our Mr Glan is happy, gave 15 per cent. He is campaigning for GOMPERS: 'Vote for him, he is a good old fellow'!
GARLAND: Ella is reducing the staff by half and threatening to close down completely. Gompers made a silly thing.
FIRST GOMPERS SUPPORTER: (*Approaching*) Garland is not happy. The yellow haven't got the permit and the salary increase.
GARLAND: There is only a hundred of the yellow but we are two thousand. Stupid politics!
FIRST GOMPERS SUPPORTER: Wow! Garland is criticizing. Do you want to vote against Gompers at the election?
GARLAND: That is my business.
(*Gompers enters with two workers.*)
GARLAND: (*Stands up fast and approaches him*) Mr Gompers, just a question.
GOMPERS: Yes.
GARLAND: Why have you decided to give the permit to Modern?
GOMPERS: What? The permit? Oh, yes! … We don't like the yellow. That is the colour of lies, betrayal and low wage rates.
GARLAND: You gave privilege to one of the competitors, and we lose our jobs. Does the Federation want this?
GOMPERS: I am ready to discuss the matter with you. You can find me every day at the Federation. (*Turns and leaves*)
GARLAND: (*Aloud*) Is that how old leaders protect our interests?
FIRST WORKER: Old fox! Elections. Is he shouting against the yellow? Yes, it gives him the votes.
FIRST GOMPERS SUPPORTER: Hey, mate, be quiet!
FIRST WORKER: Isn't it the truth?
FIRST GOMPERS SUPPORTER: The truth or not – just stop your gab!
FIRST WORKER: I don't know how to turn my tail like you.
FIRST GOMPERS SUPPORTER: Don't you know how? We'll teach you.

Episode 9

Gompers's office.

GOMPERS: You should understand. We are in the middle of the elections. Our competitors are very strong. The yellow labour is a trump card in their hands. Do you want to have your representatives in the parliament?
GARLAND: Representatives who get there in any way possible?

GOMPERS: What do you mean?

GARLAND: That not all ways are honest.

GOMPERS: (*Bangs the table*) Think what you are saying, damn! (*Comes close to Garland*) Do you think that Samuel Gompers gets the votes by pleasing the capitalists?

GARLAND: I don't want to think so.

GOMPERS: You don't want … But you do think, don't you?

GARLAND: Yes, I do. People wouldn't like to think this way but they do. Modern increased the pay and now increased the production as well. Modern has been giving a good product for two weeks but now they are selling rotten stuff. Modern never used yellow labour, but now it does. And the workers speak openly: Gompers was … bought!

GOMPERS: I? Bought?

GARLAND: Yes. And that is the truth. You didn't take the money … Old Gompers is an honest man, but he pities his nice chair in the parliament. Mr Glan is campaigning for you and the place in the parliament is guaranteed.

GOMPERS: These are intrigues. What do you want?

GARLAND: Me? I wanted to tell you what people think about you. Probably it will be good for the Federation's policy. (*Leaves*)

(*Gompers rings. Secretary comes in.*)

GOMPERS: Make an inquiry: Garland, an electrician at the factory Ella, where he worked before, who knows him, how he lives, who he is in touch with. I don't trust this guy.

Episode 10

A street next to the court.
(*Garland lights a cigarette.*)

FIRST GUY: Hello, Garland!

GARLAND: What is the matter?

SECOND GUY: Are you campaigning against Gompers?

FIRST GUY: Think of your own head!

SECOND GUY: If you bark more you will have to deal with us.

GARLAND: And how many of you are here?

FIRST GUY: Enough to break your head.

GARLAND: Is that all?

SECOND GUY: Yes! Remember what we've told you.

(*Garland leaves.*)

FIRST GUY: Follow him.
POLICEMAN: Move!
FIRST GUY: Are we bothering you, old fish?

(*Policeman whistles.*)
(*First guy kicks off his whistle; both guys leave fast.*)
(*Policeman on his knees looks for the whistle and finds it. Writes in his notebook.*)

Episode 11

At the power plant.

GARLAND: (*Working at the switchboard*) When 2,500 people are fired at once it won't be easy for any of them to find a job.
JIMMY: (*Enters. Gives Garland a newspaper*) Mr Smith was saying he'll fire me today. Can he do that?
GARLAND: Of course.
JIMMY: What for?
GARLAND: They will say you are of no need.
JIMMY: And who will work here? Are they going to employ someone else?
GARLAND: Maybe yes, maybe not. (*Opens the newspaper*)
JIMMY: If they do I will cut Mr Smith's belly.
GARLAND: (*Looks through the newspaper*) Really, Jimmy, they will put you in prison.
JIMMY: I will escape to California for the gold.
GARLAND: (*Looks through the newspaper*) To escape to California you will need money, baby, a lot of money, and we ... Damn it!... (*Reads*) Electrician Garland is called to visit the notary, Holland Street ... The matter of an 850,000 dollars inheritance!
JIMMY: Wow! 850,000 dollars! ... You've got 850,000 dollars, do you? ... (*Laughs, suddenly runs away and shouts*): Garland has a fortune, 850,000 dollars! ...
GARLAND: Jimmy! Come back!
JIMMY'S VOICE: Eight hundred and fifty thousand dollars! ...

Episode 12

Ella's offices. Director's office.

MR STROPP: (*At the phone*) What?... *The Manchester Guardian*? ... Page 4? ... An inheritance? Me?... Damn it! (*Opens the newspaper*) Electrician

Garland ... Notary's office ... 850,000 dollars? Damn it! (*At the phone*) Hello, Smith. Ask Mr Garland to come up. Left? ... To the notary? ... As soon as he comes back ask him to come to me. Yes, yes. (*Hangs up*) 850,000 dollars. He would make a good partner. (*Rings. Servant enters.*) When Mr Garland comes, let him in! Immediately! Do you understand?

Episode 13

Modern offices. Director's office.

MR GLAN: (*Walks around his office; at the office there are Adelina and Bodwen*) I know Mr Bodwen here well enough. He spent his money, but what has he made?

MR BODWEN: Mr Glan, I have enough ...

MR GLAN: Outstanding bills and gambling debts. Well, my dear. Mr Glan is an old dog and you can't fool me for the SECOND time.

ADELINA: But we love each other.

MR GLAN: Well, well, I would like to hear this in a different company. (*Approaches Adelina*) Well, my dear, if Mr Bodwen becomes your husband you will stop being my niece. And I don't give money to strangers. That is clear I hope?

MR BODWEN: I think I will manage to meet you without Adelina. And then (*Exits*) we'll have a different conversation.

MR GLAN: Bla-bla-bla! Cocks are very aggressive, Mr Bodwen, but they get fried!

ADELINA: Uncle, you abuse!

MR GLAN: And with you I want to talk big time. (*Phone rings*) Hello! Dobby? Yes, I've heard ... Big sum ... Almost a million ... Companion? Yes, not bad ... But we had a fight with him once ... We should try to talk to him ... But what is better?... Aha ... (*Looks at Adelina*) Yes? That's an idea. Good, I will think about it. (*Hangs up and approaches Adelina*) Adelina is angry, isn't she? Come now, enough!

ADELINA: You don't want to make me happy.

MR GLAN: You are wrong. (*Pause*) By the way ... Have you heard that electrician Garland has a fortune? You know him a little bit ...

ADELINA: Is he the one who got a cup from me after the football tournament between Modern and Ella? Such a guy, looks like a bear.

MR GLAN: Hmm, when a person has a million, a million dollars, he is worth making friends with.

Episode 14

At the notary's. Fifteen minutes to the end of work. Crowd waiting for Garland.

VOICES: He won't come today again.

Second day since the advert and he is still not here.

Great! A man opened a newspaper – and he is a millionaire.

Let's go!

No. Let's wait till the end.

GARLAND: (*Comes in unnoticed; approaches the clerk's table*) Hello, mister! (*Clerk is writing.*)

GARLAND: Just one inquiry …

Clerk (*Annoyed*) Yes?

GARLAND: I am Garland …

CLERK: Wha-at?

GARLAND: I am Garland. Your advert …

CLERK: You are Mr Garland, aren't you? Oh my God, why haven't you said so immediately … so much work during the day. Please sit down. (*Rushes to offer him a seat*)

EVERYONE: Garland!!! (*They rush to the chairs and offer them to Garland.*)

CLERK: I am sorry, gentlemen, but you are disturbing Mr Garland and me.

LADY: (*Approaches Garland*) Are you Garland? (*Laughs*) Oh my God, what a joy!

VOICES: Fools are lucky!

LADY: What an expressive face!

Voice: He doesn't look like a worker.

NOTARY: Mr Garland? Glad to meet you … Congratulations … Just a moment, some formalities … Your documents?

GARLAND: (*Gives*) Please!

NOTARY: Great! Everything is fine.

REPORTER: (*Writes*) Garland … Slim young man, pleasant face … good manners for a worker … modest … (*Clicks the camera*)

NOTARY: Are you going to keep the money in a bank? Or take it and invest?

GARLAND: I think I will invest.

NOTARY: What business, if it is not a secret?

VOICES: Oil?

Cotton?

Pennsylvanian are not bad …

GARLAND: My money will go for education.[1]

VOICES: Ohh!

For education?
How original!
What did he say?
What the hell!
Very interesting indeed!
Don't interrupt, please!
REPORTER: Are you going to donate all the money?
GARLAND: Up to the last penny!
VOICES: A million dollars!
What an idiot!
He's gone mad!
So young!
ADELINA: Hello, Mr Garland! It turns out that you are lucky not only at football. Congratulations!
GARLAND: Thank you!
REPORTER: Excuse me. What brought you to this decision?
GARLAND: Very easy. I am a worker. I was born and brought up in the working environment. Yes, among the working class who works, starves and sleeps not under warm blankets but under newspapers in the squares of Chicago or San Francisco.
LADY: Don't give it away; I beg you, don't give!
VOICES: Quiet, damn you!
We can't hear!
Quiet!
GARLAND: They earned this money. So, damn, I want to give the money back. I give it to educate my brothers.
VOICES: Bolsheviks' speeches!
Take him to the mental asylum!
GARLAND: And let them learn how to fight this blessed system which makes them work and starve. Point blank!
(*Everyone is nervy. First the public goes quiet and then starts grumbling. In the end voices are heard.*)

---

1 The play is thus based on the real-life story of Charles Garland, the 21-year-old son of a Wall Street broker who in 1920 inherited $1 million from his deceased father. Garland, initially, refused the inheritance and is reported as having said the following: 'It is not mine. I never did anything to earn it.' He declined from taking the money of 'a system which starves thousands while hundreds are stuffed' (quoted in Samson 1996: 1). Eventually, Garland used the inheritance to set up the American Fund for Public Service, generally known as Garland Fund, which served as a philanthropic organization to help a number of radical and left-wing organizations.

VOICES: Let the government confiscate the money!
A thousand is fine, even ten thousand, but not a million!
LADY: For God's sake, don't give all the money! Please, tell him! For God's sake not everything!

Curtain

They Tried to Hide, but Ended Up Fathers

Arkhip

Source: *Rabochii klub*, no. 5, 1924, pp. 34–7

Dramatis Personae: WOMAN, SEDUCER, JUDGE, WITNESSES.

Act 1

WOMAN: Petya! Petya!
SEDUCER: Leave me alone! What do you want? Go to hell!
WOMAN: Petya, you are as cruel as an animal! Shame on you, Petya! You gave me your word that you would marry me, and now, when you got what you wanted, you are refusing. Aren't you ashamed?
SEDUCER: Why should I be ashamed? I did promise, so what? I used to like you, but not anymore. Am I going to force myself to love you?
WOMAN: How are you not ashamed? Why did you lie to me?
SEDUCER: Who lied to you? I am telling you in plain Russian: I liked you, and I was with you. I stopped liking you, so goodbye. Are you going to hold me by my trousers? Try me!
WOMAN: Why are you talking like this, Petya? You can't leave me. You don't have any right.
SEDUCER: Phew-phew! Where are such rights, to live with a person whom you don't like anymore, written? No, my dear. Love is free. You get close, you separate. That is all, and you have no right to keep me by force.
WOMAN: But … I am … pregnant …
SEDUCER: Whaaaat?
WOMAN: Yes. You cannot leave me.
SEDUCER: It's not true. You are inventing it to keep me with you.
WOMAN: No, it's true, Petya.
SEDUCER: Okay. Let's pretend it is true. But allow me to ask you, who are you pregnant from? What proof do you have that I am responsible?
WOMAN: What are you saying!? Oh, what a rascal you are! What a sneak!
SEDUCER: You can swear all you want, but where is the evidence?
WOMAN: What a scum! I will take you to court.
SEDUCER: Go ahead, take me even to thirty courts! We shall see how it turns out.

WOMAN: Pah, you have no shame in your eyes! You are a bastard! (*Leaves*)

SEDUCER: What a damn story! But indeed, she can take me to court. I have to take action. (*Knocking on the walls*) Hey, lads, come here! I have something to tell you. Mishka! Petka! Vasil! Come here now! (*The lads walk in*)

LADS: What is going on?
- What is with all this noise, and there is no fight?
- Why call us?

SEDUCER: There is serious business, friends! I need your help.

LADS: If it is money – forget it!
- Are you going to rob somebody?
- That is a terrible situation – a serious matter!

SEDUCER: Leave your jokes! The matter is this. You surely know I have been fooling around with Natashka.

LADS: How could we not!
- You fooled around, messed up and haven't cleared it out.
- Has she left you?

SEDUCER: Worse! This malicious woman is threatening to take me to court. She is pregnant.

LADS: Woah!
- You won't have enough money to pay for all the children!
- Stay with a woman and prepare for lots of grief!

SEDUCER: So here is the thing. If she takes me to court, I take you as my witnesses. You must show that she messed around with all of you and not just with me alone. Got it?

LADS: It's clear as an orange.
- Don't fret, we'll help you!
- When you were picking up raspberries you didn't call us, and now you are asking for help!
- You love to ride, but you don't love to carry a sleigh.

SEDUCER: So, lads, I will be grateful. Just say: indeed, she is an easy woman, and she messed around with everyone.

LADS: Oh you!
- Now you are screwed up!
- Don't keep your head down. We will do it!

SEDUCER: Be certain. Easy woman, and show it at the court.

Act 2

JUDGE: So, you claim that citizen Petushkov is the father of your child?
WOMAN: Yes, your honour! I lived with him, and then he left me.
SEDUCER: She is lying. She messed around with everyone. Just ask the witnesses. And as for her claims that I am the father, that's complete nonsense, because I'm not capable of fathering a child. You can have checks carried out to verify that.
JUDGE: So you are denying that you are the father?
SEDUCER: Let God punish me! Let me be damned now!
JUDGE: Okay, okay. Witness Nosov! Your name, second name and place of birth.
NOSOV: Ivan Petrovich. The town is Yaroslavl.
JUDGE: What can you say on the matter?
NOSOV: What can I say? She was also messing around with me. She is an easy woman.
WOMAN: He is lying!
JUDGE: Okay. Witness Stameskin! Tell me, do you know the complainant?
STAMESKIN: Sure I do. You can say she is famous, as everyone is going after her, and she accepts.
JUDGE: What kind of relationship did you have with her?
STAMESKIN: What kind? Everything, as it should be.
JUDGE: Witness Artiukhin! What kind of relationship did you have with the complainant?
ARTIUKHIN: We haven't been to the Registrar, but honour with honour.
JUDGE: Witness Ivanov! What do you say?
IVANOV: She was messing around with me, as I am in front of God.
JUDGE: Okay. Witness Lupatov!
LUPATOV: I can say, your honour, what others already said. I swear I have been with her in Poltava.
JUDGE: I announce a three-minute break.
VOICES: Well, Petya, her case is exhausted.
- The court will show her what it means to complain.
- A malicious woman, she was with everyone but is putting it only on one.
- Men, you are all the same: you use and then disappear like the wind in the field.
- Petya, Petya! Shall we go straight to the beer bar? So that we wash it away.
- Which one? Bavaria?
- Nah, let's go to Green Corner.

- How they treat our man: at the Registry or court!
- They won't throw her case out.
- She's missed her target, bless.
- We shall see about that! Not all of you, son of bitches, spoil women!

JUDGE: (*ringing the bell*) Please be quiet! I am announcing the verdict:

'In the name of the Socialist Soviet Republic (of such date) 1924, the People's Court, in the presence of (so and so), in an open court heard the case of the accused citizen Petushkov – a worker of the Goznak factory – that he is the father of the child and is refusing to support him. The court has held: that citizen Petushkov categorically refused to accept that he is the father of the child, that the witnesses from the side of citizen Petushkov, citizens Nosov, Stameskin, Artiukhin, Ivanov and Lupatov confirmed that citizen Siniaeva has lived with them, and that, by doing so, and based on the revolutionary conscience and socialistic justice, the court, based on article 144 of Family Codes, has decided that said citizens should all pay one-third of their monthly salary for the support of the child.' The case is now closed.

VOICES: What is all this!
- Please, your honour …
- How am I involved in all of this?
- My money! (*Tries to hurt the Seducer*)
- You are such a bastard!
- You dragged us into this story!
- It's all because of you, you fool!
- You were taking advantage and now we must pay!
- It's not right!
- What a story!

WOMAN: You deserve it! You tried to hide, but you have all ended up being fathers!

Part Four

Production Approaches and Examples

'After the Holiday'

Platon Kerzhentsev

Source: *Iskusstvo*, no. 6, 1918, pp. 3–5

The October festivities are over and already forgotten. Posters have been removed, garlands burned, flags folded and put away in the shed. But we have not finished yet what has started, especially if the future organization of the nation's festivals is to benefit from this experience of the first, large-scale, revolutionary festival of the Soviet Union. In that matter, we are just beginners and we have to learn a lot before we can achieve a good result.

First of all, the street decorations. Only the square in Moscow produced a holistic impression because of its overall unity in the decorations. It was a Soviet square with long, red banners that densely surrounded the obelisk and with posters that stretched across Tverskaia Street. There were luxurious green garlands of austere solemnity and, I would say, even pleasant massiveness. The dark red colour of most banners suited this massiveness. I am not a fan of the obelisk, but even this, in green and purple, was in harmony with the whole view of the square and the Soviet building. Certainly, I might have disagreed with the monotony of the shields that had the Republic's signs, which were placed on the facades of the surrounding houses, but these details were lost in the background of the square.

All other squares in Moscow, despite the energies of the artists, certainly did not give the impression of a unity of design and often came as a surprise because of their complete mismatch in the decorations, even on the same building. The grandest poster was placed on the Metropole in Theatre Square, which was probably the best poster among Moscow's decorations during these October days. The facade of the Metropole was also well and tastefully decorated.

What did you see on the other buildings around Theatre Square? On the Bolshoi Theatre and the Continental there were miserable picture posters, meagre in colour, which were not positive and just gave a sad impression. On the Maly there were episodes from Stepan Razin's[1] life, portrayed in an Old-Russian Balagan[2] style, but they were so weak that they made you smile. The

---

1 Stepan Razin, known as Stenka Razin, a Cossack leader who led an important insurrection against the tsarist state in southern Russia in 1670–1.
2 Balagan, Russian fairground performances on show booths (Golub in Leach and Borovsky 1999: 279). Balagan used here implies a crude and simple form.

most important thing was that all of these separate decorations did not match each other and just created a disappointing feeling.

The same disharmony could be seen in Revolution Square. I found interesting a poster of a peasant on the old City Duma. It was a lush and joyful gamma of colours. The decoration on the building of the Food Commission was quite good but conflicted with the decoration of the City Duma. Posters in dull colours mounted in old gold frames were placed at street level, among the bright red colours of a clear sunny day. This, perhaps, was not their right place. Furthermore, the image of the Revolution was exhibited in the midst of the posters but again pictured in a different manner. Posters on the History Museum were also painted in a style which conflicted with the others.

In organizing future festivals, we will need to pay special attention so that this disharmony is not repeated. For this purpose, the decoration of each square should be given to an artist or a coordinating team.

As we are talking about details, two extremely successful decorations should be mentioned: the Okhotny Ryad booth and the fence on Tverskaia Street, close to the National. The artist who painted the tedious wooden booth on Okhotny Ryad found cheerful colours that were well suited to the tradition of Russian festivals, to the colourful Russian fair, the Yarmarka and to the cheerful paintings found in traditional Moscow houses. These flowers and bouquets, with their simple and bright patterns, unwittingly made you smile. Even now you cannot pass by these booths without giving them special attention and enjoying the colourful painting. There are no slogans and symbols, no clever inventions, but they still achieved the aim we expect from street decorations. They immediately give you a cheerful feeling, happiness and a sense of inexplicable joy.

A fence on Tverskaia Street, which has been an eyesore for ages, was painted in a different style which was almost as good. You cannot see this painting as a whole and the artist took this into consideration. He divided the painting into few separate pieces, which appear when you walk along. The best part of the painting is the one where a group of men have raised their hands, and the middle part of the picture shows the beginning of a new world from the chaos. They were so pleasant that the two best decorations were not removed to be hidden in the stores but permanently placed on the buildings.

We have to comfort ourselves with the thought that the decorations intended to remain permanently after the festival, as monuments, and which are evident in different parts of Moscow, might actually be temporary. They can be replaced because they are not as good. One of the most unsuccessful is the monument of Marx and Engels, which had to have a central position. Both figures show absolutely no shape that is familiar to us. In their poses, one feels the student's inexperience and non-spirituality. The same goes for the Konenkov memorial. The young artist failed here (possibly because of the rushed order). There is no simplicity, but too much conglomeration and diversity of colours. We would like to see something stricter, like the sculptor's previous creations.

The majority of other monuments were not removed, but they are completely ordinary and are unlikely to be recognized as worthy of attention.

The banners and posters carried in the processions had some variety and a pleasant diversity of colours. But a common style was lacking even here, and the artists created either symbolic posters or used a futuristic style which was against the proletarian world view. They drew neat images which, however, remained artistically simple. They scrupulously showed the crafted banners of the English workers.

The mass of the people during the festive procession was the active part of the festival. On the other hand, in the evenings of the 6 and 7 of October, the large crowd on the streets did not seem very active and looked tired. People have not learnt yet how to enjoy themselves with the artists and the singers.

Figure 7 May Day Agit-Automobile, undated. Courtesy of Lynn Mally.

Trucks with circus artists give rise to a sense of excitement, but, unfortunately, there were few of them.[3] Moreover, the audience did not dance, sing or play as it usually happens in festivals.

Our people still have to learn how to enjoy themselves. When organizing future festivals, we will need to pay special attention to the fact that all the people should actively participate in the festival. For example, even the selling of boutonnieres, small flags, ribbons, etc., which this time was organized by random sellers, managed to draw the people into the celebrations. This, of course, is not enough. We need to involve more activists and organizers on the streets and in the squares. We need more speakers, singers, artists and musicians, who can be part of the crowd and move from one district to another. Also, small choirs and groups of people should be organized to perform in the squares and on the streets.

People will get together around the performance groups and slowly become involved in the celebrations.

I do not have space to talk about the participation of the theatre during the October festival. It should be noted, however, that despite the rush in the preparation of the festival's theatre programme and its lack of acts, the theatres managed to put on galas and exclusive plays. Of course, if you want the theatre performances to match the spirit of the festivities, special plays and something exclusive should be arranged. This is possible with effective preparation.

It was suggested that the October committee should be turned into a regular organization, and this is an idea that makes sense. National festivals require long preparation, especially here, where we are not used to them. We will achieve excellent results for which we struggled this time if we start preparing for the 1 May celebration in January.

---

3 See Figure 7.

Performances during the Civil War

Alexander Mgebrov

Source: *Zhizn' v teatre tom 2*, 1932, pp. 365–71

Gastev[1] was included in the Proletkult's work during the first half of 1919, but no other significant proletarian poet came to us in those days. We intended to expand all the work in such a way that all proletarian poets of the time, united by the Proletkult, could see the light of the theatre and be revealed to the masses through performance.

Unfortunately, the swiftness of events, I repeat, the severity and significance of the moment, prevented the complete implementation of this plan – life forced us, with the iron logic of necessity, to rush into the thick of it all, leaving dreams and plans far behind us. Dozens of our young companions were constantly leaving; today they are still singing that 'Girls in the bright kingdom of the future will become more beautiful than the Venus of Milos', but the day after they were forced to pick up rifles and quickly rush into the struggle for the future, where people dreamt more beautiful dreams than Venus of Milos.

All this greatly ruined our work. And not only did we have to answer all the needs and cultural demands of the masses, but the Proletkult itself demanded from us performances on Saturdays and Sundays for huge numbers of workers.

The same was asked of us by almost all newly formed military units, after the appearance of the first improvised Red Army clubs and red corners. The mass, united by a single impulse, longed for inspirational words and, in these words, music. That is why we were everywhere welcomed with open arms.

[...]

And we ourselves felt needed, inseparable from the great life that was boiling, ringing around us, increasing ten-fold our strength, and making the impossible possible.

Yes, we responded, I repeat, to all the significant events of those days. Wherever a new club opened, we were the first to be welcomed. If a solemn and call of need sounded from Smolny, we were the first to be invited. When new units went to the front, we responded to their enthusiasm with our own. And we responded not only with simple concert performances. No, these were real celebrations that converged with the enthusiasm of the masses.

---

1 Aleksei Gastev, see Kerzhentsev's essay 'The Repertoire of the Proletarian Theatre' in Part Three.

How many performances did we present? It is impossible say. There were a great many of them, not only in the city, but also outside it. We went to Kronstadt and its forts, to Luga, to Kolpino, to Siversky, to Gatchina, to Moscow, to Krasnoye Selo, to Sestroretsk, and I don't know where else, and I am not even accounting for the trips to the Western and Eastern fronts. And what amazing performances they were!

I remember, for example, that in Luga I had to present an evening of Whitman's[2] work in the open air, in front of a thousand crowd. *Europe, Song of the Banner at Daybreak* and *We Two Boys Together Clinging* were performed without any decorations, just on the green hills, and the sunset provided light for the performance. The crowd merged with us.

[…]

[These performances were prepared] with completely inexperienced forces, with people who had never before opened their mouths to pronounce one line of poetry, and even more so monologues, people who never sang properly, who had never taken a paint brush in their hands. It sounds fabulous, and it was.

[…]

In addition, we must remember that all our performances were then given absolutely free of charge. They existed as a deep, comradely community, where unforgettable moods and inseparable associations between audiences and performers were sensitively intertwined. It was a continuous, solemn celebration of creativity, energy and enthusiasm.

---

2 Walt Whitman, see Kerzhentsev's essay 'The Repertoire of the Proletarian Theatre' in Part Three.

Collective Readings

Alexander Mgebrov

Source: *Zhizn' v teatre tom 2*, 1932, pp. 318–34

A lot of young people gathered at the theatre department of the Proletkult. [...] The power of the collective has never been felt as much as in those moments.

[...]

In the whirlwind of these thoughts and feelings, the first attempt at collective recitation, along its rhythmic expression and embodiment, was born among the Proletkult.[1] By this time, the literature section of the Proletkult had published with fabulous speed a number of books by proletarian poets (Mashirov,[2] Sadofev,[3] Kirillov[4] and others), and a wonderful, very original book of Aleksei Gastev's poems, titled *Poetry of the Worker's Blow*.

The music section hurriedly created songs and compositions to the words of Kirillov, Sadofev and Mashirov, but Theo (the Theatre Department) did not lag behind it and the evening programme was constructed on the calls made by the poets. But how was one to embody these poems on the stage? Didn't everyone want to participate in the celebration? Wasn't it difficult for someone to be left out from this first joyous day?

The music section seemed happier than us: there several dozen people sang together, their hearts involuntarily touched each other and, as if with a single impulse, with one breath, a powerful sound was born from a common melodious and pleasing tone. It was a choir.

What were we to do? An individual reading of a play is much more limited and less accessible to a large number of people. Reading poetry also requires a lot

---

1 These are the collective readings which Mgebrov produced at the Petrograd Proletkult. See von Geldern (1993: 30–2). Mally writes as follows about collective readings in general and on Mgebrov in particular: 'Collective readings were another innovation employed by drama studios, a solution to the problem of repertoire and to the poor preparation of Proletkult students for public performances. The head of the Petrograd theatre, Mgebrov, was an enthusiastic supporter of this technique. He adapted nondramatic material for the stage, fashioning poetry into elaborate scripts with very detailed choreography. Individuals read small parts of the poems, but the majority of the work was declaimed by the chorus. Mgebrov hailed this as an original, collective artistic form' (Mally 1990: 148).
2 Presumably this is the same Aleksei Samobytnik-Mashirov, the poet from the working classes referred to in Piotr Kogan's essay in Part One titled 'Socialist Theatre during the Revolution.'
3 Ilia Sodofev, another important name among the first wave of proletarian authors and who had started writing even before the Revolution (Mally 1990: 138).
4 Vladimir Kirillov (1890–1943) was one of the most popular among the proletarian writers of the time. His poem 'We' is considered as a typical example of Proletkult creation (Mally 1990: 99). Another poem of his, 'The Iron Messiah' is reproduced in von Geldern and Stites (1995: 4–5).

of schooling and many other things that develop by tremendous perseverance, time and work, such as voice, diction, the mastery of temperament and the ability to use it. It was impossible, of course, to educate in one month the workers in all these individual aspects.

We tried to hand out a few poems to the most capable participants, but how boring this was! It was poor and not responding at all to the impulse and inspiration that possessed everyone! And our hands dropped, and we did not know what to do.

But then one day, one happy day, it occurred to us that we should make everyone learn collectively one short poem by Ionov. To perceive it easily and quickly, we decided to put the poem to a certain rhythmic movement. It began with an ordinarily simple march, but suddenly in this march, words and phrases involuntarily began to separate themselves. At the same time ideas arose in relation to the musical combinations of the voices, within the meaning of individual phrases and words. Thus, quite by chance, extraordinary prospects opened up before us, not to mention the fact that we were able to master this relatively quickly. We had a fair amount of material through which we composed a diverse and original programme, as it was a collective, it did not lag behind the choir. This was the first experience of collective reading of poems, the first axis around which everything spun not only in separate verses but also in long poems.

[…]

On the same day, another interesting staging of Gastev's *Tower* was held. It symbolically reflected the struggle of the working class. It was staged in the following way. On a high platform, surrounded by a hundred raised hands, in a monumental pose, stood bare-chested, and with a leather apron hanging down, the reader of the poem. While reading he was accompanied by distant music and the whole scene was flooded by a strong red glow. This staging gave further impetus to a number of similar experiments.

The highlight of our first evening was a choral recitation of works by Gastev and other poets. Thus, the evening of 1 May [1918] offered a combination of performances by a vocal choir, a choral recitation, a number of separate dramatizations and the play *Red Corner* by V. V. Ignatov, which essentially was the first revolutionary play. During the same evening, besides everything else, a lot of fiery words were said about the upcoming proletarian culture, and a number of proletarian poets spoke publicly for the first time about their works: Mashirov, Sadofev, Kirillov, Pomorsky and others.

[…]

You can think and argue on this topic as much as you wish, but the fact remains that the young Proletkultists showed, from the very first days, a completely unusual enthusiasm, an exceptional upsurge and an amazing heroism. Short poems, like Gastev's *When the Morning Horns Beep*, for example, consisting of rhythmic stress on the seventh and eighth syllabi, then sounded as a whole poem.

We used everything we could: an overturned chair, a table set upside down, piles of machines and benches stacked on each other, a pole that suddenly fell into our hands, a flagpole, an unbuttoned blouse, a rolled up sleeve, an occasional ray of light, a smile that sounds full of joy.

[...]

We divided eight lines between a rather large group of young people, breaking them into separate words, half-phrases and even half-words. Some words and phrases were spoken collectively, others individually (in terms of tone and sonorous voices), others were accompanied by rhythmic movements, overruns, static poses and dynamic movement.

[...]

Enough about Gastev. Rather, I interrupt temporarily about him since what has been said is enough to show the main direction in which our work has progressed. I can only say that it was not that simple and that it required long hours of systematic exercise. However, undoubtedly, all this work developed a general sense of rhythm, of musicality, the ability to catch each other, and to keep the pace. Most importantly, it developed temperament, both individually and collectively. This method made it possible to get to know everyone quickly, for the stronger participants to carry the weaker so that the latter are not excluded from the general circle of enthusiasm.

[...]

Various proposals came to the Proletkult from everywhere: from military units, from the Red Guards and the Red Army soldiers came to us. Workers' clubs were constantly appearing at that time and they wanted us to come and perform at their grand openings; we performed in squares and in simple work places, in the open air outside the city, at grand rallies and concerts and ahead of the regiments going into battle. We were present everywhere, in the joyful, truly inspirational moments that not only the Petrograd but also the Moscow proletariat were experiencing.

'Collective Creation in the Theatre'

Platon Kerzhentsev

Source: *Proletarskaia kul'tura*, no. 7–8, 1919, pp. 37–41

I

Collective creation[1]: these are the words around which there is so much confusion, words which nowadays are being misused as much as 'proletarian culture', 'proletarian writer' and 'proletarian poetry'.[2]

Some people think that collective creation is a necessary condition for proletarian work in the areas of science and art and that there are no other ways of creating a new culture. This is, of course, a mistake. Many works created by individuals without the visible participation of the masses can be and even are the real keystones of socialist culture, since they show the genuine will of the collective, the aspirations and hopes of the working class, and the ideology and world view of the proletariat.

Some works (scientific and artistic) that reflect the great communist ideal, already included in the treasury of proletarian culture, are being created not only by individual efforts but also by people from the bourgeois environment. In the same way, many creations can be born in the future not as result of collective work but as the creation of individuals. Such individual (but not individualistic!) creativity may be more popular in the future because of the fact that the human personality itself will be more developed and better prepared to identify its ability.

Of course, in the society of the future this creativity of individuals will be infused with the stamp of collectivism to show the new communistic psychology. But in spite of the collectivism of its content and its spiritual connection with the masses it will not be collective creation.

One can notice another simplified understanding of collective creation. Any crowd, any mass is considered to be a collective, and its performance to

---

1 For an in-depth discussion of this essay and of collective creation as articulated by Kerzhentsev see Aquilina (2014). In that article a link is made between Kerzhentsev's theories and contemporary theories of devised performance.
2 This is reference to the debates that were going on about such crucial terms like 'proletarian culture', on which initially it was difficult to reach agreement. See Introduction.

be a collective creation. Therefore, people easily sum under this term the choir singing in the opera, the vociferous chanting, the crowd scenes in dramas, folk dances, etc.

In this case there is a double mistake. First of all, not all performances can be considered 'creative'. Creativity is not the performance of a learned programme, but the creation of something new (even if it is within a programme), arising, overcoming, a victory. Therefore, not every piece of art is a result of creativity – it can be created by a lazy hand of a person working for money, without fire, without the fight to achieve in a better way the planned objectives.

Secondly, not every mass can be considered a collective. To become a collective, it shall have not only inner affinity and a certain organization, but also unity of spirit, a sense of kinship, common tasks and, above all, a pervading thought for the best interests of the whole.

Any participant in a collective shall consciously seek to embody the best interests of the whole and comprehensively identify the ideal of the proletariat: communism. Specific tasks should be made clear to everyone. Finally, creative organization shall be based on the principles of partnership, while staying apart from any authoritarianism and allowing ample space for criticism.

II

To make these abstract and schematic statements more understandable, I will explain in what measure and in which form collective creation can be used in the theatre.

First of all, it is necessary to mention that under the word 'theatre' I understand all theatre art in general, including even more primitive forms of theatre like games, round dances, processions, folk festivals and so on. These public 'actions' are, despite their simplicity, especially valuable for us because they wake up the theatre instinct of the masses and give us the basis for the mass theatre of the future, where the gap between an actor and an audience disappears, where the whole mass is a collective that creates creatively.

Collective creation in theatre can be outlined in the following ways. First of all, a collective working in the theatre shall include participants of different categories and not only those directly connected with theatre activities. For example, in the case of the Proletkult one can say that for theatre creation all their studios – literature, music, painting and other ones – are to be attracted. The bourgeois system instilled strife between the arts which should have been creatively synthesized in theatre. Real literature has been cut off from the theatre, and plays are supplied by secondary writers. The best artists were also 'out of work' in the theatre and failed to merge with theatre work. The same occurred with the best composers, who were rejected by the theatre or who could not find ways to the stage. So the bourgeois theatre's 'suppliers' appeared – its own writers, artists and musicians.

Against this specialization we must propose a close fraternity on the stage between all the arts, the close work of proletarian writers, actors, artists and musicians.

It is not only this union between the representatives of different artistic areas that is important. The system of creative team organization is also essential. It shall be built on the principles of friendly partnership that excludes any sort of authority and bureaucratic hierarchy, to leave instead a wide space for criticism. A big part of the initiative is given to each ordinary member of the work.

Collective creation can work correctly and fruitfully only when there is a natural equality between its members and equal value is given to all theatre participants. The actor and stage director, prompter and stage worker, light technician and artist, make-up man and musician shall be considered as necessary creators of the scenic whole. They will have (at least potentially) a wide possibility to express themselves, provide their support for the stage, act as a critic, etc.

Experiments in collective creation are possible only if such a truly friendly organization exists.

Bourgeois theatre only knew productions of the stage directors who, although conferring with experts, rested solely on their own vision and led all the work on a play. We have to break away from this tradition and form. From all the studios involved in a staging, a special board which would include, for example, an actor, a musician, an artist, a writer etc., will be elected. This board will direct the staging ('manage a play'), constantly engaging all forces from the studios in active participation. All the details of a play will be discussed and creatively worked upon during rehearsals.

It definitely does not mean that stage questions shall be solved somehow by the majority of votes and that the managing group will give instructions to the actors. Surely the actual management will be in the hands of only one board member who, however, will consult other board members during the rehearsals. Before and after the rehearsals all principal moments in the direction of play shall be discussed both in a directing collective and in a meeting with all the members.

However, this system of work will be fruitful only on the necessary condition that each member is, if possible, a universal worker and that he not only understands clearly the general conditions of the theatre but is also familiar with all its details. To achieve this, we shall let all the participants carry out, at least partially, the work of the author, stage director, decorator and actor. Everyone shall create his own plan to direct the play, give the play his interpretation, work on the play's text (in literary terms), go over some roles (like an actor), think of the decorations and maybe draft them, take care of the musical side of a play and so on.

It definitely does not mean that all this complicated work will fall fully on the shoulders of each participant. Surely a stage director or a person who is inclined to this work will pay more attention to the staging, while a writer or a lover of literature will work mainly on the play itself and so on. But it is important that elements of work are acquired by each person and that everyone is not confined to his area but has done the work of others.

Only such universalism (which will be typical in the future system) and the conscious attitude to creative work will make the appearance of collective creation possible.

This universalism will help to identify diverse talents; it will make valuable and significant comments on all production participants, regardless of their area of specialization.

In experimenting with collective creativity in the theatre we shall abandon the timid thrill given by the play text. We shall take it only as a basis, as a suitable plot and rewarding material, and in the process of work we will expose it to significant changes and alterations. This processing of the text is dictated not only by the absence of a suitable repertoire and by the fact that many plays are unactable, but also by a need to develop literary creativity in the proletarian masses.[3]

I imagine that the process leading to the staging of a piece will be as follows. Someone chooses two or three plays. There will be a report on these plays during a meeting of the Proletkult studios, where excerpts from the plays are read and discussed. One of the plays seems to be the most attractive. After the final discussion and voting the play is chosen. After that a managing board is chosen, which can possibly consist of different studio members and specialists.

The studying of the play begins. At this point the main work is done by the literary studio, with participation from the others. The critical analysis of the

---

3 On the repertoire problem see essays in Part Three.

plays is written down, their interpretation is planned and initial notes are made. When this preliminary work is completed, the staging plan is discussed and in connection to it the musical and decoration sides of the staging.

This work is being performed at the managing board, in the studios and during the open meetings with participants. The staging group is considering all this work, but of course it can choose its own ways, agreeing not with the prevailing opinions but with those expressed by the minority.

The process of the play's rehearsal sees changes to the first plans of the staging, to the redistribution of the roles, to the musical part etc. A new literary processing is undergoing.

Thus, bit by bit, from the effort of different individuals and groups, a new play is born, ready for staging.

To make these attempts of collective creation more successful it is necessary to work not only on the universal abilities of the actors but also on their capability for improvisation. Starting with improvisations on small scenes, one can then move on to more complicated improvisations with many participants and even create whole plays in accordance to the chosen theme or plot.

Work on improvisations will promote the ability to create in a close cooperation with others. From here the ability to be an active creator of folk festivals and processions is born.

One should not forget that collective theatre work is just one of the methods of the new theatre, and it does not exclude other ways that lead to proletarian theatre. It is also important to keep in mind that we are currently at the stage of the first experiments. No relevant precedents and no developed system are available.[4] It is natural to make mistakes and to have misconceptions that can

---

4 Kerzhentsev however did value the collective processes of a number of performances which he saw during his travels abroad (Kerzhentsev 1923: 48–64). He understood that the collective creation of these performances had particular weight in the creation of a community's communal spirit, i.e. in their ethics of a shared life. Prominent among these was the performance about the life of St George staged in Hampstead, a suburb of London. The defining principle of this performance was that the greatest number of the suburb's inhabitants participated in its preparation and that ultimately all the production was sustained through the suburb's sole energies. For example, about three hundred villagers made up the cast, while others contributed by composing the music, sewing the costumes, painting the scenery, mounting the stage and so on. Kerzhentsev paid particular homage to the Hampstead villagers' competence in writing the text. A collective process was again adopted. Collective creation was also manifested during the performance itself, which drew a lot on audience participation. In fact, the production was not deemed 'ready' until the spectators (who again were members of the Hampstead community) saw the performance and filled in the details that were knowingly left out by the directors. One example involved the use of placards to delineate scene changes. The performance also stimulated audience participation, Kerzhentsev argued, because the spectator was bound to react when seeing an actor drinking from a cup which he would have painted. The communal spirit was reaffirmed in this way, as were the suburb's roots and belief in the importance of a shared life and values.

be sorted only by experiencing the ways of collective creation. In the absence of such experience we shall apply the new method with great care, all the time examining and correcting ourselves.

Collective experiments in the theatre will be fruitful only on condition that suitable literary material is chosen, meaning plays that reflect the collective interests and which, one way or another, are close to communist ideals.

At the moment such plays are rare. However, it will be possible to change some old dramatic works in the new spirit. We shall also call upon the literary studios of the Proletkult and the proletarian writers to work for the theatre. When different studios launch joint work, writers from the working class will be naturally interested in the theatre and get involved. And for now we need to use the old repertoire for collective creation while necessarily refining and reworking it.

In the theatre work of the Proletkult, as well as in all other areas of activity, the most important thing is the main purpose sought by the activists of proletarian culture. Methods of work to achieve this main purpose are of significant but secondary importance. Therefore, in applying collective creation the activists of the Proletkult shall not forget the main purpose. Collective creation will be useless and will be killing itself if it does not create pure individual works. The harmonious combination of the new methods with this new high purpose is the only formula for success of Proletkult work.

'Strife between the Arts'

Platon Kerzhentsev

Source: *Vestnik teatra*, no. 19, 1919, p. 2

The art of theatre takes an exclusive and fortunate place in relation to a number of other arts because it is in theatre that they can combine creatively. In theatre, the arts approach each other and become related. A true and genuine theatre always unites the poet and the actor, the artist and the musician, the architect and the dancer. The majority of the arts live separately outside the theatre. Painting sometimes (though not often) combines with architecture but never with music. Music shuns architecture. Poetry does not communicate with painting.

With no scene or theatre, and if the art of spectacle did not exist (the same as theatre art), the entire family of the arts would not meet. It would stay without communication, without connection. The theatre's roof is the parental roof under which all the arts come together and become a family. Theatre art is unique in its form and methods, because it synthesizes all other arts.

There is no theatre without words. It is only on the stage that poetry becomes loud. There is no theatricality without colours, without painting and without sculpture. The art of architecture goes hand in hand with the decorator's. Music is inseparable from the stage because human speech must be rhythmic if it is to become theatrical and artistic. Dance also has to have a place on the stage because the movement of the actors must be harmonic and rhythmical.

Theatre workers are happy to have the opportunity to creatively combine the different arts on a stage. However, and unfortunately, over the last few years, we have not seen a genuine combination in the theatre of the arts.

The era of bourgeois domination created separation, disconnection, insularity, specialization, individualism and severed the family of the arts. Each art got cut off from the others and became individualized. Even the ones which were close to each other got separated: we nearly lost the fresco (the combination of architecture and paining); the sculptural decoration of a building moved to the craftsmen, etc.

In the era of capitalism, theatre was not the synthesis of the arts, but it came in the shape of an old, used, cheap product that was being sold at a cheap price, with the label of 'Art' stamped on it.

The separation of the arts in the bourgeois system is noticed everywhere. The greatest writers are unable to create something good for the theatre, or the theatre simply cannot incorporate their creations. Tolstoy was pushed to the theatre by chance as he wanted to write a play for his home theatre. From his dramatic works, only two fitted the theatre. Tolstoy instinctively felt all the lies and the historical judgement expressed by the bourgeois culture. He had an inner fight with modern theatre. Chekhov and Gorky became dramatists only because of a special and exclusive theatre.

The same story occurred in the West. The great writers communicated with the theatre only by chance, or they wrote plays which never appear on the theatre stage. I can mention Verhaeren, Wells, etc.

Everywhere the main producers of plays were secondary and peripheral writers-craftsmen of pen and scenes. The bourgeois theatre was not a suitable place for genius playwrights, and it created the environment for semi-talented or semi-worthless writers.

The same happened with painting. All the decorations were and are drawn by painters of little talent who 'adjusted' to the theatre. Masters of the paint brush are left behind. Such great decorators as Cézanne and Gauguin remained in the theatre backyard. In Russia, only random and private initiatives gave us the interesting decorations of Roerich, Benois, Bakst, Dobuzhinsky, etc.

Great musicians like Scriabin or Berlioz did not contribute anything, or nearly nothing, to the theatre. Debussy's relation with the theatre was incidental. The doors were, however, open for Massenet, Puccini, Verdi and, especially, for writers of the operetta.

We should also mention masters of dance like Isadora Duncan, who remained out of the theatre and left space for the old-school ballet masters.

The bourgeois theatre did not unite the different arts. It even created enmity between them. However, it used for itself 'its own' writers, decorators, musicians and dancers.

We are especially feeling the pain of this situation in this current era of destruction and creation. In the period of revolution, the need for creation and unity is urgently felt. Not without reason, Wagner started dreaming of a new coalition in theatre between drama and music after he was shocked by the revolution of 1840s. Now we want to see the large-scale progress of this synthesis. Theatre should become the grand master of the united arts. As in the periods of the greatest theatres, it has to join the processes of creation of the writers and decorators, of musicians and dancers, of all the masters of the arts.

Till now, only a little has been done in this direction. In fact, the problem has not been grasped or even set. Our artists are still going in separate ways. In the theatre administration and directories, there is still no place for the creators of the different arts but only for pure theatre art. There are no organizations that unite closely all the artists, regardless of their speciality. There are no projects in which such unification could be carried out in practice. We have kept an old style.

There are attempts to unite opera with drama and ballet and to create a versatile actor, but literature and painting are forgotten. In all truth, the Moscow Proletkult is attempting to direct all studios (theatre, music and literature) to work on plays. But it is only the beginning. There is no widespread and conscious intention to create a new actor.

And, undoubtedly, that is one of the main aims of the modern theatre masters.

'On Futurism'

Fyodor Kalinin

Source: *Proletarskaia kul'tura*, no. 7–8, pp. 41–3

We shall not use the usual way to talk about futurism. This way is used to show examples of its specific manifestations, examples which demonstrate the entire meaninglessness of futuristic tricks. These tricks are often unclear even to the 'creators' themselves. The futurists produce plenty of such material. However, we cannot shake them out of balance this way. The futurists are not embarrassed when they are shown their senseless gibberish, and it does not stop them from moving from defence to attack. Futurists strike a majestic pose of contempt; they grab history by its coat-tails – by the way, when it is to their benefit, they even deny history – and begin to say through gritted teeth: 'What about the Symbolists? What about Cézanne or Picasso? Did you understand them when they were entering the stage?' Often the one to whom the question was addressed would get embarrassed and think to himself: 'Hell knows, maybe I really am mothballed and behind the times?' Feeling more and more embarrassed, the one denying futurism would begin to see something in it and fall silent.

Thus, pointing out to futurists their own baboonery is, to a significant degree, a monkey business. The important thing for us is to clarify the social nature of futurism and its social meaning. But before this let's dwell on their understanding of artistic form.

In issue 17 of *The Art of the Commune*,[1] form is considered as 'determining consciousness'. In this case, the writers of this newspaper absolutely do not understand that form in art is simply a frozen ideology that cannot define content and that it only serves as a way of organizing it. Development and changes to forms happen in the process of their overcoming with the content of being, when the material that is being organized does not correspond or fit in the form set.

---

1 *Iskusstvo Kommuny* in Russian.

In the same issue, they mention Alexander Veselovsky,[2] who laid the foundation of the history of the literary form. This is being used to prove freedom of form from substance, from everyday life, etc. It is true that the history of literature can be studied as a history of form; art can be looked upon as predominantly an issue of form, but it does not follow and it cannot follow that form is defined by form and not by content. Not a single wise guy proved that forms grow out of forms without any connection to content, and no one will ever prove it. To consider form on its own means is to engage in metaphysics, in idle talk, and, of course, this will have nothing to do with Marxism.

The mode of production of material life defines economic relations between people. This way content is created, which, in turn, defines form. What is futurism then? This is a social phenomenon of the capitalist system, bourgeois ideology that reached the limit of its final development. This is the death throes of the bourgeois spirit, craziness as it foresees its perdition. All the quirks, wild dances, quackery, whims and 'feast in the time of the plague' come from here. According to popular belief, the devil fears holy water and, in the same way, the bourgeois ideologists in the arts and other areas, in the time of decrepit capitalism, fear and shun the consciousness of the mind. The material foundations of the bourgeoisie – private property and private means of production – during the period of imperialism were developing into the socialized form, which created inside the bourgeois system the contradictions denying private property and the whole system of relations between people and their ideology. Naturally, in such conditions there is reason to shun the mind and its logic.

The way to develop ideology has been defined by the mode of production, which in the capitalist system has already started turning into a socialized form represented by trusts, cartels, etc., and behind those the silhouette of the socialist economy had already loomed – such way could not turn the eyes of bourgeoisie to the consciousness of mind. The bourgeois ideologists' hopes and trust in the power of the consciousness of mind were undermined. The logic of consciousness summarizing and generalizing the developing mode of production showed the picture of the impending doom of private property – the foundation of bourgeois capitalism. From there comes the passionate, 'in your face' love for sophistry, for over-sophisticated word and speech. The futurists

---

2   Alexander Veselovsky (1838–1906), an essential name in nineteenth-century Russian literary theory who, using interests developed from the social sciences and comparative folklore, argued that the main object of study of literary and critical scholarship was to be directed towards themes, motifs and plots (Stacy 1974: 100).

rave about their own brilliancy and specific greatness. This raving, individually and en masse, expresses the despair of deadly melancholy and the foreboding of their own perdition. Aching and nagging melancholy rises from the deep dark bottom of their soul and forces futurists to silence it and to persuade everybody, including themselves, about things in which they don't believe. You remember, reader, the excellent description of this type of people given by the genius of Dostoevsky in *Notes from the House of the Dead*. He has one of the characters whose only business is to walk from cell to cell and repeat the same phrase over and over again: 'But he is lying about everything, he is lying!' No one listens or pays him any attention; this makes the pain of his melancholy even more tormenting, but he is still trying to repeat the meaningless phrase in a hoarse and tired voice, and this is what probably saves him from an immediate and final madness. Our futurists scream for exactly the same reasons.

In issue 8 of *The Art of the Commune* they talk about 'the torn consciousness' of 'the great poet of our time Khlebnikov'.[3] For the futurists the absence of an elementary logic of the consciousness in their fellowman is the highest achievement.

Torn consciousness, as you see, gives boundless and unlimited space for the intuition to wonder around the forms. The poor writers of *The Art of the Commune* took upon themselves the unhappy task to be the theoreticians of futurism, and the even unhappier task to attach futurism to Marxism, to its historical materialism. (See the issue above of *The Art of the Commune*.)

Poor authors of *The Art of the Commune*! Don't you see that you 'sew your black fabric with white thread',[4] and a rotten one at that! This is what the 'torn consciousness' means exactly – some kind of pink elephants in the eyes, when everything looks the other way round.

Marxism is a teaching that shows to humankind the way from anarchy and chaos towards the triumph of the logic of consciousness.

Remember Engels's words: 'The proletariat will jump from the kingdom of necessity to the kingdom of freedom.' The Marxists have a simple understanding of this: power in a socialist society will triumph over anarchy and chance. However, your intuition will not have the freedom to wander around from one form to another; consciousness will establish a strict control over it; overly wise guys will be sent to a mental asylum. But here we cannot help your grief. The

---

3 Velimir Khlebnikov (1885–1922), futurist poet and playwright with a far-reaching influence. For a detailed discussion see Leach (2018: 81–6).
4 Translator's note: this is a Russian idiom that means 'poorly disguised'.

march of historic necessity, with its steel measured pace, not only shackles your weak and feeble intuition but grinds to dust such a fat and seasoned beast like the imperialist bourgeoisie.

'Attaching themselves to socialism in the revolution', the futurists like to single out as the sign of their kinship with socialism the fact that the bourgeoisie also bullied and persecuted them in the same way that they did the socialists. The issue of the futurists and the socialists should be taken with a pretty big pinch of salt; as for the persecution by the bourgeoisie, that did happen but for entirely different reasons when compared to the persecution of the socialists. The bourgeoisie understood too well what the futurists are not, but it instinctively sensed that the harbingers of its doom lurk in the form of the futurists' performances, in their baggage – just like Oleg's death which, according to the legend, was hidden in the skull of his favourite horse.[5] For the bourgeoisie the futurists were a mirror, which showed, ahead of time, its destiny, the prospects of its degradation and death. The bourgeoisie was turning away from the futurists and squinting in order to avoid seeing its fate, the sight of which squeezed its heart with the deadly cold of the impending doom.

The futurists are against the routine of everyday life. Nevertheless, futurism, the way it exists in every country with its national specificity, *is* the routine of everyday life. In the West, where capitalism is much better developed and where it has deeper roots in communal life, futurism did not show such riot and debauchery as here. This way the bourgeois ideologist, who in order to obscure and slow down the future collapse of capitalism, invented and adapted more refined and diverse theories of intuition, philosophical mysticism and other fine matter, which they used to screen themselves from the shining path of the theoretical development of human society.

Russian futurism is a completely different story. Our capitalism was weak and underdeveloped; in this situation futurism subconsciously served as a screaming barometer that gave a bright reflection of the sense of the upcoming disaster in capitalist society, which had to happen quicker than in other countries. There was no time or strength to invent refined theories; this is why the tossing about of our futurism was so unbridled and crazy. Its intuition sensed the underground roaring of an oncoming explosion. In this way futurism is a historical necessity but already a passed stage. What is left of it is the need to adjust the wreckage

---

5 Translator's note: this is a reference to the famous poem by Alexander Pushkin 'The Song of Wise Oleg'.

which spreads the dust that infiltrates the lungs of the proletariat with tuberculosis. We have the duty to carry out the disinfection and to install state-of-the-art ventilation.

Can the proletariat follow futurism or its trail? Clearly not, as the proletariat and futurism are opposites. The proletariat cannot follow the path of turns and twists and perform dislocations of the torn consciousness, which is foreign to proletarian ideology and does not in any way fit into it. The proletariat has in front of it a rich field of creation in the manner of harmonious logic. It anticipates grand constructions built out of the rich reserves of subconscious experiences, intuitively expressed, covered in the juice of feelings and connected by the powerful force of a coherent logic – the cement of consciousness. The prospects of developing the human spirit are infinite; the complexity of its ornaments is countless; the expression of artistic creation has to be made a conscious ideal. You can fill it with whatever intuitive material you like, but all of it has to be strictly and tightly connected to an ideal under the keen scrutiny of consciousness. The path of overly sophisticated language and overly sophisticated colours is the path of charlatanism and lying to oneself, cowardice in front of the shining ideal and the prospects of humankind moving forward – cowardice for the sake of preserving today and running away from tomorrow.

'Creative Play. The Improvisational Method of N. F. Skarskaia'

P. P. Gaideburov

Source: *VO*, no. 6–8, 1919, pp. 36–40

About two years ago I followed a workers' request and organized a theatre studio at the Ordnance plant. This studio did not pursue strict professional tasks, and staging a production was not a goal of our work, but rather its natural consequence. At that time, if I am not mistaken, such a type of studio work was the first attempt to introduce the working masses to artistic creativity on the basis of their general cultural development. The leader of this initiative was N. F. Skarskaia.[1] It was there that she used for the first time the method of dramatic improvisation created by her.

Theatrical improvisation has existed for a long time. The actors in the early Italian theatre made it the foundation of their art, now known as 'commedia dell'arte'. A number of attempts – up to recent times – to revive this type of scenic art did not influence the professional theatre or any of its creative methods. Moreover, 'creative play',[2] as I allowed myself to name the Skarskaia Method, finds itself not in the past, which cannot be artificially revived or brought back, and not in our modern improvisational technique, which we now see in theatre schools as an additional means to develop both the actor's ability to express individual feelings (fear, pity, happiness, fright) and the transitions from one feeling to another. Based on the nature of theatre, at least the way it is understood at the Mobile Theatre, of which N. F. Skarskaia is a founder and leader, her method has a wide breadth and integrates within it universal cultural aspirations – the latter are inherent in any truly modern and artistic theatre, which brings its creative work closer to the cultural ideals of the people. This method defines the independent role of improvisation as a truly creative

---

1 Nadezhda Skarskaia was one of Vera Komissarzhevskaya's sisters. Before the Revolution she organized productions in St Petersburg intended to elevate the cultural level of the workers. With the support of the philanthropist Countess Panina, she founded the Popular Theatre in 1903, with her husband Pavel Gaideburov (Swift 2002: 73 and 156). Under the name of the Mobile-Popular Theatre, this theatre was where 'the first and strongest impulse for mass spectacles arose in Soviet Russia' (von Geldern 1993: 119).

2 In Russian, the word used is *igra*, which can be translated to 'play' or 'game' but also 'performance'. It is related to the word *igrishche*, or the genre of dramatic play that developed after the Revolution. These involved the elaboration of popular games into political propaganda (von Geldern 1993: 109–10).

play that provokes intense interest among its participants, as it had immediately become clear after the first attempt at the Ordnance plant, and regardless of the fact that the improvisation method there was only used as a creative approach towards the performance on the stage.

Almost simultaneously with the classes for the workers, a professional studio at the Mobile Theatre was organized and led by Skarskaia, which helped to further develop and deepen her method. Another contributing factor was that the member-collaborators of the studio took the creative method out of its walls to different audiences. In this way, new experiences, observations and forms of application for the method were found. Thus, some of Skarskaia's students started teaching foundational lessons in her method at a labour school, others in the evening schools for teenagers, the third group in various proletarian and children's clubs. For example, N. G. Vinogradov[3] taught practical lessons in the short-term courses for instructors that later became the Institute for Extracurricular Education. Later, he organized a theatre 'workshop' for the Red Army soldiers, where his work was a direct continuation of his studies at the Mobile Theatre studio. He produced the whole tragic saga *The Overthrow of Autocracy* by using the method of 'creative play'.[4]

At the short-term courses for the Red Army soldiers at the Institute for Extracurricular Education, I involved a member of the Skarskaia's Studio, D. Shcheglov. He led practical lessons, and notes about his teaching and its meaningful results were published. His description also shows, to some extent, the method he used. He also gives examples of improvisations he borrowed from other sources. It is to be pointed out that the interpretation of the improvisation method and its possible use are Shcheglov's, that is according to his personal tastes, habits and inclinations which do not always coincide with the character, direction and interpretation adopted by the studio and its leader. Naturally, such thing may be legitimate, but it does not help the full and clear understanding of the method in its pure form, as they say.[5] This fact, however, does not diminish our interest in the story of the practical use of the method of 'creative play'.

---

3 For a detailed description of N. G. Vinogradov's work see von Geldern (1993: 122–9).
4 The performance was produced with soldiers of the Red Army who had themselves taken part in some of the revolutionary events staged. For more information, see von Geldern (1993: 125–6).
5 The criticism raised here happened in other instances. D. Shcheglov was often criticized for taking unique directions that were contrary to official measures, as articulated by the Petrograd Proletkult for example (see Mally 1990: 118–9).

It is another matter when improvisation classes are taught only from hearsay, as it happens in various studios and clubs. The quick and wide expansion of such classes is explained by the strong interest from the masses. However, in the overwhelmingly majority of cases, this kind of practical or studio work has only one thing in common with the Skarskaia method – the word 'improvisation' in the title.

We do not need to go into the details of what makes the method of creative play dramatically different from any other type of improvisation. The most significant one is that creative play serves as a foundation to develop artistic consciousness and to create works of art. It also reveals the creativity which to a greater or lesser degree is inherent in every human being. However, the type of improvisation that is familiar to us, just like any other, is more or less accidental in the production of a studio performance or even the professional education in theatre.

[...]

One may consider Shcheglov's work not rounded enough, or missing some parts, but the principle of creative play as a basis for his lessons raises the question of bringing an individual towards creative action in a new way. I repeat, additions to this plan are possible, but basically it cannot be changed in the slightest way without collapsing the whole work altogether. The basis is the principle of creative play, which has to be either accepted in full or not at all.

Does the above mean that we cannot question our practical work and its theoretical development? Of course not. In involving collaborators[6] in our artistic and cultural search, it is inappropriate to deny their possible use to develop and strengthen arts and culture. On the contrary, the comparison of various plans and methods of work promotes new creative rays and leads to the elaboration of independent devices better suited to the personality of any leader. Different activity should take place.

[...]

It is useful to add a general description and work plan of the method of creative play. N. F. Skarskaia is preparing a book dedicated to her 'system', but unfortunately this work is currently far from seeing the light of day. Therefore,

---

6 Translator's note: The specific word that is used here is *poputchikov*, which in early Soviet Russia meant someone of the wrong descent, someone who was neither a proletarian nor a peasant, but who had knowledge that could be useful for the construction of the new state and who therefore could be forgiven for being from the noble classes, religious etc.

I take the liberty to tell what I know about it and how I use it in my pedagogical practice.

The Skarskaia Method of improvisation is a system of dramatic acting divided into five types of exercises or five levels of improvisation. Together they lead towards creative action, but separately they do not become creative play. Moreover, none of the five types of improvisation can be seen as a technical exercise. Each of them is an organic link in the development of the general system of artistic sensitivity and acting, of feelings and their physical embodiment. Each carries a seed of genuine creative possibilities.

Speech is inherent to a human being. A person uses speech to express accumulated thoughts and emotions, recognized to the extent that they have to be expressed. The first level of creative play reveals the connection between the inner world of a human soul and mind and the external world – this is done through the use of the spoken word. A performer is given a piece of text describing thoughts, emotions and conditions which he is experiencing as a character and which brings him to say his words. For example:

> He was writing at the table. It was quiet. Suddenly a buzzing sound came from the street. He listened closely – no, nothing there. He started writing again. A moment later there was the buzzing again. He was listening: yes, some real noise can be heard … He let it go and returned to his writing. But now the shouts of a huge crowd are clearly heard, and they grow louder and louder. He jumped on his feet and opened the window: 'Hey, what is this shouting about?'

The second level of improvisation is a combination of two or more experiences, which bring people to a *dialogue*, to an *exchange* of their thoughts and feelings that *matured* into words. Performers are given this kind of exercise, this theme:

> The term of his exile finished two years earlier than expected; to get home quickly, to cheer up his father and sister; they are so lonely without him … What has become of them? It is the end of May now: the father, of course, spends all his days in the garden … The trip from the station seemed never-ending; he kept asking the coachman to rush his horses … finally … he ran straight to the garden – nobody there … he ran through the terrace into the dining room: his sister is near the window, sewing … she turned to him … looked at him as if he was a stranger …
>
> – Masha …
>
> She startled … got up … threw herself at him with a cry, embraced him and started weeping.

– Darling, I am home, home …
She laughed through the tears.
– Oh God, what is happening?
She embraced and kissed him again.
– Let's go to father.
She moved away and drooped, then looked up at him and took his hand in hers.
– Lyosha, we don't have a father …
– Did he die?
She nodded and covered her face with her hands. He slowly moved to the door leading to the garden and stopped to think.
– He never saw me return.

The only part performed from this whole description is where the action begins; the rest serves to introduce an improviser to the circle of emotions and moods needed for the action and for sensing the atmosphere in which it happens, and on which it largely depends.

The third level is improvised play on the theme set out in the narrative, the dramatized performance requiring improvised dialogue. An example:

'A husband comes back after a year in jail. His brother came to pick him up. His sick wife and sister are waiting at home. His wife is very excited. At last, steps are heard on the stairs. One more minute, and after a year apart they will meet.'

The fourth level of improvisation sets up a task for performers to decipher feelings, situations and images hiding behind a dialogue (conversation), which we imagine overhearing in real life or reading in an unfamiliar piece of dramaturgy. The interpretation of the task and its creative embodiment through the living characters is already a truly creative process of scenic action, *acting* based on a previously composed dialogue. An example of such dialogue without any suggestive explanation is the following:

– Has he come?
– He went to him.
– Masha, I am scared … what is it? …
– He moved an armchair.
– Did you hear?
– Calm down for God's sake.
– He is coming, Masha, I am scared …
– So?
– Say it!
– He calmed down and called for us all. Let's go.

In an exercise like this the gender, age, the number of participants, their family and other relations depend entirely on artistic imagination, on the inventiveness and resourcefulness of the performers. The only rule for the casting and distribution of the lines is the logical and psychological justification of the dialogue.

The fifth level is quite independent to and externally undetermined by the creative process of the performers; it is when their art meets with the art of the author (his creation and literature). Performers are given a theme, an abbreviated formula, which contains the potential for improvisation. For example: 'The end justifies the means', 'Haste makes waste', 'Children's wisdom finds answers to the most difficult questions', 'Sincerity and truthfulness effortlessly break the most complex intrigue', 'Often the most insignificant event provokes a loud quarrel with very sad consequences', etc.

The play of the performers, without any preparation, preliminary agreement or a predetermined topic, is completed by this fifth stage.

All the examples given above are borrowed from N. F. Skarskaia's work at the Studio of the Mobile Theatre.

Every leader should begin by giving participants his own examples of improvisations (assignments) on each of the five levels. Later on the improvisers may compose improvisations of their own, for themselves or for their colleagues. This new task not only facilitates the development of their imagination – the foundation of any kind of creativity – but in some cases it may also help the discovery of a new stream of creative ability in the sphere of literature.

All improvisations have to be performed without any additional objects, apart from those needed to sit or lie down on. This develops in a performer a sense of the objects, the logic of manipulating them and a sense of gesture. It teaches economy of movements, which is the necessary condition for expressive performance.

The importance of the method of creative play, and the diverse forms of its application, is such a curious subject and one which has a strong practical value, that in the future I will take liberty to propose to my readers several articles on the subject. Now I would like to conclude by underlining naturalness and simplicity as the distinguishing features of this method. Every truly new and important step in the field of cultural achievement, every significant discovery, is simple and natural because they have a single source and foundation – the laws of nature, which are essentially always simple and organic.

N. F. Skarskaia's method reveals, through simple, almost routine occurrences, and through the use of simple and natural means, the core qualities which up to now remained uncultivated and unused. When applied these qualities enrich human activity with new creative possibilities and approaches and, in combination with E. Jaques-Dalcroze's[7] discovery in his system of rhythmic gymnastics, it will bring man closer to the enchanting image of the future 'Creative Human'.

---

7 Émile Jaques-Dalcroze (1865–1950), whose system on Eurhythmics had at its root the experience of music through movement. Eurhythmics provided a reference point to the training of amateur actors – see, for instance, 'A Unified Studio of the Arts' and 'On Theatre Work at the Clubs' in Part Five.

'Experiment in the Staging of Émile Verhaeren's Poem "Insurrection"'

Valentin Smyshlaev

Source: *Gorn*, no. 2–3, 1919, pp. 82–90

In our work to create the proletarian theatre, collective criticism on all our achievements and the ways to reach them is very important[1].

The opening evening of the Moscow Proletkult took place on 6 November [1918], and the programme included a dramatization of Émile Verhaeren's poem 'Insurrection'. My task here is to introduce comrades working in the field of proletarian theatre the techniques and methods of our work that led to the creation of this dramatization.

At one point a student of the Drama Studio in the urban district brought a collection of Verhaeren's verses to the lesson and invited everyone to stage something through them. A general conversation about the staging began. The most significant aspects of theatre are action and dialogue. Therefore, the staging requires the composition of a scenario or the writing of a play on a topic that has to include these two theatrical essentials. Hence, the task was to choose a poem that would easily turn into dramatic action. We chose 'Insurrection' as this poem expresses in a highly artistic way the feelings of the masses, the feelings of the revolutionary crowd who through the destruction of slavery is building a new joyful life. We immediately read this poem together, and it made a tremendous impression on us. It seized us, and we wanted to perform it. I would like to emphasize that the enthusiasm for the desire, which is the basis of artistic work, arose here.[2] We began to think immediately how the poem could be produced when the impression from the reading was still so bright in our minds. We raised the following question: 'What should the viewer take and what is his first impression?' And someone said the word 'chaos'. Chaos – this became the common thread that we tried to transmit through the staging: the chaos of

---

1 Elsewhere, I discuss this essay as an instant of amateur-professional hybridity (Aquilina 2020: 125–9).
2 In his acting manual Techniques to Process a Stage Performance, Smyshlaev goes in substantial depth when discussing the initial impression which a text or a theme makes on the actors, be they professional or amateur. He likened this moment to the fascination of reading a new book. The initial enthusiasm is not fleeting but actually serves as the very real and tangible material with which the actor works (Smyshlaev 1922: 13).

sounds, lines, movements, the chaos of hope; the chaos in which one can find both the groaning of those dying and the enthusiastic ecstasy of the creators of the new life.

During the same evening we drew together a picture of the staging as it was initially imagined. The theatre is immersed in complete darkness. Somewhere, formless and broken sounds of music are heard. They gradually turn into an ecstatic hymn. The curtain slowly moves apart, but the viewer still cannot discern anything on the stage. Some streams of golden sparks break the darkness and merge with the stars. There is the roar of a formless, excited crowd, the trampling of running feet. Little by little the red reflections of the fires scatter in the darkness. The spectator starts to distinguish some lines, resembling corners of houses, window edges, doors, but these are not definite lines, but trembling, broken, rebellious ones. The spectator sees a bustling and excited crowd ... And over all this chaos, the words of Verhaeren's poem are heard ... Groups of people merge together and split ... human bodies fall down ... there is someone above the crowd who delivers a speech ... somewhere the enemies appear ... fight ... and victory ... And through the sparks of burning buildings, everyone is alarmed by the worrying call of the bells, and the enthusiastic and determined crowd is slowly coming forwards towards the audience:

> Through killing create and update,
> Or else fall down and die.

The curtain is drawn and separates the crowd from the audience ... That is, in general, how we initially pictured the staging, how we thought it would be. Then we had to develop a text. Here again we did a lot of teamwork: we used to gather together, read the poem and everyone who wanted took part in the work on the text of the script. In the course of this work, of course, the text of the script changed many times. A lot of new editing was made, and more than once. Eventually the scenario was worked out.

[...]

The text of the script was not developed at a desk. It was not developed through imagination either. It was elicited all the time from the live feelings of the participants. After reading the poem we started working with études first, which consisted of improvisations on topics close to the theme of the poem and, at the same time, close to the life experiences of those involved. Among us there were many who had taken part in the October Revolution. We shared our memories with the comrades and tried to reproduce into dramatic action the episodes of the great battle we had experienced. Besides, among us were participants of the 1905 uprising, and we also used their memories as themes for our sketches. We built our dramatization on these vivid feelings. Naturally, these sketches were not exact copies of the experience; they were not photographs of reality – no! Warmed by the imagination of the creative artists, these memories turned into a reality very similar to the truth; from genuine truth they turned into a work of art.

Through improvisation we also found the mise-en-scène, and the whole form and colour of the staging.

Certain roles immediately became obvious once the text became more or less clear, and together we chose suitable actors; after all, a whole crowd consists of separate roles, because in the crowd there are workers, students and townsfolk. Besides, everyone has their own personal life, each one sees the events in the poem in different ways, and everyone has his or her own character.

And then we had a lot of work ahead of us. I invited all the comrades to think who they wanted to play, and in this way the roles in the crowd described by Verhaern were outlined. There were workers from different professions (metalworkers, masons, drapers, tailors, dressmakers, unskilled workers, etc.) and soldiers, clerks, managers, cooks, maids, telegraphers, old and young, people actively leading the uprising, and people who accidentally happen to be in the crowd; in short, the infinite variety of human individuals we can observe in any crowd.

Having outlined the roles, it was then important to give them life. It was necessary to give everyone a series of actions, which would create a common performance line. Here the so-called method of today helped us a lot.

In general, this method means the following. The actors, coming to a rehearsal, would imagine a whole day of the persons they are playing. This method, in addition of developing the actors' imagination, is also remarkable as it affects in a certain way the actors' souls. From 'rich' emotional impressions, it brings the feelings necessary for a given part.

Every participant in the crowd did this work. Some even recorded it, and here I will give some of these 'dreams', as we call them, so that the reader can see what we mean by the 'method of today' and how we can use it. Here is the fantasy of the student playing the worker:

> It was morning; as always I woke at 6 o'clock, had a cup of tea in a tavern, and went to the factory, to work. My thoughts drifted far away from reality. I imagined that the time had arrived when the worker is not under the oppression of his master. When everyone feels a free citizen … and so these tempting pictures opened up more and more in front of me. Evening. On my way home I noticed a lot of people in the streets, and the faces of passers-by were very excited. I hurriedly

drank some tea and visited my friend to find out what was the matter. But before I reached his apartment, I suddenly heard shooting. There was shooting in the city centre. At first, these were timid and solitary shots, but then they became more vigorous, and rifle volleys took my attention. I went to the main street and saw a truck passing by, then another one with workers and soldiers armed with rifles and machine guns. I asked them to take me with them. The car stopped, and I was already with a rifle in my hands sitting with my comrades. We raced to the centre, where there was non-stop shooting. Our red banner, the emblem of freedom, equality and the brotherhood of nations, spread as a broad strip, and we flew as if we had wings to the battle site. No fear, no hesitation. We were strongly determined to either win or die. But here the battle is near; and the bullets are flying and buzzing. We make our way to the barricades. The dead and the wounded were falling down around us. But there was no fear, and we rushed forward with the shouting of 'Hurray' and the singing of the Marseillaise. We rushed to the attack ...

And here is the fantasy of a student playing a soldier:

An acquaintance of mine, a worker and member of a political party, told me of the day of the uprising. On the day of the uprising, I was appointed, with two other soldiers from my squad, to guard the money box of the district's headquarters. My comrades knew that there would be an uprising, but they did not know exactly when. From talking to them I realized that they were ready to openly join the rebels and support the uprising. Seeing that the comrades were sincere, I told them that the uprising would begin that night. The three of us decided not to return to the squadron, but to move together with the workers. During the whole day we were very excited. I wanted to run to the streets and accelerate the moment of the uprising. Finally the shift came to an end and we were informed that the city was not safe, that the people were assembling in crowds and that they were being shot by armed riders. On leaving the building, we noticed that in one of the streets a crowd of several thousand people passed singing revolutionary songs. My comrades and I immediately decided to join them and together with the crowd we quickly went to the square ...

The reader probably already noticed that in these fantasies everything is very similar to the truth; I think that in them there is a lot of genuine, real truth and that the comrades who wrote these 'dreams' experienced once again what they had once experienced in reality. The significance of these fantasies for the staging is enormous: here is found the foundation of the role, where all further knowledge of the image is built.

[...]

In these dreams, the students, without knowing, approached the most important thing that had to be shown. I could give an endless number of very interesting and curious fantasies (more than 100), but it seems to me that the method of internal approach that we applied in our work is clear. We tried to touch our souls, to light them up with the fire of desire, desire very close to what we once experienced in reality, but completely different than it really was.

So, with a series of sketches, a series of fantasies, we guided our attention to the stage problem created by ourselves and the author. But this task was still not clear to us, we could not yet grasp its exact meaning, we could not clearly express it; we had a premonition, but we could not name or define it, and therefore we could not even recognize it. We could not find yet what K. S. Stanislavsky calls the 'through action' of the whole work. But we did not despair; we persistently continued to work and search. We were interested in expressing not only the individual feelings and attitudes of other individual roles, but also the feelings of the crowd, the all-encompassing feeling which engulfs every person in a large group of people. […] In our work on each individual character from the crowd, we did not forget the magnificent folk scenes of the 'Court' from *Brothers Karamazov* and the scene of Act 3 of *Woe from Wit* in the productions of the Moscow Art Theatre. We approached our task from the awareness of that special feeling, when one person in a crowd is linked to the whole group through some very special strings.

The most vivid and frequent expression of such states emerges in moments of panic. In order to 'consolidate' this feeling, we did a lot of improvisations. I remember one particularly successful improvisation. It was a sketch on the topic 'Fire'. We gathered in our rehearsal room and suddenly began to smell smoke, but we continued to work, not paying it any particular attention; but the smell was becoming stronger and stronger; anxiety took over our souls; someone ran to find out what the matter was and rushed back in horror screaming that the entire building was on fire. Everyone rushed to the exit, but there was no way out; the fire cut us off. Everyone started rushing around the hall. This improvisation was especially successful, and almost everyone felt this connection between a person and crowd. We all had one basic desire, which connected everyone together: to find a way out as quickly as possible.

From a number of other sketches we found material for future use; for example, some parts of the poem were read out by several persons, others by everyone involved. This is only one external form that expresses collective feelings, but first of all we tried to find these feelings, these enormous and powerful feelings known only in a crowd. Everyone is connected to each other, shoulder to shoulder, merged like iron – a team can read only this way, and everyone then feels how their word becomes the word of all and their throat, producing the sound, is the colossal throat of the collective hero. And not only through the word, but also through the movement, through the action, one's solidarity with the whole is manifested, a special rhythm of the crowd: as if the feet of more than one man step on the ground, as if not one hand rises, but thousands, and thousands of feet move like one.

It seems to me that we managed to find this in our performance, and this was especially vivid in two episodes. The first was the part of the poem that begins with the words 'Death automatically aims at … '. Here the poet himself gives us the rhythm of the march – one-two, one-two. After all, the march is one of the main rhythms of the collective action. We noticed this, and we interpreted it in our scenario: the retreating crowd, pushed into the corner by the hail of the enemies' bullets, carrying death, suddenly straightens up and bravely, as one, attacks the enemies with a desperate desire for victory. The second was in the final episode, when everyone in the crowd, with one strong feeling of great creative ecstasy – as if flying above the theatre hall – raises their hands, partly armed with sticks, scraps and whatever they could find. They stand still, strong, welded together, confident and mighty.

But would it be right if this synchronized rhythm – synchronized words, synchronized steps – continued throughout the entire production? Maybe for some other performance it would have been right, but, it seems to me, not for 'Insurrection'. The poem was born out of chaos; it was born out of the collective feelings which carried people from peaceful suffering to joyful action. Just like animals when they are drawn by an 'unknown force' and spontaneously move in crowds to new places, so are human crowds carried away by this 'unknown force' … hurrying forward! And the synchronized rhythm in this spontaneous movement can be born only when the crowd begins to merge through the desire to help and support each other. This rhythm is the action and meaning of an organized crowd. The moment of the insurrection is, if I may say so, not rhythmic; the memory of the past is still too strong and the elements of the future are still not clear. At the time of the insurrection, when the old forms are breaking down, when a social development that was determined by law is being destroyed, chaos still reigns. That is why in our first reading of the poem we realized the impression of chaos. That is why this definition was our guiding thread. But even this did not give us the right to build the entire performance on a particular rhythm, despite its clear character. It would not be at all true. But, as in all spontaneous movement, there are hints of the future. In our work there are moments that manifest organized rhythms, elements of the future construction of life.

So little by little, from rehearsal to rehearsal, we groped for the form to reveal the actions and feelings of the masses on the stage. I emphasize: all the time we moved on according to the content of the stage tasks (given by the author and ourselves). Our analysis was needed for the sake of a new synthesis, one which was our own. And now, proceeding from the main thread, i.e. the staging of the mass action, proceeding on the fact that the play is written in a poetic form and thus it is full of exaggerated emotions, unusual in our daily life, we had to merge the actions of separate characters (the leader, his friends) with this mass, with these intense emotions. It was so striking to us that every small, unfinished and indefinite gesture or word of individual persons completely breaks the entire form. I hoped that everyone, even when talking separately, could be completely filled with emotions that rise to the point of an extreme. I wanted for every action to be not only completely finished and defined, but also significant, magnificent – so that everything would emphasize the grandeur and importance of the feelings of the creative crowd, so that everything would be in harmony with the rhythms of the new life that is coming. And here, apart from the acting, we needed the creativity of the artists and of the musicians. The artist with his lines and colours, the musician with his sounds and rhythms, helped us to complete the dramatization. And not only to supplement it, no – they brought us their own thoughts and feelings, which were new to us, and we absorbed them, and they merged their creativity with our own.

Unfortunately, we had to show our work before it was finished, but the process itself already gave us a lot. It convinced us, above everything else, that we are on the right track, that we believe in the spark of proletarian culture which attracts all of humanity and that we are already trying to find the way.

The Results of the New Theatre

Platon Kerzhentsev

Source: *Tvorcheskii teatr* 5th edition, 1923, pp. 123–36

The experience of the last two years has shown us that the revolutionary creativity in the art of the popular masses is capable of achieving great victories. A lot of that which two years ago appeared utopian is starting to become a reality. Moreover, the collaboration of the spectators, which the theatre masters had so ridiculed, is now being noted. This collaboration is still very primitive, and at the moment it is only seen when spectators, for instance, join the singing coming from the stage, or in the large mass scenes, but even these examples were unknown to the bourgeois theatre. It is important to note that the participation occurs in a completely spontaneous manner, without preparation, constrictions or soliciting.

The following is a characteristic example recounted by a Proletkult collaborator at Starogorkinsk (under the Moscow Governorship).

A dramatic text that treated the theme of the revolution was collectively created by the workers, the majority of whom had never set foot in a theatre before. One particular scene depicted the workers bringing down a wall that represented the old times. As the actors onstage shouted and hurled themselves against the wall, the spectators instinctively and together stood from their seats to help the actors in their struggle. The victorious notes of the Internationale were played when the wall was destroyed, to which the whole hall joined.

Similar examples were also reported during the Congress of the Worker-peasant theatre.[1]

Such participation is possible only on two essential conditions: that there is class homogeneity across the public and that the dramas staged have a particular impact on the spectators, therefore, mainly through revolutionary dramas.

Another type of participation is the collective creation of a dramatic text by the actors and the spectators. And in this way another of my proposals which appeared utopian has now been realized.

The performance by the Starogorkinsk Proletkult referred to above was created collectively. The theme was also elaborated collectively. The staging was

---

1 See Piotr Kogan's essay 'Socialist Theatre in the Years of the Revolution' in Part One.

devised in detail by the whole group. The actors were the ones who composed the text and the director only needed to make some observations and edit the piece as a whole. The leader described the performance arising from the collective efforts as follows:

> A suffocating and low-ceiling hall. A small stage. There is no proscenium or prompter. Part of the auditorium is separated by grey panels and the side entrance is hidden. Right in front of us there is a grey wall. The stage is in semi-darkness. A silent attention can be felt everywhere. A buzzing of voices is then heard, voices of men, women and children, which little by little become louder. A group of tired and starving women directly cut across the auditorium and move towards the stage. Children are running after them. The men appear. They move in a stoop, slowly, and a soft cry accompanies their movements. The men arrive to the grey wall. Among them there is a group who though bent low are still indomitable and strong. The women, with their babies in hand, crawl on their knees and shout, 'Bread! Give us bread!' They stretch out their hands and beg for pity. The men are murmuring darkly, and their first lines amass underneath the wall. Silence is everywhere.
>
> A voice starts a prayer: 'Great God, you are seeing the suffering of the people. You can see that they have no strength left!' Other voices join in and the entire crowd implores on their knees the invisible God behind the grey wall.
>
> The prayer ends. On its last moments the notes of a waltz are heard from behind the wall. It gets dark. A window appears in the wall. It is strongly lit and couples dancing can be seen. Men and women are fleetingly sharing magnificent toilettes. Someone from the crowd raises his head and looks inside. Behind the windows the couples become agitated and look over onto the crowd.
>
> Among the guests at the feast there are the servants offering delicate food. The crowd feels how that useless congregation of cheerful invitees mock their tired bearing and torn clothes. The crowd start to murmur dully. The burghers are afraid but someone calms them: the workers are stupid and cowardly. They are not organized and will not dare to lay hands on the capital. They have strong faith in the wall's divine origin.
>
> The men's rumble becomes menacing. They slowly move forward. It gets dark again and in front of them stands the strong wall that hides the unknown.
>
> An agitator tries to stir the crowd. He tries to destroy the legend. The men want to believe him but the women are scared and hold back those who want to fight. However, a small group of brave men still manage to hurl themselves against the wall.
>
> The scene changes to a splendidly decorated hall. This is the hall where the bourgeoisie's global high council meets. The leader reports to the council the disorders of the workers and the appearance of the agitators among the workers.

The bourgeoisie discuss a plan to prevent an insurrection. The army has to be strengthened, the agitators arrested, while other agitators are to be sent in the midst of the people. For this end, science and especially religion need to be taken advantage of.

The crowd hears all this and hurls itself with even more agitation against the enemy. The wall becomes higher. They are initially scared and retract, but the bravest again throw themselves forward. The entire crowd follows them. The alienated soldiers appear. They push back the first lines but not all of the attackers. A preacher tries to hold back the assailants with false speeches. The women hesitate but the leaders resolutely hurl themselves forward and pull down the wall with their strong hands. The wall collapses.

The shining sun comes out. On a hill there is a strong and fearless worker, with a hammer in hand. He incites the crowd to move forward towards the rising sun. His call is powerful:

'Forward! Towards Socialism!
The road is difficult and full of thorns.
But the hour of a new prosperity is near.
The kingdom of a new fraternity is near.'
A resounding Internationale is heard. The sun shines brightly. The waving red flags also shine.
The whole hall sings the Internationale with the actors.[2]

The work of the Moscow Proletkult also substantiates my ideas.[3] The 1919–20 winter was dedicated to the interesting attempt to create the cycle *Popular Revolutionary Movements in Russia*. The cycle covered the following historical moments: (1) Bolotnikov's riot, (2) Razin's revolt, (3) Pugachev's revolt, (4) the Decembrists' revolt, (5) the peasant's revolt that followed the manifesto (the episode that occurred in the village of Bresdna, under the Governorship of Kazan, in 1861), (6) 9 January 1905 and (7) the December days in Moscow.

The work proceeded as follows. The leader introduced the theme of each movement and then identified the most significant episodes and figures. The group first immersed themselves in the atmosphere of each epoch and understood its social causes, after which the work shifted to improvisation in order to reproduce the determined episode. In contrast to conventional improvisation where the interpreters have complete freedom, the improvisation in this case

---

2 A footnote in the original reads as follows: 'Socialist Construction for 1919', no. 4, pp. 95–6.
3 See Figure 8.

was complicated because the leader kept the interpreters together by 'directing' and guiding the improvisation. This he did by giving the improvisation the necessary orientation when it steered away from the right path and its rhythm dropped. The strong material that emerges from this work is integrated to the leader's scheme. The result of this entire work is a dramatic text.

In Petrograd the drama *The Red Year* was staged by the dramatic workshop of the Red Army. The division between stage and auditorium was eliminated. The action started at the back of the hall. It is 9 January 1905. Passionate speeches are being made; angry shouts are heard. It is immediately clear that this is a spontaneous creation. The February Revolution is then represented: the destruction of the barricades and the abdication of the Tsar. Everything is concluded with the funeral of the old world accompanied by carnival songs and dance. The last part is dedicated to the October Revolution. Volleys of shots are heard. The tension of the spectators reaches the climax. The leader of the workers asks who is for the Soviet. The spectators rise from their seats. The victory is now clear. 'All Power to the Soviets!' And the whole auditorium joins in the song. The Internationale is played.

This dramatic composition is made of eight episodes: (1) 9 January 1905, (2) a student's family in Moscow, (3) a mutiny in the military prison, (4) the arsenal, (5) the police station, (6) the barricades, (7) at the front and (8) to the General Staff.

The repertoire of the performances is elaborated collectively. The dramaturgy is defined along general lines first while the details are specified by their own accord during the performance.

The actors are young professionals or worker-actors. Despite this, the improvisation develops without difficulty and pushes the spectators to participate directly.

The audience participated in a particularly heated way during the performance of *The Overthrow of the Autocracy* at the House of the People at Rozdestvensky. This occurred during the third episode that represented the mutiny at the military prison. Some spectators even forgot that they were being presented with a theatre action and were ready to run in assistance of the mutineers.

Improvisation is widely used at a theatre circle in Veliky Ustyug (under the Sev. Dvina Governorship). The majority of the participants in this case are sailors. Variations on the theme 'at the barricades' are often created, and these improvisations are performed with great passion and enthusiasm.

Figure 8 The First Workers Theatre of the Proletkult. Scene from the performance *The Road Ahead*, 1926. © A. A. Bakhrushin State Central Theatre Museum, Moscow.

Even in the most isolated villages, the members of the peasants' theatre are transported by the enthusiasm for the improvised performances and for collective theatre creation. Without the help of any instructors, the peasants of the Busuluksky district staged performances based on popular Russian songs, like *Uchar the Dealer*. Local authors have also themselves written and performed dramas.

At Kostroma there is a workshop of proletarian study which makes excellent work that does not need the participation of professional actors. The members do everything themselves. They attentively read the dramas, distribute the parts and choose the director from among their cohorts. These performances are enjoyed very much by the local populace.

News of dramas composed by the peasants and the workers continue to come in. They are responsible for the renovation of the ageing repertoire. The Petrograd Proletkult staged with great success the drama *The Legend of the Communards*, which was composed by a worker. In the east, the drama *The Battle of the Red Ural* was composed in the trenches by a Red Army soldier whose occupation was that of a shoemaker. In Astrakan the drama *The Sacrifice of Freedom* was presented in the Tartar language. It was written by a certain Sattarov, a worker. The drama *For the Red Soviet*, written by the worker Arsky, was performed with great success in Petrograd.[4] This drama was performed at the rear of the front by the Commission for the Fight against Army Desertion. After seeing the performance, 500 deserters who had been sentenced to labour expressed their wish to return to the front.

Experiments in open-air theatre have also been made. Such performances were staged in Petrograd (the drama on the revolution, *The Legend of the Communards*), in Kiev (*The Taking of the Bastille*, performed in the S. Sofia square) and in certain other cities.

The open-air performances were not created along the lines that I have already drawn attention to, but even the fact that a shift occurred away from the closed theatre building will give a new impulse in the creation of theatre art.

Local theatres and also those in the workers' district have developed in all the large localities of Soviet Russia. The successes of the professional dramatic art are shown in these theatres. Slowly, however, these theatres are shifting to the service of the local circles to whom they opened the way for the new art.

It is interesting to note the attempt made in Tver along those lines. The aim was to create a 'theatre of the neighbourhood'. We can read the following in the journal *Tverskaia Pravda*, where there is also a reference to the author of this book [i.e. to Kerzhentsev]:

> A similar 'theatre of the neighbourhood' truly represents the 'circle for the extra-curricular formation of the districts of Yamsky under the Tver Governorship'. The anniversary performance of the circle did not only celebrate those on the stage but also those sitting in the auditorium. The 'stage' always knew that it could count on the help and the support of the 'auditorium', while the spectators knew that one day they will also have the opportunity to perform on the stage. The whole context was a collective, a circle, a family with their grandmothers and grandchildren.
>
> The majority of the spectators had contributed with the actors in the organization of the performance. Both spectators and actors were members of the Yamsky Circle, who made equal payments. These are the 'Friends of the socialist theatre' which were spoken about at the First Conference of the Proletkult, those 'Theatre Promoters' about whom Kerzhentsev spoke.

---

4 See Introduction.

The circle of extracurricular formation at Yamsky has dedicated its activity to a theatre understood in a broad sense. The sections of theatre (headed by Comrade Polunin), music (headed by Comrade Prokofiev) and art (headed by Comrade Novoselov) together form a collective where they complement each other in their work. The anniversary performance created an organic artistic effect. *Contrary to performances staged in other Tver theatres, no prominence is here given to any individual actor. However, something much more important can be noted: the Yamsky circle has its own physiognomy.*

This physiognomy was achieved by the fraternal work of all the Circle's members: the scenographer also performs, puts the make-up on the actor and, if necessary, serves as the prompter, etc. On similar lines, the Circle can count on the sacrifice of each member. There are no prominent or obscure members. Here everyone is equal in the work.

Proletkult cells in many cities have made a big step forward in the field of theatre. Their work is concentrated in the workshops for dramatic study, where the actors are prepared. A number of groups of proletarian actors have already been formed. They perform their repertories to the public and dedicate particular time to the work at the front.

From as early as the spring of 1918, and as the director of the Moscow Proletkult's theatre section, I had elaborated a project for this new field of proletarian work. The following general scheme was agreed upon: theatre workshops for workers are to be set up in various districts, the best among the participants are to join special and central workshops that would carry more developed work, and theatre groups would be formed from both central and district workshops; the best performances would be staged in the capital, where a large theatre would need to be prepared for this purpose. It can be seen that this programme has now been almost completely realized. The Proletkult's importance is also increasing in other cities.

It can be easily affirmed that in two or three years the best theatres in the Soviet Republic will be occupied by proletarian theatre groups who will seek the new theatre art through the path of the Revolution.

The Proletarian Actor

Valentin Tikhonovich

Source: *O Teatre*, 1922, pp. 89–96

The working class was for long estranged from all art. It was accustomed to look at art's centres and creators from the bottom up. Even after almost five years of the Soviet system, bewildered by theatre politicians, specialists and ideologists, this class has not yet found its class-based path and is treading water at the crossroads between a ramshackle academism, the agitation of the Theatre of Revolutionary Satire,[1] technical apprentice, everyday philistinism and the 'last cries' of theatrical fashion.

The proletarian class has not yet recognized its path of proletarian art. Maybe this is being somewhat tried out, but the stitches are still general and timid, and the samples are few and weak.

[...]

Talking about the ideological objectives of the proletarian theatre is the same as talking about the ideology of the working class: the most common task is the deepening, dissemination and further development of these objectives. Everything that bears the stamp of pessimism, passivity, of the static, anarchism, scepticism, mysticism and individualism contradicts this ideology. Optimism, activity, revolutionism, organization, self-affirmation, positivity, collectivism – these are the characteristics of proletarian ideology.

[...]

Antithesis of the professional and proletarian actor. The professional actor was contemptuously opposed to the workers and peasant theatre because of the latter's basis in amateurism. This opinion is now obsolete. But since 'professionalism' is equated to '*skill*', we will not be afraid of professionalism. But the fact remains that professionalism also means something else, the separation from one's own class, and the *declassification of the* proletariat. This is the danger of professionalism, the danger of distorting the ideology and psychology of the new actor by the mores and views of the intellectual from the petty-bourgeois environment. Moreover,

---

1 This was an agit-prop theatre popular during the Civil War, but which quickly faded once the New Economic Policy was introduced and at about the same time when this essay was published. Members of this theatre joined Meyerhold's troupe in 1922 (Senelick 2007: 397–8).

the professionalism of the actor that we know is associated with an art that is saturated with the *old* ideology and clothed in the *old* form.

What is the new look of the proletarian actor?

The actor as a gramophone of the author's text gives way to an actor who can himself be an author, that is, an *improviser*.

The actor as a puppet in the hands of the director is replaced by an actor-*creator*, a participant in the creation of a single performance whole.

Instead of an actor-specialist in speech (drama), gesture (pantomime), singing (opera) or dance (ballet), a *synthetic* actor is capable of fully fledged, action, expressed both tonally, through speech and song, and plastically, through gesture and dance.

Instead of an experiential actor who transfers his personal and random emotional experiences to the performance plan, or the actor in a performance based on established laws and the traditions of the old art, the proletarian actor is one who *reveals* class psychology. He uses the whole range of his mental strength and creates his proletarian intuition and fantasy on this foundation.

A conservative actor who respects traditions, who has mastered the clichés, and who imitates his great predecessors and contemporaries is constrained by crystallized forms. He will give way *to a revolutionary actor* who is building a new theatre and for whom the old is only material.

The actor, in spite of his conservatism and anarchism ('genius and rowdiness!'), with ready access to his power of 'inspiration', 'guts', 'moods' and so on, is replaced by an actor *organizer*, who forms the limit of his stage images within the general plan of the director's composition.

Instead of the individualistic actor who puts himself at the centre of the performance, thinking only of himself, an actor-poser, the proletarian actor is a *collective* actor, a true comrade in his creative team.

Instead of an actor-priest who looks down on the crowd from the top, while at the same time voluntarily or involuntarily serving its tastes, he is the actor-*ideologist* of his class and, at the same time, its servant.

'The Dramatization of a Living Newspaper'

Moscow Proletkult

Source: *Iskusstvo v rabochem klube*, 1924, pp. 66–71

1

The living newspaper originated in Russia during the Revolution. It is its essential acquisition.

Thanks to its flexible form, the living newspaper is an excellent instrument of agitation, propaganda and social work. The two components of the term – 'newspaper' and 'living' – are equally important. It means that even an illiterate person can 'read' such a newspaper.

Considering that the main audiences of this newspaper are

- coordination cells in factories,
- workers' clubs,
- workers' faculty halls,
- military units,
- peasant houses etc.,

and that the largest number of readers are from:

- the proletariat,
- Red Army men,
- and, often, peasants,

the significance of the living newspaper in the political and social education of the masses becomes evident.

The success of the living newspaper, its **circulation** (audience attendance), always depends on the liveliness and sensitivity of the material organized and on the methods and ways by means of which the problems and questions of the day (and a living newspaper, as any other newspaper, should be based on today) will manage to touch the audience, arouse it, stir it, interest it, and, at the very least, get noticed, especially because the purpose of a living newspaper is to **show** rather than to **tell**.

2

Not so long ago living newspapers in Russia were so popular that there was not one club or military unit where a living newspaper was not 'issued'. And to be honest, the initial circulation of such newspapers was more than satisfactory. The masses flooded the auditoriums and devoured everything that was shown to them.

The organizers of the living newspapers often acted instinctively. The newspaper issues were made in an extreme rush, to the extent that any one issue of the newspaper was similar to the others. That model quickly became a barrier. The novelty of the work and the novelty of the such agitation and communication methods with the masses were in the beginning saving this situation. A big part was played by the eagerness of the masses, their incomparable thirst for knowledge.

But it could not last long: the **number of newspapers** was growing every day, while their **quality** stayed at a freezing point. Improvements were needed, but nobody provided them. Instead of variety and anarchism in the organization, a system was needed, with a definite and accurate structure. However, there was nothing like that. As a result, the interest in the living newspaper cooled everywhere. And how couldn't it get cooled? Instead of being punchy and sharp, instead of lasting an hour and a half or two hours in total, living newspaper 'issues' were filled with hour-and-a-half-long speeches by several participants, **besides which there was nothing else**.

There can be no doubt that the previous methods of the living newspapers have become outdated and that there is need for correction and, partly, change. The technique of the living newspapers must be improved, for now it is extremely poor. This technique was of such low and ridiculous quality, especially in the countryside, that only dacha performances of the past could be compared to it.

Therefore, the immediate goal is the reorganization of the living newspaper (its improvement), and the most important thing is the renewal of its methods and devices.

3

First of all, a living newspaper is not a Workers' Faculty. A Workers' Faculty teaches. A living newspaper does not refuse to teach, but teaching is not its most important feature. A living newspaper demonstrates. Its general material is typical of newspapers, but it needs a different kind of elaboration. The elaboration of such material must be made in order to fill in a 'reader' on the events and arouse his interest. In such an elaboration a newspaper must **nudge and prompt**. And the most important thing is to avoid chance and spontaneity in the organization. A newspaper issue must be based on very accurate calculation rather than the participants' spontaneity.

In brief, a good living newspaper demands a **director as a precondition**. It requests a certain coherence; it must be prepared and demonstrated clearly. It needs to impress, excite, activate, attack and draw the audience in the sphere of a pressing question of the day. In other words, a living newspaper must be **theatricalized**.

4

An active living newspaper that is like a meeting in its form should take **something from the theatre,** from theatrical vividness, especially when the theatre itself is based on political meetings, mass demonstrations and public festivals. The recent staging of Martinet-Tretiakov's play *Earth Rampant* at the Meyerhold Theatre proves this best of all. A theatricalized military camp or a theatricalized meeting – that is, in the main, how the play was perceived.[1]

The main forms of the living newspaper resemble both a meeting and a demonstration and, therefore, there is nothing left but to actually dramatize living newspapers.

5

Those who happened to be at the anti-Curzon mass demonstration in Moscow probably remember the components that where involved in it. These were

- procession of the masses,
- banners and posters,
- topical speeches,
- clear-cut slogans,
- caricature,
- painted dummies of the enemies,

---

1 On this popular success at the Meyerhold Theatre see Braun (1998: 188–93).

- choral singing of *chastushki*,[2]
- declamation and
- information.

Although in this case it was the peoples' spontaneous explosion that was organized, the demonstration had many theatrical features in the finest sense of the word. It means that the demonstration was bright, expressive and retained in memory. (Notice: the theatre begins with demonstration, manifestation, mass celebrations.) Its very construction as an agit and political-educational moment made this demonstration a kind of giant, all-Moscow, living newspaper.

There can be only one conclusion: every club worker should understand that a living newspaper's political, industrial or cultural topics must be **deliberately and clearly dramatized**.

6

Propaganda theatre can take the following forms:

1. Oral newspaper,
2. Living newspaper,
3. Agitational play.

A living newspaper is placed in the middle. It differs from an agitational play because it has more variety, flexibility and, perhaps, topicality. It differs from an oral newspaper because it has more focus: every issue of a living newspaper must have a striking moment, a sensation and a main theme.

Every issue of a living newspaper must strike home; there should be no blank and boring parts. In view of this, and differing from the oral newspaper, every issue of a living newspaper should be timed to a certain event, date or anniversary.

Each issue should be unique and different from the other ones. The material should be streamlined and without repetition. It certainly can and must stay on related topics (inculcate ideas in the listener-viewer), but in a new way, in a new framing and formulation.

The order of the demonstration is not always the same. It changes depending on the situation. Generally, you cannot release a number without having thought

---

2 Translator's note: a traditional and short Russian humorous or satirical folk song.

through the **task**. The task (today is anti-Curzon, in a week it will be Dobroliot,[3] in a month it will be *Make the new way of everyday life!*) should define the material and its order, especially if this task is agitational and current.

The newspaper should be made from above rather than below and its consistency should be achieved by the communist component of the workers.

7

A living newspaper issue can start with a **cover**. The role of the cover is to provide a kind of living picture consisting of the actors and the demonstrated things.

The cover should be followed by **compèring** – one or two compères or clowns, whose funny remarks immediately catch the attention of the audience.

Generally, compèring should accompany a living newspaper, if possible, from start to finish. For example, an issue can feature a **headline** (brief, shocking and sharp) that can be listened to with due attention only in the frame of the compère. These headlines are followed by remarks and pure theatrical digressions to warm up the attention of the audience.

After or before the headline (on the main topic of the issue) there can be a series of **slogans** that will detail the topic. Slogans on the main topic can be pronounced later (and not once), but the most important thing is not to **overuse them**.

Slogans must be short and articulated in the same way as proverbs. Slogans should be associated with the issue's main idea. But there should not be too many of them.

To focus the attention on them, slogans should be presented, like everything else, in an outwardly theatrical way. For example, a few people can go on the stage with a horn (that can be made of cardboard) and blow to the audience:

A – **Bread must be cheap.**
B – **But when will bread be cheap?**
A – **Bread will be cheap if we reinvigorate farming.**
C – **But what should we do for that?**
A, B – **We should collect general civil taxes.**
Everyone *(approaching the footlights)* – **Comrades, together, to spite the**

---

3 Translator's note: an early Soviet aviation company.

bourgeoisie, don't hesitate, pay immediately the general civil taxes!

Slogans can often use quotations from Lenin, Trotsky, Radek and other leaders, but the purpose is to **pronounce** them in theatrical way, using the mouths and the horns of the special heralds.

After this a **performance** follows. It is better if every issue consists of not one but two to three short performances, or two performances and one performed, short dramatized feuilleton.[4] Performances must be prepared very carefully and rehearsed many times.

All the props must be prepared in advance. The fewer the decorations the better. Much more necessary are the real things or parts which were made in a factory, rather than the bright trifles and painted scraps of cardboard that usually occupy the stage. The magic of painted decorations is over. The real things (on the stage) are located in the frame of the actors' play and of the compère. In the end, these will be much more effective than the old-fashioned props.

Figure 9 Living newspaper, Central Club of Builders, *Building Site*. Source: *Rabochii i teatr*, 1927, no. 15, p. 18. From the editor's private collection.

---

4 A section of a newspaper that offers fiction, criticism or light literature.

Figure 10 Living newspaper, Union of Textile Workers, *The Weaver*. Source: *Rabochii i teatr*, 1927, no. 15, p. 19. From the editor's private collection.

Between one dramatization and another there must be breaks (maybe even intervals). The breaks can be filled with **messages from the local worker-correspondents**, again delivered in a highly theatrical manner, pronounced from different corners of the auditorium, and certainly prepared beforehand and followed by the compères' remarks.

The same thing can be said for the **news** and the **telegrams**. The latter can be received directly on the stage **by telephone.** In this way, they will always look theatrical enough.

We now present the living newspaper issue on the topic *Make the new way of everyday life!*, which was based on the ideas listed above.[5]

---

5 For visuals of living newspapers see Figures 9 and 10.

'On Staging Agit-Trials'

Moscow Proletkult

Source: *Iskusstvo v rabochem klube*, 1924, pp. 96–9

The agit-trial is one of the more interesting, entertaining forms of mass work.[1] It is easily grasped by the audience. Everything – from the minor problems of daily life (although far from insignificant) to questions on the international workers' movement – can be put in the form of the trial. The intriguing content of the indictment, the debates from both sides, the questioning of the witnesses, the performance of their roles with make-up on – as well as the introduction of comedic moments in different parts of the trial – all of this fixes the attention of the spectator and compels him to think about the separate cases, speeches, etc. The spectator feels either sympathy or antipathy to this or that character, guessing in advance the final ruling of the court, the sentence and so on. In a word, the spectator, one way or another, actively perceives the whole process of the political trial. It very often happens, especially if the trial is well staged, that a part of the audience goes from being spectators to active participants, contributing a number of witty, sensible remarks from the floor. In the practice of staging agit-trials, there are often occasions when someone from the audience crosses over onto the stage and gives a speech for the defence or prosecution. In such a case, the improvised speech, penetrated by sincerity, and the connection of the stage to the audience, creates an exceptionally favourable environment for the achievement of the trial's aims.

From the above, it follows that the agit-trial as a form should occupy a worthy place in the general scheme of political-educational work. However, the principles of club work state that this form of mass work is insufficiently developed in the workers' clubs. Allegedly, the absence of pre-written trials, technical difficulties and so on do not allow for the development of a system of trials in clubs.

The aim of this article is to provide a series of methodical and technical instructions to this end.

There are some who mistakenly think that the staging of some trial-that-never-was requires the presence of a pre-written text. There is often the need to stage a trial on such a topical and current theme that to waste time writing out

---

[1] Secondary sources that tackle the agit-trials include von Geldern (1993: 110–11) and Mally (2000: 42–3, 61–5).

a script would dampen the pertinence of the topic to the point that by the time it was ready it would no longer be worth staging. Such topics could be the trial of Curzon, the trial of the Japanese government that refused to accept a Russian steamer carrying bread for earthquake victims, etc. Trials of this kind expose the general and the whole essence of the imperialistic politics, the cunning of capitalist governments and so on. It is not suitable to stage such things three or four weeks after the event.

If it is possible at all to stage them, then all the material must be adequately refreshed.

However, any telegram significant to the given trial and additionally introduced into the indictment requires corresponding changes to the questioning of the witnesses, a different presentation of the case from the part of the defence and prosecution and so on. Because any pre-written script is constructed on the close connection of its different parts, the introduction of significant additions to the text entails a whole series of changes and additions to the whole text. The work is not small and of little reward.

The conclusion of this: it is possible to write a script for a trial only when the topic will not change and is considered from a more or less static point of view.

The only thing that is needed **in advance** is the **indictment**. The latter should be thought up and written out beforehand, because the whole proceeding of the trial is defined. The indictment is so important that its task is to immediately sketch the whole picture of the accused's activities for the spectator.

From the indictment, the spectator should be able to clarify for themselves the following: (1) the nature of the accused, (2) from what milieu, (3) the exact order of the crimes or misdemeanours committed and (4) how the crimes or misdemeanours were uncovered.

All this should be sufficiently convincing, while the script should be maximally compressed and well written.

After acquainting themselves with the indictment, participants in the trial must agree **in advance** on their actions. They do this by dividing themselves into witnesses for the defence and for the prosecution. It is not recommended for either side to prepare questions beforehand.

This restricts the whole trial of its sincerity and will not give opportunities to the defence and prosecution for cross-examination.

Witnesses should know only two things: (1) who they are playing, including the age of the character, their social position, their name, patronymic and surname, material status, etc., and (2) what they are striving for with their answers (to compromise or to rehabilitate the accused).

The defence and prosecution, knowing upon which of the witnesses they can most rely on, must only acquaint one another with the main arguments of their speeches and no more.

The accused is one of the roles of greatest responsibility in the trial.

His behaviour plays an important role and influences both the general proceedings and the relationship of the spectator to the trial.

The accused should have a significant amount of freedom of behaviour, but again, this is closely connected with a number of conditions: he should understand the general predicament of the character and should be particularly familiar with the role he is playing. A short cue (2–3 words) should be pronounced with the applicable intonation and should completely reflect the condition of the accused, both in its content and pronunciation. It is important to note that even in the case where the accused has nothing to say, he still remains a central figure of the trial. Whether with sympathy or animosity, the spectator always observes the accused. Therefore, every word said for or against the accused is unavoidably reflected on the latter. And because the accused is being spoken about almost all the time, he must always **act** and must act well.

The speeches by the defence and the prosecution should be a summary of all the evidence gathered from the statements of the witnesses, those of the experts and so on. Neither the prosecution nor the defence should make anything up or use any material that is not known to the trial or to the spectator. Each component of their speeches should be clear and accessible to the understanding of the spectator, who should be prepared in advance for each phrase. Therefore, the case from each side should be short and should have the aim of summarizing everything and concretizing all that which has been said in the course of the trial.

The sentence can be written in advance. But this is not obligatory. The process of the trial itself defines the sentence. The latter is the finale, the logical ending. The sentence is the moral that proceeds from the whole trial, but especially from the debates of the two sides.

Therefore, a good sentence is one which goes without saying after the conclusion of the debate. It only remains to confirm it in an easily perceptible form. In such case it is desirable to invite a few people from the audience for the pronouncement of the sentence. The others find this extremely engaging.

There are still a few general words to say about the engagement and the active participation of the audience during the trial. It is very necessary to engage them. How can this be achieved? Primarily it can be achieved in the following way:

1. by inviting expert and witnesses directly from the audience;
2. by including a spectator as the defence or prosecution (besides participants already playing those roles);
3. by inviting spectators to participate in the indictment;
4. with an interlude, played out by the audience between the separate parts of the trial and with speeches from the audience (see *The Trial of Fabkom Member N. I. Egorov*).[2]

All the moments given above significantly enliven the proceeding of a trial and bring the spectator into close connection with the active participants.

We can call the trial described above a 'simple scenario of a trial'. There are trials that, on the formal level of maximizing impact and interest, use all the means at the disposal of the modern theatre. Such a trial is called 'theatricalized'. It takes the following form.

The indictment is broken down into points, which are not read but played out by actors in the form of separate sketches. This produces the proceeding and the conditions of the crime, in the form of a living cinema or pictures accompanying the corresponding text.

The role of the secretary of the trial, who reads the indictment, becomes the role of a compère, who leads proceedings and connects one scene (the indictment) to another.

In scenes of this nature, it is possible to use polyphonic reading, music, songs and so on.

The questioning of witnesses in a theatricalized trial are enlivened through (1) a projecting screen, acting as a silent witness and (2) slogans, placards, speeches from both sides in the form of rumours, etc.

The sentence unfolds in the form of an epilogue-apotheosis, with music, sound and decorative and light effects.

All these moments – the chorus, the staging, the acting and the construction – substantially intensify the impression and consequently have an exceptional organizational significance.

---

2 This is the example of a trial given in the volume after this theoretical text.

'Club Stage – Competition of Living Newspapers'

N.N.V.

Source: *Rabochii i teatr*, no. 15, 1927, pp. 16–17

The Red Avrovets *(Avrov Club)*

The usual club newspaper. The participants are the tram depot workers: they write all the material themselves and regularly release a new issue of their newspaper. Pluses: well-developed work with the masses (up to eight performances of every issue); all materials are locally rooted and immediately relevant; general clarity in the staging. Minuses: cliché directing.

The Houseworker *(13th Group of SRKH)*

An amateur newspaper of the most backward workers – street cleaners, bath house-staff, etc., and of an older age – up to forty years old. The text is their own and mostly far from smooth. Obviously, the theatricality is primitive.

The Latch Bolt *(Otcomhoz)*

The amateur living newspaper of the workers' youth from OTCOMHOZ. It is used by the Cultural Department of the Workers' Union of the Public Utilities and is sent to factories. This way it carries out work with the masses (up to 10–12 performances per month in away locations). The level of immediacy is the same-day staging of the *Smena* morning issue. Good success.

The Filter *(The Waterworks)*

The usual club newspaper, with the nominee instructor. The material is all amateur, of a quite good literary level. The content is local. Their record of immediacy is the presentation of telegrams from the evening issue of the *Red Newspaper*, although quite primitive.

'Of the County Department of Soviet Sales Clerks'

The text (commissioned) is weak and inexpressive; the staging is poor – a few original moments give way to unbearable clichés. The newspaper was not successful even among its own audience.

'Of the First Group Committee of Soviet Sales Clerks'

A completely different impression is produced by the newspaper of the First Group Committee; thanks to its leadership it can be placed among the normal club newspapers. As they say, it is well cut and, apart from some exceptions, firmly sown. The text is decent and strong in places.

Of Prombank

Weaker than the previous one but amateur. Good singing. Young fresh voices. The text is not as good, sometimes too long, but some numbers are good. The performers often do more recitation than they act; even the master of ceremonies chants.

The Probe *(The County Department of Soviet Sales Clerks)*

An old and experienced newspaper, which has only been working under the union for a month. The long touring left some hokey-pokey mark on this collective but they have formed a good ensemble.

Of the club named after Kaznitsky

A normal newspaper but without a name and still searching for its own face. Their strength is in the reflection of local life, and if the young and bold newspaper fully commits to this road, it will become a useful worker. Their success is moderate.

Of Kronoprodraikom

A district newspaper that enjoyed some success. In some moments, it is stronger than the Kaznitsky guys. It overwhelms with singing and choral chanting but the content is only interesting when it reflects local burning issues.

The Metallist *(T.S.G.R.)*

A normal newspaper of the higher rank – at the Union's Central Club, the newspaper tours to various places. Good casting. The production has a number of successes and failures.

The Traction
(Department of Transport)

The only newspaper of the transport workers (local transport) but perhaps the weakest. Half of it is rally chanting and the other half is the naivest and also primitive. The text is unclear, apart from the couplets.

Of the County Department of Carpentry

Of the higher rank but the content and production are of the average club level. There are good participants but no director's hand, although the newspaper is led by an instructor, a methodologist of the Department of Culture.

The Red Utility Worker

The Red Utility Worker is an amateur newspaper; however, it is part of the Union Cultural Department. The newspaper was passing with flying colours; the audience demanded encores but we do not have to hold our breath. With the strong witty text and trade union content, the newspaper suffers from 'overacting'.

The Young Smirnovets *(p. Smirnova)*

The pioneers' newspaper. Excellent beginning and a bad ending that would be more suited to an adult newspaper. Their own pioneer life is not shown enough due to general adult subjects.

The Chisel *(Trotsky Uprofbureau)*

The Chisel falls into two parts. The first one is slogans and long foxtrots. The second is couplets and local life. The first one falls out completely; the second one, presented with some skill, hits home and provokes loud reactions from the audience.

The Tram Signal *(Skorokhodov Trampark)*

The amateur newspaper of the Red Corner. No theatrical skill but the newspaper hits its target with very simple means that are performed quite well. The content is flawless, purely local, up to the chronicles: production meetings, production competitions, living wall newspaper and witty ads.

On the Red Signal *(Blokhin Trampark)*

The amateur newspaper at the club. It is performed with a full Russian orchestra, which does not happen often. Strong cast and solid ensemble. Everyone wears a tram work uniform. It has original content: industrial poetry, 'poetization' of the work of the tram service. This is the first newspaper of this kind with a general satirical background, and worth a closer look.

The Blue Blouse *(Variety)*

The last newspaper of the competition is of the new variety type and, for the first attempt, successful, even if it has a few flaws. Such endeavours need to be encouraged in every way. Together with the undeniable achievements in content and directing (the newspaper is amateur, with a dance teacher), the shortcomings are the uneven level of participants, with two or three underworked exits.

The article about the outcomes and the detailed results of the contest will be given in the next issue.

Part Five

Training

'On the Work of the Theatre Department of the Moscow Proletkult'

Valentin Smyshlaev

Source: *Gorn*, no. 1, 1918, p. 54

The Moscow Theatre College of the Proletkult emerged according to the general plan of works of the Proletkult in the sphere of the creation of proletarian culture.

It was formed on the group's initiative, consisting partly of Communists and partly of theatre professionals who responded to the invitation to work on the creation of a proletarian theatre. Our main task is creativity, i.e. seeking those forms of theatre which would correspond to the new content. But before looking for and creating the new, it was necessary to inform the workers who wanted to work with us of the theatre culture and techniques (internal and external) which we inherited from the theatre of previous eras. Hence, the need to carry out pedagogical work is also obvious.

This work should be organized in the following form: a Theatre Board, which includes, apart from the initial group, the instructors – in most cases these are the best among the young actors of Moscow's theatres – and the representatives of the workers.

A special instructor, who is also a member of the Theatre Board, is tasked with the management of each studio; his main responsibility is to examine the area to which he is appointed. The dramatic studios of the Proletkult are organized in all districts of Moscow, and their main task is to acquaint students with the theatrical technique of dramatic art. The fact is that after the liberation of the proletariat from the chains of slavery, its own creativity also manifested itself in theatre work. Drama circles emerged almost in every factory, in every plant. But the work there was organized chaotically, disorderly. The leaders of these clubs were mostly provincial actors, hardened in stencils, patterns that are alien to creative energy – these were, in most cases, the losers, who got the chance to take advantage of the situation. But the workers did not have any experience; they were groping in the dark. And then an instructor from the Proletkult looked at these circles and informed them of the Proletkult's intention to help the amateurs from the working class, of organizing this chaotic but strong and relentless movement of the proletarians in creating their own theatre. The instructor arranged general meetings for these groups, during which he explained our goals and objectives and proceeded to record who wished to work at the studio. In most cases there were no exams and tests. We accepted whoever wanted to join but warned them that those who were clearly unsuitable for the stage would be informed directly so as not to waste time and to try and work in some other field.

The instructor started lessons when a group had enough candidates (30–40 people on average). The instructor's plan was worked out during a meeting of the Theatre Board. A Committee elected by the workers themselves runs all the administrative work of the studio. In addition, studio members arrange general meetings to decide on certain issues related to the internal life of the studio. Each studio elects a representative on the Theatre Board, who becomes a full member of the Board; besides, a representative of the studio is elected on the general Council of the Proletkult.

Thus, the legislative and executive body is the Theatre Board: this is made of the Head of the Department, who is approved by the Executive Office of the Proletkult – this is a responsible instructor-organizer in charge of the general management of the pedagogical work at the studio – a Secretary of the Department and another member who communicates with other districts.

In addition to these individuals the Board appointed a Commission in charge of editing the materials received by the general magazine of the Proletkult. Whenever required the Board also organizes temporary commissions to perform certain tasks.

The Board has already done certain things in the field of education. During the past two months the studios organized work in the following subjects:

1. Diction – the aim of the training was to teach how to speak properly and clearly.
2. Recitation – to teach an understanding of the rhythm of verse, its construction, how to read poetry, etc. There have been experiments in choral recitation.
3. Placing the voice – to develop voice so that it sounds loud and clear.
4. Plastiques – to develop freedom of movement and to subordinate facial expressions to one's will. Classes are conducted in accordance with the system of Jacques-Dalcroze and the Rabenek[1] school.
5. Theatre make-up – to teach how to emphasize the characteristic features of an image using paint and wigs.

---

1 Ella Rabenek, Russian dancer influenced by Isadora Duncan.

6. Decorative art – using simple tools to accomplish specific decorative tasks, getting familiar with the technology of the modern decorative arts, learning how the stage is organized, including its various systems, etc.
7. Stage exercises – to teach students to get involved in stage tasks; here we applied extensively the method of improvisation, which shows the imagination, creativity and artistic feeling of the students. These improvisations included charades played out by the studio students. In addition, the students became acquainted with the modern methods of working on a play. These methods were primarily based on the work of the Moscow Art Theatre, which generally provides room for initiative and self-revelation.
8. Lectures on theatre theory and history.

The instructor would distribute these subjects across the weekly schedule, with the main emphasis made on stage exercises (see the approximate timetable attached at the end of this article). In most cases, the instructor himself teaches one or two courses (mostly the stage exercises). To teach other subjects we invited special experts (not members of the Theatre Board), who therefore serve several regional studios.

But as I mentioned earlier, we are teaching only as a necessity, because our main task is creativity. Even the student-workers obviously and understandably would rather proceed directly to the creative work. In this case, the instructor tried to do everything that was in his power. For example, in some districts of Moscow they are already working on plays which, when they are more or less formed, will eventually be shown in all districts of Moscow and perhaps even in the province. But this work is used by an instructor to show in practice, while working on a play, the methods of work and to convince the students of their validity. The work of the studio-school still continues parallel with the rehearsals of the plays.

Following the performances of these plays we plan to arrange a special evening dedicated to them, where everyone in the studio would share their impressions and criticisms. In addition, 'second day performances' are planned, which means the following: studio students who watched a performance but without participating in it play an improvisation in accordance with their impression of the play and the acting. Apart from the direct benefit to the participants of the 'second day performances', these improvisations can clearly point out any shortcomings in the performance. Such a critical and creative test will undoubtedly have a great impact on the artistic growth of the students, on the development of their imagination, initiative and taste. In addition to these plays, there are attempts made and a search for new performing arts forms. At the moment we are working on a dramatization of the poem 'Insurrection' by Verhaeren,[2] and the painting *Do Not Go*; the work is based on the method of improvisation, which means students create themselves a number of sketches on these topics, and then, under the guidance of their instructor, some sketches are selected. This is the way to develop very unusual and interesting forms of stage action. And here the principle of collective work is carried out in full. At the moment the creative work in the dramatic studios of the Proletkult is actually limited to these attempts, because our main focus is, again, teaching.

P.S. We receive many requests from the provinces to help in the organization of theatre work among the local proletariat, by sending instructors or lecturers, for example, or by organizing concerts, etc. So far we (taking into account our short existence) cannot fully meet these requests. Keeping the provinces, where there is a shortage of local instructors, in mind, we will use this magazine to share our experience and the results of our work with our friends. Any doubts and questions can be directed to the Theatre Department of the Moscow Proletkult (Moscow, Vozdvizhenka, 16, Theatre Department).

Approximate timetable for the Drama Studio of the Moscow Proletkult

(Evening Classes)
Monday: 7 p.m. – plastiques; 9 p.m. – lecture on the history of theatre (or any other of the theoretical course)
Tuesday: 7 p.m. – stage exercises
Wednesday: 7 p.m. – diction and voice training; 9 p.m. – make-up
Thursday: 7 p.m. – decorative arts; 9 p.m. – recitation
Friday: 7 p.m. – stage exercises
Saturday: 7 p.m. – plastiques; 9 p.m. – diction and voice training
Sunday: trips (visit Moscow theatres, art galleries, museums, walks etc.)

---

2 See an account of the work going into this production in Part Four.

Dramatic Laboratories

Platon Kerzhentsev

Source: *Tvorcheskii teatr* 5th edition, 1923, pp. 88–94

The immediate and practical work to create the proletarian theatre will concentrate, first of all, on the formation of proletarian actors.

Every theatre is based on the creative actor, in the same way that literature is based on poets, paint on painters, etc. We have to admit that at the moment we have no actor for the proletarian theatre. But we are expecting him and working to create him.

[...]

To truly create the new theatre and the great revolutionary movement in this area it is necessary to lean onto actors from the proletarian milieu. The creation of the proletarian actor is the first and most important task to accomplish.

For this it is necessary to follow the example of the Moscow Proletkult and create dramatic laboratories in the workers' districts. These laboratories will welcome all those proletarian elements who are inclined towards theatre and who are capable of creative work in this field. The entire country has to be covered by such cells in which the invisible but extremely important work to create the new actors is carried out. During the Revolution, a marked increase of proletarian dramatic circles could be noted.[1] This was incontestable proof that the proletariat's creative forces had been awakened and that proletarian expressive forms in the field of art were indeed being found. Unfortunately, the majority of these circles were led by professional actors of the third grade, who had joined the workers for commercial interests and to serve their own ambitions. For this reason the majority of the circles succumbed to the worst kind of bourgeois influence. Many dramatic circles of the workers became spaces for dilettante hobbies. They had a dubious repertoire and staged work that showed little care for quality. Instead of training the actors, these circles corrupted the workers' masses by exposing them to base and vulgar bourgeois dramas. They promoted carelessness, petty ambition and superficiality.

The dramatic laboratories are to declare a ceaseless war against such circles. However, the war against the dramatic circles does not entail their destruction.

---

1 This is a reference to the 'theatre epidemic'. See Introduction and relevant essays in Part One.

On the contrary, the laboratories are to be born from these existent circles. The laboratories need to choose all those participants of the circles who have talent and who want to carry out serious work. The circles will still exist, but under the influence of the laboratories their work will become more serious. In time, all valid members of the circles will stand to gain in one way or another from the laboratories. If currently (and provisionally) the laboratories are composed primarily of members coming from the dramatic circles, then in the future the circles will admit only those who are trained at the laboratories. Obviously, the laboratories will admit not only the members of the dramatic circles but anyone who wishes to join. If for some reason someone is not accepted at the laboratory (lack of space, negative attitude towards the theatre, etc.), then he will still have the right to learn by attending the laboratory as a listener and spectator because the hours of teaching and training will be accessible to all. This, in fact, is the general principle adopted broadly by, for example, the Moscow Proletkult. We refute the bourgeois principle which says that true creation can only take place in the *sancta sanctorum* and closed hours of rehearsal.

In order for the teaching to move forward the help of professional actors will be called upon. But in most cases the theatre youth will be used, because they are less fossilized and more animated by the desire to create. They are in a tight union with the proletariat and with the new theatre. These youngsters will teach the workers the ABC of theatre technique, such as the use of the voice, diction, declamation, precise knowledge of the scenic rules, the art of make-up, etc. At the same time, they will also not weigh down the work by imposing their own authority or their own professional model. They will be the ones to subject themselves to the influence of the work environment, and even though they are not strict communists, they will show an attentive sensitivity to the research carried out and to the proletariat's objectives. In such an organization the professional bourgeois actor will not pervert or corrupt the worker-actor: that fear is unfounded. On the contrary, the work environment will assimilate the professional actor. It will subject him to the cause of the working class and force him to merge spiritually with it, the class to which he transferred in order to exercise the teaching profession.

At the dramatic laboratories the worker will first of all learn the technique of theatre art. The worker can successfully work in the field of proletarian theatre only when he has appropriated this technique. Sometimes one hears the opinion that technique is not necessary for the workers, that it is a bourgeois prejudice, that one only needs to develop the revolutionary temperament, and that the rest will follow of its own accord.[2] A consistent application of this point of view will precipitate the young theatre proletarian in the abyss of the most deadly dilettantism. Many dramatic circles adhere to this point of view, and as a result they corrupt the masses of workers with superficial and ill-considered theatre dilettantism. One has to fight with all means against the contempt for the school, the studio and serious work. It has to be understood that the art of the actor, like any other art, does not only need enthusiasm and skill, but also serious and persistent work. Our demands from the members of the circles need to be great.

The proletariat needs to act strongly against every superficiality, against all dilettantism and against every shallow interpretation of the tasks of the theatre.

Experience has shown that those who oppose theatre schooling on grounds that it is a bourgeois residue have themselves fallen under the influence of the most deadly dilettantism, one that is in itself highly bourgeois. They reject theatre training or a theatre system because they see them as futile. They renounce the pedagogical advances in the field of theatre technique and fall under the influence of the worst professional actors or the most vulgar among the amateurs.

The proletarian theatre school, like its theatre, must evidently elaborate a technique of its own.

Valid elements from the technical arsenal of the bourgeois theatre need to be appropriated after they are processed by a highly rigorous criticism. These elements are to be used when searching for new inroads, in the same way that at elementary schools we make use of old books in order to utilize the experience of the past, but without ever losing sight of the creation of new teaching methods and tools.

The work at the laboratories must stimulate in all possible ways the students' initiative and autonomy. The technical formation must be a kind of teaching in the ABC, which opens possibilities for further work.

For this reason, it is indeed possible to have instructors with diverse theatre orientations, as long as they do not hinder the critical development of the students' intelligence. First and foremost, they must encourage autonomous work. The laboratories do not only have pedagogical and preparatory tasks. They are also laboratories for new attempts. It is where the first attempts to create the proletarian theatre are carried out.

---

2 Contrast to the very different opinion which Kerzhentsev himself expressed in the essay 'The Creation of the Proletarian Theatre' in Part Two.

The laboratories must be organized as a sort of artistic community, in which the members live a common and comradely life. The laboratory instructors are simply older comrades. The organization of the laboratories falls in its entirety on the participants' shoulders. This organization includes the discussion on the plan of work, the choice of the repertoire and the actual staging. These are activities that concern the laboratory as a whole or a board chosen from within its members.

Instructors from the laboratories of a city will form, together with student representatives, a special board which will coordinate the Proletkult's theatre work. It is also important to bring together students from different laboratories and have them carry out common work like, for example, shared lessons, but also, and especially, the staging of a piece that would become the focal work of the laboratories of a particular district. These, so to say, central productions are prepared in the separate laboratories and the results are then harmonized together at the central place.

Such productions of dramas with a large number of actors not only demonstrate the results of the work carried out at any one particular time in the laboratories but also pave the way for real collective theatre creation.

The first step is to create, with the help of the Proletkult's dramatic laboratories, a number of well-trained groups, after which we can then tackle certain problems like the adaptation of existent theatre buildings to the needs of the proletarian theatre. The Soviet government will put the best theatre buildings at the disposal of the proletarian theatre groups.

Certainly, the proletarian groups will not be on the same level of the professional actors in terms of technical proficiency or training, but they will compensate through their revolutionary temperament, their militant class psychology and their heated enthusiasm for anything which is new. Their dramatic abilities will also make them succeed. Workers of little experience and with little training were successful in the political and economic fields, and they achieved this success in a short period of time. The workers will be successful also in the field of art, and in particular that of theatre art, where the proletariat can expect great victories.

The Proletkult's dramatic laboratories will lead towards the real proletarian theatre, which will revolutionize the scene, create a new theatre art and conform to the epoch of the socialist revolution and the spirit of a socialist society.

'A Unified Studio of the Arts'

Moscow Proletkult

Source: *Iskusstvo v rabochem klube*, pp. 9–16

1

Two provisions form the basis of the work at a unified studio of the arts: **(1) the concept of art as life-building (the development of new modes of life) and (2) the utilization of the most influential art forms as a form of social impact.**[1]

The artwork at the workers' clubs must be determined and directed on the basis of these provisions. We must consider the specific tasks which must be solved by this work.

A workers' club is not an institution that trains specialists in the various areas of art creation. The goal of a workers' club is the harmonious and comprehensive development in its members of those conditions that are necessary for building a proletarian life. An immediate emphasis on a specific reality is the basis of all its work.

In connection to this, art activity is understood, primarily, as a force which organizes the material value of the clubs (in terms of the highest expediency of the material equipment and its practical use); secondly, as a factor that produces socially productive and environmentally oriented skills in a club collective; and, thirdly, as an instrument of mass education and comprehensive development to be used in solving the artistic and militant tasks of the working class.

The basis of practical work

1. **A number of disciplines are obligatory** for the artistic work of a club (see further). This follows from the fact that in studying these disciplines the attention is not on a purely aesthetic upbringing and education, and not on specialization, but rather on the direct implementation of these disciplines in everyday life. Studying these obligatory disciplines becomes the foundation on which all further artwork at the club is built.

---

[1] Elsewhere, I give a detailed exposition of this essay, framed around the theories of Henri Lefebvre and Robert M. Gagné, to argue that the transmission of artistic training can impact on and transform everyday life (Aquilina 2020: 118–25).

2. With such a condition, **all the sections will have one common root,** which is firmly embedded in the depths of life itself. For example, literature classes in the old system (still common in clubs) could in no way be regarded as obligatory for all club members.

   We do not see literature classes as a factory of poets and writers, but as work to acquire skills in verbal and written language or, in other words, as development in club members of the skills necessary in the practical and verbal use of words. On the basis of this work, which is common to all club members, we enable further more productive literary work in separate workshops for those members who are especially interested in verbal mastery.
3. **The artistic work carried out in specific fields (theatrical, literary, musical, fine arts) is organically linked to and carried out by all club members, with whom it shares a common ground. These fields must also work in connection to one another.**

A common link is obtained, first of all, through the unity of tasks put forward by the artistic work of a club. These tasks are formulated in the process of club development. This obliges us to orient ourselves towards the practical work that the club demands, especially when selecting the disciplines that require separate study and when developing the study programmes. The unified work cannot, however, be simply regarded as the work that solves common tasks, regardless of the manner in which this work is carried out in separate sections. It is necessary to plan the work in such a way so that in every separate case there is a general strategy that allows every section to be considerably familiar with the problem-solving methods of the others. Only with such a layout will interrelationship and mutual assistance be regarded not as alien, and for the common work to become truly organic and thus yield the best results.

Thus, **the differences and fragmentation of the artistic work in a workers' club must be ended. A number of disciplines will become obligatory. Sectional work is seen as additional to the common work. It will take a specific character with a specific aim. These will be developed on the principles of 'close cooperation'.**

These are the main lines under which the concept of a 'unified studio of the arts' at a club can be understood.

The obligatory disciplines include physical education, eurhythmics, voice training, verbal and written speech, choral singing and ideological subjects. Other work is planned in the theatrical, literary, musical and fine arts sections.

2

From the subjects usually taught in theatre workshops, eurhythmics and voice training (techniques) will become obligatory. Voice training techniques mostly aim at the development of vocal qualities for their direct application to volume and intonation in everyday life.

Eurhythmic exercises are obligatory because they help develop psychomotor abilities.

Theatre work will, undoubtedly, be carried out through the dramatizations of current events, agitation speeches, entertainments of a theatrical nature, revolutionary cabarets, organization of living newspapers, theatrical trials and so on.

Its main goal must be the development of those theatrical forms which would be the most flexible and expedient both in the life of the club and also in the public arena. Another significant task of the theatrical section is the effective organization of parades, celebrations, demonstrations and, generally, all mass performances. The aims of the theatrical work coincide in various ways with those of physical education.

3

Physical education must also be obligatory. It is obvious, however, that these classes should not have the goal of preparing record-breaking specialists in some sports discipline. The main aim is to produce a normal, healthy, physically fit person (gymnastics, active games, sports). This aim is 'biological' in nature, but this does not fully describe the work in the field of physical education. There is also another goal, which is 'social' in its character: the development of effective orientation skills within an environment, in everyday life and in work.

There is also a third factor, inseparable from physical education, which is the 'demonstrational' (somewhat theatrical) aspect. Examples of these are the athletes' parades, their demonstrational exercises and games.

4

Verbal and written speech will become obligatory from the discipline of **literature**. Verbal material can be adapted to solve various tasks arising from everyday life. Linguistic work does not depart from practical speech but places the organization of speech as its main task, making it flexible, expressive and straight to the point. Other work, more specific to the literary section, must also be developed on this basis. Its starting point becomes, therefore, not 'poetic' forms of language, but rather the forms provided by everyday practices (protocol, statement, letter writing, speech, report, newspaper, journal and so on). The work in the so-called correspondence clubs will acquire a special meaning because of this.

In its further development, literary work will inevitably touch upon dramatizations, agitation speeches and in general all those forms the necessity of which is highlighted by the club's practices (live and staged newspapers, trials and so on).

5

Choral singing, taken from the field of music, is obligatory for all members. In this case, choral singing is regarded in its constant application in everyday life and as an organized way to begin work on collective performances like celebrations, parades and entertainments.

In the choral singing work with all club members we must, obviously, again avoid the pursuit of preparing specialists in this area. We are not talking about choral acapellas here, but rather about the ability of every member to be active while singing. It is quite obvious, however, that a main choral core, i.e. a certain group of members who are specifically interested in choral singing, is necessary if the other singing work involving all the club members is to provide the desired results.

A complete revision of the repertoire is needed. The pace and rhythm of everyday life demand a song that is sprightly, dynamic and saturated with revolution. A national (peasant) song could be used in its most lively forms, such as in dancing songs, satirical and bandit anthems. Necessary topical material could be provided by labour (factory) and city songs, in couplets (limericks) for example, if the necessary work on their collection and sorting is carried out. Classes (obligatory and in the musical section) in choral singing provide the full musical programme in a workers' club.

The classes in solo singing, piano, violin and so on, though popular today, cannot be considered suitable to club work due to the fact that a club is neither a music school nor a conservatoire that prepares solo singers and specialists in the playing of an instrument. This does not exclude, of course, the necessity of introducing piano classes, for example, as an ancillary field of choral singing.

6

The classes in **fine arts** must serve the club's needs in the creation of posters, diagrams, slogans, inscriptions, placards, banners and so on. The fine arts material can be shared between the everyday classes and the extraordinary events. For the latter, it is propitious to include all members of the club in the preparation of the premises.

7

Special attention must be given to set-up classes in ideological subjects (political education, political economics, Marxism, cultural history and so on). It is precisely these subjects that give club members the link on the basis of which their activity in the various fields of club work can then develop. The understanding of the life around the workers, the industrial relations, the class tasks and, specifically, the club tasks forms the invariable line of work in this area.

Lesson plan

On the principle of a unified studio of the arts.

Obligatory subjects

1. Physical education. Gymnastics, sports, active sports games
2. Eurhythmics
3. Spoken language. Breathing, voice training, oratorical speech (subjects which organize voice and speech with the goal of utilization in everyday life)
4. Written language. Grammar (studying the mechanisms of language) and style (utilization of different grammatical antitheses for different purposes)
5. Choral singing (as a constant requirement of everyday life)
6. The equipment at the premises and stock inventory (on a general club scale and specifically for certain sectional work conditions)

Section work

I. Theatrical section

1. Body gymnastics
    (a) physical education (with acrobatics)
    (b) eurhythmics
    (c) biomechanics (if a qualified teacher is available)
2. Voice gymnastics
    (a) voice and breathing training, diction
    (b) declamation
3. Production work
    stage exercises (as preparation for further production tasks)

II. Literary section

1. Grammar and style: assimilation of techniques for practical and written language; spoken language
2. Common printing knowledge: typographic newspaper content
3. Practices of mounted and living newspapers

III. Fine arts section

1. The formation of hand and eye
2. Study of texture, colour, form, composition
3. Construction (applicable mainly to theatrical productions)
4. Production work: study of specific artistic forms and their particular tasks (inscription, slogan, poster, banner, etc.)

IV. Choral section

1. Musical literacy
2. Practical sessions (in choral singing and reading of scores)

'On Theatre Work at the Clubs'

Moscow Proletkult

Source: *Iskusstvo v rabochem klube*, pp. 17–24

1

Our main position is the following: the theatre work at the workers' clubs does not aim to prepare professional actors. It is only one of the ways to solve the general tasks of the club and, more specifically, a way to solve these tasks in theatrical manner.

The tasks which are faced by a theatre collective at a working club are unique due to their particular character. For example, a dramatization must be set up because of an event, a number of performances during street celebrations and demonstrations must be organized, a living newspaper must be staged, a trial must be worked out and so on.

These forms are exactly what justifies the use of the energies of the club members on theatre work and what makes this work useful and vitally necessary. However, regular demands for dramatizations, trials and so on are generally regarded by the theatre collective as intrusive to the general course of their work, as something that violates the programme of the classes.

This occurs when the collective considers the staging of those plays (usually from the classical repertoire) that do not have a direct relation (and more often none at all) to the tasks of the day and of our whole epoch. Sometimes, dreams to open a separate theatre follow. This approach is, undoubtedly, erroneous, and work in such a manner would not differ in any way from the work of a professional theatre and of professional actors. In this case, there would be no other option but to put an equals sign between the latter and the members of a theatre collective at a workers' club.

However, the task of the workers' theatre club is not to create separate theatres, nor is it to create any sort of conservatoire or art school. Ergo, theatre art, as one of the approaches to solve the tasks of a club, is the foundation for all the theatrical work at the workers' clubs.

2

In accordance with this, there immediately arises the question of establishing a solid connection between production (demonstrational) and studio work. The question boils down to whether members of a theatre collective need to be professionals. The opinion exists that the acquisition of mastery through regular work is not necessary, for it would separate the club members from the direct tasks of club life and turn them into professionals who are concerned only with their specialized work. Thus the unity with club life would be lost, and the unity of a club's tasks and its ambitions would be misunderstood. This point of view is undoubtedly correct, of course, if the theatre collective fails to orient itself towards the direct needs of club life. The situation, however, changes if this orientation does take place. Indeed, if we agree with the definition of theatre work given earlier – as one of the way to solve the tasks provided by club life – and, if we take into account the fact that any way can be 'convincing' (i.e. it can reach its goal), then we must admit that none of the tasks can be solved without the ability to wield theatrical material. Those who speak against the necessity of mastery cannot, of course, disagree (and in practice they do agree) that certain 'skills' and 'abilities' must be present. The question that arises is the following: where should the line between 'skills' (abilities) and 'mastery' be drawn? In general, those who stick to the slogan of fighting against mastery miss their point. It is not mastery that should be attacked, but rather the direction that theatre work is headed to when it is separated from the direct needs of a club. And, if we manage to steer it correctly, if the focus of all aspirations is located at the core of club life, then even mastery will cease to be frightening. Clarity of a task plus the mastery in material execution: that is the formula for any successful action.

3

It is necessary to highlight here another factor. Even if a club has the correct set-up for its theatre work – i.e. one that shows an ambition to serve the club's direct needs through agitational speeches, living newspapers, trials, stage parties and so on – misunderstandings will inevitably rise on the grounds that the theatre collective will fail to satisfy all the requirements demanded of it. It will often happen that these requirements are so common and framed by such limited time constraints that the collective will fail to find within itself either the necessary strength or the flexibility to cement in a theatrical format its opinion of the questions provided by life, highlight their own point of view and propose a certain direction. In such a case, how can urgency and mastery be united?

The solution to this question can, once again, be found in the fact that all studio work must be directly oriented towards production (demonstrative) work. A constant check of the expediency of the skills obtained through the studio work must take place, and this expediency is determined, of course, by none other than the ability to utilize all the skills in the solution of production tasks. This constant check will invariably straighten the line of theatre work, and the collective will develop within itself the ability to use to the maximum the minimal level of mastery that it has acquired. These remarks are directed, primarily, towards the execution of stage activities; even when the singularity of theatrical work in the workers' clubs is more or less determined, the classes are still taught mainly to stage agitation plays, while the practice of club life already puts forth other kinds of theatrical action which do not coincide with the format of 'plays'. These new formats demand a special set-up, special skills and special approaches in material organization. They cannot be ignored, of course, because in that case they would definitely be separated from the general direction of the life of the club.

4

The development of new theatre forms at the workers' clubs is given in two articles of this (first) compilation. The article about the organizational methods for staged evenings (evenings of recollection, celebratory meetings, agitation parades, etc.) will be published in the second compilation, which is being prepared for print. Therefore, we will focus primarily on that side of theatre work at the club which results in the production of plays.

5

Those tasks which appear before a whole club (and, therefore, before the theatre branch as well) naturally follow from the general revolutionary tasks of the proletariat. Moreover, these tasks also have their own purely local character. In light of this, the club's tasks are most complex. They demand a solid ideological background from the collective, a knowledge of the surrounding environment and the ability of a quick and precise orientation. It is not enough, however, to feel the task, to understand it with precision: for a theatre collective the understanding of a task is inseparably linked with its presentation, with its elaboration through theatrical material.

Here comes the question about the methods necessary to treat stage material.

In the theatre, the material is the actor's body and voice. The first necessary condition is the general training of this material. Therefore, physical education becomes the basis of theatre work. These exercises obtain special meaning for an actor, primarily because his work is of a physical nature, often long and tiring. This work is unfathomable without physical flexibility, without the endurance of the body. The next stage (theatrical in its sense) is the treatment of stage movement. Here we already come face to face with the question of an acting system, for we must first of all regard those methods with which theatrical material is brought out of its usual state and into the active state demanded by stage action. To this question there exist two main points of view. One of them is conducted by the school of psychological naturalism (the Moscow Art Theatre); the other is explained through the biomechanic system that is developed in V. Meyerhold's theatre workshops.

To construct a performance (or any theatre action) on the system of psychological naturalism is to base it on 'experiences'. This school believes that an actor must experience, in the most realistic manner, everything that the character experiences in the play. If an actor fails to summon within him these experiences then his acting becomes erroneous, 'unable to reach' the audience.

To summon these emotions, the actor must rely on his own life experiences, on everything that was truly felt by him, as a person, in his life. A successful portrayal of a part is wholly dependent on the extent to which the experiences and emotions of the character become those of the actor. 'The actor-creator', says V. Nemirovich-Danchenko, one of the directors of the Art Theatre, 'uses the word (and gesture?) so naturally, so lightly, so effortlessly, that it does not even have to be thought about. It becomes a portrayal of his own experiences'. This phrase fully highlights the importance of experiences in the theatre system of psychological (spiritual) naturalism. From here, for example, comes the peculiar 'initial rehearsal without words, while sitting down; the search for the inner scheme of the part, the careful eye contact'. From here come the exercises ('pranas') based on the commandments of Indian yoga, from here come the evangelical words recalled by V. Nemirovich-Danchenko: 'I assure you, most solemnly I tell you, that unless a grain of wheat falls into the earth and dies, it remains alone by itself. But if it dies, it produces many others and yields a rich harvest.' While admitting that in its time and in a certain social environment the system of psychological naturalism had its own great meaning and was, probably, the best system to show the characteristics of the repertoire of its time (Chekhovian, for example), it also cannot be denied that as the basis for the theatre work at the workers' clubs it would have been a most unforgivable mistake. (It is enough to remember the 'self-hypnosis', which is introduced by this system, as acting's main virus.) Working with this system is simply unthinkable in cases where the theatrical tasks are dramatizations of the stinging events of the day, agitation speeches, living newspapers and street performances. Work in the theatrical scheme of 'spiritual naturalism' is fundamentally unacceptable for a club member who has completely different tasks before him, different from the 'forcing' of all sorts of 'experiences'. Those theatre collectives at workers' clubs which still 'lean' in this direction must, finally, realize the comprehensive damage of their mistake.

The main principles of **the biomechanical system** can be encapsulated as follows. In contrast with basing the actors' work on nervous self-hypnosis or unorganized physical excitement, the necessary requirement for playing the part is the neutral, working, heightened excitement of the actor, which can be compared to the excitement an athlete feels before the beginning of a competition or that of a worker before commencing a difficult task. This excitement demands utmost concentration and precision. This necessary condition is the result not only of general physical training but also of biomechanical exercises. Biomechanical exercises systematically develop various movements as a basis for an actor's work. The concept of movement is central and most important in this system (the organic sounding of voice, for example, is derived from movement): (1) muscle strain, (2) discharge and (3) cry, which is viewed as the necessary tuning fork that defines the sound of words and phrases. Movement is split into its elements, clarified in its structure and further developed depending on the given task.

The work on a part (the general task) is divided into two main factors: (1) the study of the plot (to determine a number of positions, movements and gestures that are sequenced by the given task) and (2) the presentation of the material (the work on every element according to motoric, biomechanic laws). The biomechanic system of acting cannot be called a fully developed one. The value of its experimental achievements demands a precise and detailed study. However, as a principle of work, and developed in a certain direction, the system that must be implemented is that of biomechanics as a method for staging a play on the basis of the construction and analysis of movement (of course, along with all the necessary and inevitable corrections and improvements).

Stage exercises are also important sectional classes. As was shown before, these exercises must take place during production work. When planning stage exercises, it is necessary, therefore, to consider the possible character of the production tasks and figure out what kind of skills could be used, for example, in dramatizations, improvisations on a political subject, for living newspapers, the organization of theatre trials, the performances during parades and so on. The approach here is the following: start from simple exercises with a restricted theme, which boil down to the performance of even just one movement-gesture that has a connection with the sound of the voice, and move to exercises of increasing difficulty. The most important factor is the necessity to orient towards the audience certain conditions of perception and a certain environment, because theatrical action obtains its final goal only in the perception of the viewer. As strange as it sounds, this is something that theatre workers often forget.

Parallel to the stage exercises is the training in a number of disciplines that have a specifically educational character. These disciplines and subjects are also evident in the theatre sections. They include eurhythmics, acrobatics and voice training. It is important to highlight the futility, or rather, the damage even, of the **plastiques** exercise. The main characteristic of this sort of physical training is its aestheticism, a purely visual beauty. It shows a lack of precision in the separate actions and a constitution that is dictated by chance. We believe that for club work plastiques cannot yield anything except a waste of time.

Eurhythmics. Of course, eurhythmics demands a different attitude. It is included in the curriculum of a unified studio of the arts (see related article), and it gains a special meaning in the work of the theatrical sections by being obligatory to all club members.

Acrobatics. The need to practise this discipline is seen, on the one hand, in the fast tempo an action acquires when based on acrobatic movement and, on the other hand, by the agility and precision of calculation given by this training.

Voice. Voice training, also included in the curriculum of a unified studio of the arts, necessarily obtains further attention and emphasis in the sectional theatre work. The special goal of these exercises is to develop consistency between 'sounds' and movement exercises.

Character of theatre forms. In the practice of modern theatre art, it is impossible, of course, to highlight all the methods and directions on which to base the theatre work of the workers' clubs. Each theatre collective must act as a kind of pioneer in this field, a constant explorer, a creator of new forms. Material (in the sense of different forms of influence) must be pulled out of various theatres, including those of the so called low genres (cabaret, music hall, farce, circuses and so on). This should not be embarrassing at all.

This material proves to be quite valuable. The point is to use in the correct way the force and character of these various theatres. We cannot, of course, talk here about the indiscriminate recognition of some form or other. However, an opposite point of view, one which denies any sort of utilization, would be equally incorrect. The problem is solved with the appropriate setting – using and being influenced by other forms in the interest of the proletariat.

Moreover, forms from the 'low' theatre are sharp, flexible and real in their nature and often become the most effective in reaching their goals.

Organization of spectacles in everyday life. The solution of the propagandistic tasks through theatre is not wholly satisfied by the activities of theatre collectives in the workers' clubs. The task of organizing consciousness is followed closely by the task of organizing everyday life. And since we are talking specifically about theatre collectives, there comes the following question. Mass celebrations, demonstrations, sport games and communal competitions – all of this is becoming an inseparable part of everyday life. The masses are here not in the role of an audience, but rather as direct, active participants. Spectacles can and must be, of course, ingrained into the flow of organized masses, but the centre of everything, undoubtedly, must be the life of the mass itself. And here, great value is gained by groups that lead the crowd into action, giving it rhythm, awakening its initiative. Within the limits of a celebration's general plan (parade, demonstration) there exist dozens of variations which enliven the scheme, flesh up the plan and make the everyday pulse beat with true life. The tasks of theatre collectives are their integration into the general flow so as to initiate it, thus becoming the organizers of activity in everyday life. These are difficult tasks that require great imagination. Experiments directed towards the solution of this matter must be placed on the list of work of the worker clubs' theatre collectives.

Epilogue: The Construction of Amateur Theatre

Nikolai Evreinov

Intervention during the conference on theatre organized by the Agitprop Division of the Communist Party

Source: *Puti razvitiia teatra*, 1927, pp. 261–77

We were just now engaged in fierce and heated debates about the professional theatre. These disputes are caused by the fact that we have a well-known crisis in theatrical business and professional theatre. We have exactly the same crisis in the area of our club theatre. Disputes take place there as well, and we also have two more or less distinct policy lines to follow. True, the disputes here are not as great, not as fierce. Maybe the points of view and positions were not revealed so clearly, but still, there are known disagreements. Therefore, let me identify the main line that we must now lead in the field of club theatre and those opinions and disagreements that have emerged on it.

I must, at least for a short while, dwell on the current state of our club scene and on its significance.

First of all, a few numbers. What is the club theatre? What audience size does it command? We have 3,200 trade union clubs. These clubs have auditoriums that together hold about a million spectators. On the club stage there are 127,000 productions in one year. If our summer theatres are also included, we will have figures of approximately 40–50 million visits every year. Now, I cannot compare these with the numbers of the professional theatres, because I do not have them at my fingertips. Probably there are more spectators visiting the professional theatres, but in terms of influence and service to the working masses the club theatre is more important, as it serves spectators from the working classes.

The tasks of club theatres

Now, let me talk about the challenges facing the club theatre scene and the features that distinguish it from professional theatre.

Our club theatre scene has two challenges. The first is to serve the worker-spectator, and the second is to educate cadres of workers in the field of stage art and art in general.

Forgetting one of these tasks would undoubtedly be wrong and hinder the development of club theatre. The first task prevails in our country – the massive work of serving the worker-spectator. But at the same time this task cannot be separated from the second – the artistic education of our circle members' cadres working on the club stage.

The club stage has a number of features that distinguish it from the professional theatre. The first feature is that the club theatre is much closer to a worker-spectator than a professional theatre would ever be. In the auditorium of the club we have, more or less, a uniform composition of the visual mass. Therefore, the club scene can be more adaptable to the cultural level and needs of this spectator, something which a professional theatre working for the masses cannot do for a spectator who comes from the street. The second feature is the closeness between club actors and the audience.

These moments give us reason to say that the club theatre can be much more flexible to adapt to the education needs of the working masses. It is more likely to catch their mood, to influence them in a stronger manner and to come closer to them.

Finally, the club stage, as an example of amateur theatre, is the most important support and source of creativity for the new theatre – the theatre of socialist culture. It is not just a source, but one of the most important to create a socialist culture, to create a new theatre. That is why it would be harmful and incorrect to contrast the amateur theatre to the professional one, and a theatre of the workers to the rest of the Soviet theatre. Therefore, we need to emphasize the need for the professional theatre to connect with the amateur one, especially now when we are setting ourselves the task of expanding the area of our influence, through art, on the working masses. We also need to point out the importance of using our club theatre to raise the level of socialist art.

The repertoire of club theatres

One of the main issues of the club theatre is the question of the repertoire. This repertoire is extremely poor. […] Of course, there are decent things in the club's repertoire that have stood the test of time. But along with every good play there is such trash, against which we and the professional theatres rebel. […]

The second main drawback of the club theatre is that the performances are not artistic, their elaboration is weak and the preparation of the circles is poor. This is because of the poor team of directors. The quality of this team is low, their qualifications are weak, and they often do not understand or do not know the basic techniques of stage art. Hence, the poor staging in the work of the drama circles. No one teaches them, and therefore they neglect to develop the artistic arrangements of the performances. That is why the worker says: 'Enough agitation, enough of your home-made concoctions, give me theatre.' But he does not only speak. He also fulfils this requirement by producing a whole series of full-length and good plays. These new phenomena were born in our club theatre as opposed to the old ways of the amateur theatre. In the struggle for quality we now have, in a number of clubs, serious productions of plays that have appeared on the stage of the professional theatres. [...]

Of course, we cannot just stage full-length plays on the club stage. We must not forget the small forms that have a good past and which we can use in the future. There is the so-called living newspaper, popular music, folk forms such as the booth, petrushka, artistic storytelling. The production of short one-act plays is at the moment in full swing. It would be wrong to say that we should only stage full plays on the stages of the club theatres. We must make full use of the small forms. They are more accessible for the club stage, more flexible, and they can be more adaptable to political agitation. But we also believe that it would be wrong to drive out productions that are staged after a long period of preparation, such as [Vladimir Bill-Belotserkovsky's] *The Storm*, *Mermaid* and a number of other plays through which the worker must improve his cultural level. That's why I believe that in relation to the repertoire of our club theatres, we must pursue a policy of combining different forms from the performing arts: full-length plays (drama, comedy) and small forms (living newspaper, variety and so on). [...]

Practical measures

What practical measures are needed to improve the club theatre? First, we consider it necessary to strengthen public attention, in particular the party's, on the pertinent issues of our club theatre. If we give a lot of attention to our professional theatre, if around it there is a struggle and a dispute, then the Committee for Club Theatre, as the leader of the workers' masses, should be given more and not less interest.

Second, club theatres must be given a repertoire. This can be done in two ways: (1) select a number of plays from those staged in the professional theatre and recommend how they ought to be adapted to the club stage. The example here is that of Comrade Bill-Belotserkovsky, who remade his *Storm* for the club; (2) order a number of new plays specifically written for club theatres. This is indeed possible, although, unfortunately, playwrights are not particularly willing to do so.

Third, we must make it easier for our clubs to stage plays. It is not enough for the club to be given a play; it must also be given the means to stage it. After all, in the clubs there aren't experienced directors. Therefore, it is necessary to develop widespread models for the club stage, widespread instructions and directions, production notes and so on. [...]

Fourth, it is necessary to improve the qualifications of the club members through the publication of a magazine, manuals on stage art and a number of other ways.

Fifth, we need to review and improve the quality of the leaders of the club circles. This is one of the main difficulties in improving matters in the field of club theatre. The quality of the leaders is poor, their qualifications low. Obviously, it is necessary to take a number of measures: create courses for them and use the instructors from the available schools. It is necessary to bring professional theatre closer to the amateur theatre. This rapprochement is going on now, but it needs to be accelerated so that the assistance to the club scene from the side of the professional theatre is put on a firm ground.

The next step is to raise the quality of our productions by creating united groups. These groups would collect the best forces, which would become exemplary ones. Their performances would go in a number of clubs and thereby teach their members how to produce artistic products of a higher quality.

It is also necessary to prepare instructors from our circle members and maybe even artists. Talented circle members should be sent to theatre courses to receive more solid training. Then we would have leaders for the dramatic work and maybe even artists. So far, little attention has been paid to this.

Finally, it is necessary to release clubs from a variety of compulsory performances, from performances during various celebrations and so on. The clubs are forced to prepare performances for all kinds of political campaigns and holidays, from the 8 March to the commemoration of the Paris Commune, 1 May and so on. Because of this, the drama circles cannot work seriously. It is necessary to focus the attention of the circles only on some productions so as to give them the opportunity to improve their quality.

These, in my opinion, are the main points that should be put under the spotlight. They form the measures necessary to improve the quality of our club theatre products, provide good directions, achieve more for the working masses and overcome the crisis that we have in our club theatre scene.

References

Anrusenko, S. ed. (2004), *The Moscow Art Theatre in Diaries and Notes*, Moscow: Avantitul.

Aquilina, S. (2012), 'Stanislavsky and the impact of studio ethics on everyday life', *Theatre, Dance and Performance Training*, 3 (3): 302–14.

Aquilina, S. (2014), 'Platon Kerzhentsev and His Theories on Collective Creation', *Journal of Dramatic Theory and Criticism*, 28 (2): 29–48.

Aquilina, S. (2020), *Modern Theatre in Russia: Tradition Building and Transmission Processes*, London: Methuen Drama.

Benedetti, J. (1989), *Stanislavski: An Introduction*, London: Methuen.

Blum, V., E. Beskin, B. Ferdinand, A. Gan, I. Aksenov, V. Tikhonovich, M. Zagorsky, B. Arvatov, O. Blum, V. Rappaport and L. Sabaneyev (1922), *O Teatre*, Tver: Tver Publishing House.

Braun, E. (1998), *Meyerhold: A Revolution in Theatre*, London: Methuen.

Braun, E. ed. and trans. (2016), *Meyerhold on Theatre*, 4th edn, London: Methuen Drama.

Brovkin, V. (1998), *Russia after Lenin: Politics, Culture and Society, 1921–9*, London: Routledge.

Clark, K. and E. Dobrenko, with A. Artizov and O. Naumov (2007), *Soviet Culture and Power: A History in Documents*, trans. M. Schwartz, New Haven: Yale University Press.

Crane, R. (2011), 'The Performance Historian as Cold Case Detective: Reopening Nikolai L'vov's Investigation of the Blue Blouse Movement', *Performing Arts Resources*, 28.

Evreinoff, N. (1927), *The Theatre in Life*, ed. and trans. A. Nazaroff, New York: George G. Harrap and Company Ltd.

Fitzpatrick, S. (1999), *Everyday Stalinism*, Oxford: Oxford University Press.

Goldman, M. ed. (1977), *Modern Chinese Literature in the May Fourth Era*, Cambridge, MA, and London: Harvard University Press.

Gourfinkel, N. (1979), *Teatro Russo Contemporaneo*, trans. M. Turano, Roma: Bulzoni Editore.

Gauss, R. B. (1999), *Lear's Daughters: The Studios of the Moscow Art Theatre 1905–1927*, New York: P. Lang.

Gvozdev, A. A. (1987), *Teatral'naya kritika*, compiled and annotated by N. A. Tarshis, Leningrad: Iskusstvo.

Hellebust, R. (1997), 'Aleksei Gastev and the Metallization of the Revolutionary Body', *Slavic Review*, 56 (3): 500–18.

Ilinskii, I. (1984), *Sam o sebe*, Moscow: Iskusstvo.
Kerzhentsev, P. (1918), *Revoliutsiia i teatr*, Moscow: State Publishing House.
Kerzhentsev, P. (1923), *Tvorcheskii teatr*, 5th edn, Moscow: State Publishing House.
Kiaer, C. and E. Naiman eds (2006), *Everyday Life in Early Soviet Russia. Taking the Revolution Inside*, Bloomington: Indiana University Press.
Komisarjevsky, T. (1929), *Myself and the Theatre*, London: William Heinemann Limited.
Krylov, S. M. ed. (1927), *Puti razvitiia teatra*, Moscow: Kinopechat'.
Leach, R. (1994), *Revolutionary Theatre*, London and New York: Routledge.
Leach, R. (2018), *Russian Futurist Theatre. Theory and Practice*, Edinburgh: Edinburgh University Press.
Leach, R., and V. Borovsky eds (1999), *A History of Russian Theatre*, Cambridge: Cambridge University Press.
Mally, L. (1990), *Culture of the Future – the Proletkult Movement in Revolutionary Russia*, Berkeley, Los Angeles, Oxford: University of California Press.
Mally, L. (1993), 'Autonomous Theater and the Origins of Socialist Realism: The 1932 Olympiad of Autonomous Art', *Russia Review*, 52 (2): 198–212.
Mally, L. (1996), 'Performing the New Woman: The Komsomolka as Actress and Image in Soviet Youth Theater', *Journal of Social History*, 30 (1): 79–95.
Mally, L. (2000), *Revolutionary Acts – Amateur Theatre and the Soviet State*, New York: Cornell University Press.
McReynolds, L. (2003), *Russia at Play: Leisure Activities at the End of the Tsarist Era*, New York: Cornell University Press.
Mele, G. (1991), *Cultura e Politica in Russia – Il Proletkul't 1917–1921*, Roma: Bulzoni Editore.
Mgebrov, A. (1932), *Zhizn' v teatre, tom 2*, Moscow: Academia.
Pitches, J. ed. (2019), *The Great European Stage Directors Volume 3: Copeau, Komisarjevsky, Guthrie*, London and New York: Bloomsbury.
Pletnev, V. ed. (1924), *Iskusstvo v Rabochem Klube*, Moscow: All-Russian Proletkult.
Rigby, T. H. (1979), *Lenin's Government. Sovnarkom*, Cambridge, New York: Cambridge University Press.
Rudnitsky, K. (1988), *Russian and Soviet Theatre – Tradition and Avant-Garde*, ed. L. Milne, trans. R. Permar, London: Thames and Hudson.
Samson, G. G. (1996), *The American Fund for Public Service – Charles Garland and Radical Philanthropy, 1922–41*, London: Greenwood Press.
Sen Gupta, K. (2005), *The Philosophy of Rabindranath Tagore*, London and New York: Routledge.
Senelick, L. (2007), *The A to Z of Russian Theater*, Lanham, Toronto, Plymouth: The Scarecrow Press.
Smyshlaev, V. (1922), *Tekhnika obrabotki Stsenicheskogo zrelishcha*, 2nd edn, Moscow: All-Russian Proletkult.
Stacy, R. H. (1974), *Russian Literary Criticism: A Short History*, New York: Syracuse University Press.

Stanislavski, K. (2008), *My Life in Art*, trans. J. Benedetti, Oxon: Routledge.
Stourac, R. and K. McCreery (1986), *Theatre as a Weapon*, London and New York: Routledge and Kegan Paul.
Swift, E. A. (2002), *Popular Theater and Society in Tsarist Russia*, California: University of California Press.
Tucker, S. (2006), *World War I: A Student Encyclopedia*, Santa Barbara, Denver, Oxford: ABC Clio.
Von Geldern, J. (1993), *Bolshevik Festivals, 1917–1920*, Berkeley, Los Angeles, Oxford: University of California Press.
Von Geldern, J. and R. Stites eds (1995), *Mass Culture in Soviet Russia*, Bloomington: Indian University Press.
Wilson, K. M. (1991), *An Encyclopedia of Continental Women Writers, Volume 1*, New York and London: Garland Publishing, Inc.
Worrall, N. (1989), *Modernism to Realism on the Soviet Stage*, Cambridge: Cambridge University Press.
Zolotnitskii, D. I. (1976), *Zori teatral'nogo Oktyabrya*, Moscow: Iskusstvo.

Index

Academic Theatres 3, 56, 89
acrobatics 29, 198, 204
agitation 25, 160, 165, 167, 168, 171, 195, 196, 200, 201, 203, 208
agitki/agitational play 17, 170
Agitprop Division of the Communist Party 30, 206
agit-trial/trial 11, 17, 28, 29, 57, 174–7, 195, 196, 199, 200, 204
amateur actor 1, 2, 25, 26, 27, 77–9, 151
amateur theatre 1, 2, 4, 5–12, 16, 17, 18, 20, 21, 24, 25, 26, 29–30, 42, 45, 47, 55, 78, 85, 86, 207, 208, 209
amateurism 11, 12, 52, 74, 78, 165
Ancient Theatre 14, 30, 85
Andreev, Leonid 53, 54, 91
Annenkov, Yuri 9
architecture 47, 70, 136
Arsky, Pavel 17, 53, 163
autonomous work 2, 5, 6, 27, 36, 191

Bakst, Léon 137
balagan 121
ballet 3, 59, 137, 138, 166
Balmont, Konstantin 76
Belaia, Sofia 53, 54, 89
Benois, Alexandre 137
Berlioz, Hector 137
Bessalko, Pavel 14, 15, 17, 94–7
Bill-Belotserkovsky, Vladimir 208
biomechanics 28, 29, 198, 203
Blue Blouse viii, 22, 23, 24, 181
Bogdanov, Alexander 2, 3, 4, 14, 18, 36, 41, 42
Bolshoi Theatre 56, 121
bourgeois art 39, 63, 67, 68, 69, 74, 75
bourgeois culture 31, 45, 51, 63, 67, 68, 69–70, 137
bourgeois theatre 32, 77, 78, 79, 132, 137, 158, 191
bourgeoisie/bourgeois class 46, 48, 54, 65, 66, 69, 94, 95, 140, 142, 159, 160, 172

Bourrillon, Henri 92
bytie 57

cabaret 25, 195, 205
Calderon de la Barca 92
capitalism/capitalist 64, 65, 69, 72, 73, 81, 90, 136, 140, 142, 175
Cézanne, Paul 137, 139
Chekan, Viktoria 85
Chekhov, Anton 1, 4, 13, 53, 137, 203
choral singing 27, 170, 180, 194, 196–7, 198
circus 25, 124, 205
Civil War 5, 17, 18, 25, 86, 125, 165
class struggle 27, 36, 39, 53, 69, 70, 72, 74, 75, 95, 99, 128
club theatre/club stage 6, 27–30, 89, 178, 199–201, 206–9
club theatre scene 30, 206–7, 209
collective creation/collective creativity/collective work 4, 18–20, 42, 51, 130–5, 158, 162, 192
collective criticism 4, 44, 151
collective readings/collective recitation 4, 19, 55, 127–9
collectivism 20, 21, 36, 42, 43, 44, 72, 73, 74, 130, 165
Commedia dell'arte 22, 92, 144
Committee for Club Theatre 208
Communist Manifesto 50
Communist Party 12, 30, 37, 206
content 9, 12, 14, 18, 32, 35, 43, 47, 70–1, 72, 75, 130, 139–40, 157, 174, 176, 178, 180, 181, 182, 185, 198
Countess Panina 144
criticism 4, 13, 18, 20, 21, 26, 36, 44, 131, 132, 145, 151, 172, 187, 191

dance 25, 89, 124, 131, 136, 137, 140, 161, 166, 182
de Vega, Lope 13, 55, 92
Debussy, Claude 137
devised performance 5

Dickens, Charles 88
diction 26, 28, 128, 186, 188, 190, 198
dilettantism 7, 56, 57, 68, 90, 191
director 9, 13, 14, 19, 20, 25, 30, 48, 52, 77, 92, 132, 133, 134, 159, 162, 164, 166, 169, 180, 202, 207, 209
Dobuzhinsky, Mstislav 137
Dostoevsky, Fyodor 59, 141
dramatic circles 27, 58, 185, 189–90, 191, 209
dramatic laboratories 27, 189–92
Duncan, Isadora 137, 186

Ebert, Friedrich 64
Eisenstein, Sergei 17, 102
Engels, Friedrich 123, 141
eurhythmics 27, 29, 150, 194, 195, 197, 198, 204
everyday life 7, 28, 49, 54, 56, 57, 85, 140, 142, 171, 173, 193, 195, 196, 197, 205
Evreinov Nikolaevich, Nikolai 30, 48
Evreinov, Nikolai 14, 30, 48, 58, 206

farce 25, 54, 205
Fascism 29
festivals 51, 121, 122, 124, 131, 134, 169
First All-Russian Conference of Proletarian Cultural and Educational Organisations 3, 36
First Studio 20, 56, 88, 91
folk 25, 55, 131, 134, 155, 170, 208
form 12, 14, 18, 31, 32, 39, 40, 42, 43, 47, 51, 54, 70, 72, 71, 79, 81, 99, 121, 127, 131, 132, 136, 139–42, 145, 149, 153, 155, 157, 166, 167, 174, 176, 177, 185, 188, 189, 193, 195, 196, 198, 199, 201, 204–5, 208
Freud, Sigmund 58
futurism 18, 139, 140–3

Gaideburov, Pavel 24, 144
Galsworthy, John 90
Gan, Alexei 7
Gastev, Aleksei 19, 92, 125, 127, 128, 129
Gauguin, Paul 137
gesture 149, 157, 166, 202, 203, 204
Gogol, Nikolai 1, 53, 54, 92
Gorky, Maxim 4, 14, 53, 54, 86, 91, 137

Gras, Felix 92
Gvozdev, Alexei 8
gymnastics 28, 150, 195, 197, 198

Hampstead 134
Hauptmann, Gerhart 4, 53, 55
Heijermans, Herman 14, 53, 55, 91
  Wreck of the Ship 'Hope' 86
Heroic Theatre 86

Ibsen, Henrik 13, 92, 94
ideological subjects 27, 194, 197
Ignatov, V. V. 128
igra/creative play 144–9
Ilinsky, Igor 1, 27
Imperial Theatres 3, 31
improvisation 21, 22, 24, 26, 29, 30, 32, 51, 55, 57, 92, 93, 134, 144–9, 152, 153, 155, 160, 161, 187, 188, 204
independent initiative 6, 37, 46
intelligentsia 3, 11, 35, 48, 49, 53, 66
Internationale 16, 158, 160, 161
Iskusstvo v rabochem klube 25, 27, 28, 29, 167, 174, 193, 199

Jacques-Dalcroze, Émile 150, 186

Kalinin, Fyodor 9, 14, 18, 37, 63, 73, 139
Kamerny Theatre 31, 56
Kerensky, Alexander 37
Kerzhentsev, Platon 2, 4, 5, 10, 31, 37, 40, 42, 45, 54, 63, 77, 88, 98, 121, 130, 136, 158, 189
  Tvorcheskii teatr 10, 11, 55, 63, 77, 89, 158, 189
Khlebnikov, Velimir 141
Kirillov, Vladimir 19, 127, 128
Kogan, Piotr 8, 50, 89, 127, 158
Komissarzhevskaya, Vera 14, 144
Komissarzhevsky, Fyodor 1, 8, 31
Komsomol 12
Kozlov, P. 17

Lady Gregory 91
Lebedev-Poliansky, Pavel 14
Lenin, Vladimir 2, 5, 6, 172
literature 5, 7, 9, 20, 21, 25, 27, 45, 46, 47, 50, 52, 54, 70, 89, 90, 91, 99, 127, 131, 132, 133, 138, 140, 149, 172, 189, 194, 195

liubitel'skii teatr 6
living newspapers 24–5, 28, 167–9, 170, 171, 172, 173, 178–81, 195, 198, 199, 200, 203, 204, 208
London, Jack 92
Lunacharsky, Anatoly 2, 3, 4, 7, 14, 35, 36, 37, 45, 50, 80
Lvov, Nikolai 8, 13, 48, 58

Maly Theatre 56, 121
Marx, Karl 71, 123
Marxism/Marxist 18, 35, 38, 39, 43, 64, 66, 140, 141, 197
Maslovskaya, S. D. 9
mass demonstration/mass performance/mass scenes/mass spectacle/mass theatre 6, 7, 9, 19, 21, 31, 51, 55, 58–9, 89, 96, 131, 144, 158, 169, 195, 205
Massenet, Jules 137
metaphysics 18, 140
Meyerhold, Vsevolod 5, 9, 13, 14, 29, 31, 85, 98, 165, 202
Mgebrov, Alexander 2, 4, 14, 16, 17, 18–19, 21, 55, 85, 92, 94, 95, 125, 127
Miasnitsky, I. I. 53, 54
Mirbeau, Octave 91
mise-en-scène 153
Mobile-Popular Theatre 24, 144
modern theatre 137, 138, 144, 177, 204
Molière 13, 54, 92
Moscow 1, 3, 7, 12, 16, 17, 22, 23, 31, 36, 40, 49, 55, 89, 121, 122, 126, 129, 158, 160, 161, 162, 169, 170, 185, 187, 188
Moscow Art Theatre 3, 8, 20, 26, 29, 31, 32, 56, 88, 155, 187, 202
Moscow Children's Theatre 56
Moscow Institute of Journalism 24
music 3, 5, 6, 19, 20, 25, 27, 59, 70, 80, 125, 127, 128, 131, 134, 136, 137, 138, 150, 152, 164, 177, 196, 208
music hall 205

Nadson, Semeon 71
Narkompros 2, 8, 12, 24, 37, 45, 51, 52
naturalism 29, 91, 92, 202, 203
Nazarov, Georgy 86
neighbourhood theatre 6, 77, 78, 79–81, 163

Nemirovich-Danchenko, Vladimir 202
Norris, Benjamin 92
Noske, Gustav 64, 65

Olympiad of amateur theatre 12
opera 31, 131, 138, 166
oral newspaper 170
Ostrovsky, Alexander 13, 53, 54

St Petersburg/Petrograd/Leningrad 4, 7, 9, 14, 31, 37, 50, 55, 58, 80, 85, 86, 87, 127, 129, 144, 145, 161, 162, 163
petrushka 80, 208
physical education 27, 194, 195, 197, 198, 202, 204
Piotrovsky, Adrian 8, 56, 58, 89
plastiques 29, 186, 188, 204
Pletnev, Valerian 2, 7, 9, 11, 12, 14, 17, 25, 29, 30, 37, 47, 63, 67, 102
Popular Revolutionary Movements in Russia 160
prana 202
professional actor 27, 47, 56, 63, 78, 79, 81, 151, 161, 162, 165, 189, 190, 191, 192, 199
professional theatre 4, 9, 19, 21, 30, 52, 81, 144, 145, 199, 206, 207, 208, 209
professionalism 3, 8, 11, 42, 47, 55, 63, 64, 66, 67, 68, 69, 71, 72, 74, 75, 76, 165, 166
proletarian actor 18, 20, 27, 51, 132, 164, 165–6, 189
proletarian art 2, 18, 35, 36, 40, 43, 46, 66, 68, 70, 72, 165
proletarian artist 11, 12, 68, 69, 70, 71, 72, 74, 75, 76, 132
proletarian culture 2, 3, 4, 5, 36, 37, 39, 41, 46, 50, 63, 67–70, 72, 76, 128, 130, 135, 157, 185
proletarian theatre 2, 4, 6, 7–8, 9, 11, 12, 13–14, 19, 27, 30, 42, 50, 63, 67, 77–81, 88–93, 125, 134, 151, 164, 165, 185, 189, 190, 191, 192
proletariat 2, 3, 4, 12, 18, 32, 35, 36, 37, 38, 39, 40, 43, 46, 50, 63, 68, 69, 72, 73, 81, 90, 91, 92, 97, 98, 99, 100, 101, 129, 130, 131, 141, 143, 165, 167, 185, 188, 189, 190, 191, 192, 201, 205

Proletkult 2, 3, 5, 6, 7, 9, 11, 13, 14, 16, 19, 20, 21, 24, 25, 26, 36, 37, 40, 45–7, 49, 50, 55, 67, 68, 80, 85, 86, 94, 98, 125, 127, 129, 131, 133, 135, 138, 145, 151, 158, 160, 162, 163, 164, 167, 174, 185, 186, 188, 189, 190, 192, 193, 199
propaganda 2, 25, 38, 65, 144, 167, 170
Provisional Government 37
psychology 35, 72, 73, 74, 99, 130, 165, 166, 192
Puccini, Giacomo 137

Radek, Karl 172
Razin, Stepan 121
realism 35, 57, 91
Red Army 1, 9, 13, 16, 18, 24, 56, 57, 125, 129, 145, 161, 162, 167
rehearsal 1, 26, 101, 132, 134, 153, 155, 157, 187, 190, 202
repertoire 2, 3, 4, 12, 13, 16, 17, 30, 52, 53, 55, 79, 81, 83, 85, 88, 89, 90, 91–3, 98, 102, 125, 126, 127, 133, 135, 161, 162, 189, 192, 196, 199, 203, 207–8
Revolution 1, 5, 6, 12, 13, 17, 18, 29, 32, 37, 38, 50, 51, 52, 53, 54, 57, 69, 70, 71, 81, 88, 89, 91, 92, 96, 101, 122, 127, 144, 152, 161, 164, 167, 189
Roerich, Nicholas 137
Rolland, Romain 4, 9, 89, 90, 91

Samobytnik-Mashirov, Aleksei 50, 127
samodeiatel'nost' 6, 20
Scheidemann, Philipp 64, 65
Schiller, Friedrich 56, 92
science 3, 4, 36, 38, 39, 43, 44, 45, 46, 47, 50, 51, 130, 160
Scriabin, Alexander 137
Serezhnikova, V. K. 55
Shakespeare, William 13, 55, 92
Shaw, Bernard 91
Shcheglov, D. 145, 146
Shchuko, Vladimir 9
Shklovsky, Viktor 8, 56, 58
Sinclair, Upton 92
Skarskaia, N./Skarskaia Method 24, 144–9
small forms 208
Smyshlaev, Valentin 1, 2, 20, 21, 26, 27, 30, 55, 151, 185

Method of Today 21, 24, 153
second day performances 26, 187
Techniques to Process a Stage Performance 20, 151
Social Democratic Party of Germany 64
socialism 40, 46, 64, 69, 71, 142, 160
socialist theatre 6, 47, 50–5, 81, 89, 91, 92, 127, 158, 163, 207
Sodofev, Ilia 127
Sologub, Fyodor 85
specialists 9, 11, 68, 70, 72, 74, 76, 78, 133, 165, 193, 195, 196, 197
specialization 3, 19, 28, 42, 132, 133, 136, 193
speech 27, 87, 136, 140, 147, 152, 166, 168, 169, 174, 176, 177, 194, 195, 196, 197, 200, 203
stage exercises 26, 28, 29, 187, 188, 198, 204
Stanislavsky, Konstantin 3, 11, 20, 26, 32, 155
studio work 40, 144, 146, 200, 201
symbolism/symbolists 14, 16, 48, 76, 85, 91, 94, 98, 139

Tagore, Rabindranath 85
technique 12, 20, 27, 43, 63, 66, 67, 68, 69, 70, 71, 72, 74, 75, 78, 79, 127, 144, 151, 168, 185, 190, 191, 195, 198, 208
The Battle of the Red Ural 162
The Legend of the Communards 17, 162, 163
The Overthrow of the Autocracy 9, 145, 161
The Red Year 161
The Sacrifice of Freedom 162–3
The Taking of the Bastille 163
theatre epidemic 18, 27, 29, 189
theatre form 12, 14, 18, 29, 32, 50, 51, 54, 99, 131, 136, 170, 201, 204
Theatre of the Revolutionary Satire 165
Tikhonovich, Valentin 20, 51, 165
Tolstoy, Leo 53, 54, 89, 137
training 1, 2, 11, 12, 26–9, 49, 72, 150, 183, 186, 188, 189, 190, 191, 192, 193, 194, 195, 197, 198, 202, 203, 204, 209
Trotsky, Leon 172

unified studio of the arts 27, 28, 193–8, 204

vaudeville 13, 53, 58
Verdi, Giuseppe 137
Verhaeren, Émile 21, 55, 85, 92, 98, 99, 100, 137, 152
   'Insurrection' 14, 16, 20, 21, 55, 71, 86, 94, 151–7, 188
   The Dawns 14
Vermishev, Alexander 17
Veselovsky, Alexander 140
Vinogradov, N. G. 9, 145
voice 19, 26, 27, 29, 128, 129, 186, 188, 190, 194, 195, 197, 198, 202, 203, 204
von Hofmannsthal, Hugo 14, 86
Voynich, Ethel 92

Wagner, Richard 137
Wells, Herbet George 92, 137
Whitman, Walt 19, 85, 92, 126
worker-peasant theatre 6, 51, 52, 54
workers' club 1, 25, 27, 28, 129, 167, 174, 193, 194, 196, 199–205
working class 2, 5, 13, 36, 37, 40, 42, 46, 47, 63, 64, 66, 89, 90, 91, 92, 95, 97, 113, 127, 128, 130, 135, 165, 185, 190, 193, 206

Yeats, William Butler 91
yoga 202

Zola, Émile 92

www.ingramcontent.com/pod-product-compliance
Lightning Source LLC
Chambersburg PA
CBHW062221300426
44115CB00012BA/2162